BONNEVILLE SALT FLATS

"LAND SPEED" LOUISE ANN NOETH

MBI Publishing Company

Dedication

Dedicated to Tom "Mr. Motor Head" Senter, who gave me salt fever and Bob "Mr. Salt" Higbee, because no one could, or has, loved Bonneville and its people more than him.

First published in 1999 by MBI Publishing Company, 729 Prospect Avenue, PO Box 1, Osceola, WI 54020-0001USA

MBI Publishing Company books are also available at discounts in bulk quantity for industrial or sales-promotional use. For details write to Special Sales Manager at Motorbooks International Wholesalers & Distributors, 729 Prospect Avenue, PO Box 1, Osceola WI, 54020 USA.

Library of Congress Cataloging-in-Publication Data

Noeth, Louise Ann.
    Bonneville Salt Flats / "Landspeed" Louise Ann Noeth.
         p. cm.
    Includes index.
    ISBN 0-7603-0605-2 (hardbound : alk. paper)
    1. Automobile racing–Utah–Bonneville Salt Flats.
    2. Automobiles, Racing–Speed Records–Utah–Bonneville Salt Flats.
    I. Title.
GV1033.5B66N64   1999
796.72–dc21   99-28378

On the front cover: In the foreground is Al Teague's black *Spirit of 76,* a lakester he converted to a streamliner. Teague set the world land speed record for wheel driven cars in this car in 1991 at 409.986 miles per hour. Directly behind it sits the 1953 Studebaker Champion of 200MPH Club member, Bruce Geisler. Number 219 has run every SCTA Bonneville Nationals since 1960 and set over 40 SCTA records through the years. The 1948 Crosley, built in 1950 by Howard Johansen, is the oldest running car at Bonneville. The yellow streamliner in the rear was built by racing veteran Joaquin Arnet, and is owned and operated by the Bean Bandits Racing Club. *Louise Ann Noeth*

On the frontispiece: Bonneville is one of the few places on earth where a full, 180 degree vivid rainbow can be viewed without any obstructions. Here, a red roadster is 1 mile from the starting line, and the driver is no doubt one of the happiest people on earth. *LandSpeed Productions*

On the title page: "We were young and perfect and had all the time in the world for everything. Sigh," recalled Jean Perry, a close friend of Bob Brissette, the man at the wheel of the belly tank lakester. Brissette and Howard Eichenhofer both joined the 200 MPH Club in 1958 by piloting the Cadillac engine-stuffed lakester. *Bob Brissette*

On the back cover: **Top:** Bonneville's history is one of triumphs in spite of adversity. Jim Lindsley's twin Chrysler-powered roadster is one such example. Beset with synchronization problems, it only managed to clock an initial run of 158 miles per hour. Lindsley got things sorted out in 1954 and ran a 202 miles per hour average. This was the first roadster to do so, giving him entry into the "2" Club. Sadly, on the way home from this record-setting event, the trailered car and tow vehicle were demolished when the driver fell asleep at the wheel. *Tom Medley*

Bottom: The formula for a Bonneville moment combines the mountains and the smooth salt flats with shear power embodied on at least two wheels. One of the most successful designs in Bonneville Racing history was the Larsen & Cummins Class D streamliner. Galloping down the course, it pulled on all 183 cubic inches from the blown Chevy engine, and eventually gave the team a decade-closing 289.50 mile-per-hour record. *George Calloway*

Edited by John Adams-Graf
Designed by Tom Heffron

Printed in Hong Kong

Contents

Acknowledgments

This book made it to print because people pulled together and helped make it so. With my deep appreciation, I would like to thank: God; Alice and Cy Noeth; Chuck Abbott; Art Arfons; John Baechtel; Keith Ball, *Easyriders*; Howie Balogh, Gray Baskerville, Bean Bandits; Glenn Barrett; Ron Benham; Glynne Bowsher; Dave and Judy Brant; Genelle Brimhall; Bob Brissette; Warren Bullis; Bill Burke; Steve Burke; Betty and Gene Burkland; Burly Burlile; George "dah mayor" Calloway; Fred Carillo; Ellen and Ron Christensen; Hugh Coltharp; Penny and Mike Cook; Ron Cook; Roy Creel; Fast Fred and Patty Dannenfelzer; Wilford and Reaona Day; Jim Deist; Billie Ann and Michael Devine, State Line Hotel; Bob D'Olivo; Richard Dixon; Tom Eiden; Cecile Faulconer; Don Francisco; Nye Frank; Jim Fueling; Steve "Pinhead" Garcia; Bruce Geisler; John Goepel; Stan Goldstein; Talmage (Tom) Green; Tom Groh; Tanis and Seth Hammond; Shari Hannah; Herb Harris III; Jack and Warren Harvey; Lesley Hazleton; Carl Heap; Holly Hedrich; Dottie and Bob Higbee; Stu Hilborn; Marcia Holley, *HOT ROD* magazine; Deke Houlgate; Dave Howe; Scott and Diana Howey; Gordon Hoyt; Wes and Wendy Hutchins; Kong Jackson; Wendy Jeffries; Charlie and James Jenkins; Noma and Marv Jenkins; Joyce and Jim Jensen; Harold Johanson; Helen and Bruce Johnston; Gene Jones; Ben Jordan; Kay Kimes; Lew Kirkman, BLM; Amelia and Montie Lanigan; Mick Lanigan, LandSpeed Productions; Les Leggitt; Burke LeSage; Ron Leslie; Vicki Linares; Jim and Larry Lindsley; E. Michael Littlefield; Leslie Long; Kenny Lyons; Mike and Pam Manghelli; Verlin Marshal; Dale and Lonnie Martin; Jim Mattison; Mike McGhee; Ro McGonegal, *HOT ROD* magazine; Duane McKinney; Tom "Stroker" Medley; Jack Mendenhall; Walt Metcalf; Akton "Ak" Miller; Jim Miller; Alison Moore, CSAA; Frank Morimoto; Barney Navarro; Richard Noble; Lois and Bob Opperman; Wally and Richard Parks; Jean Perry; Dave Petrali; Robert G. Pruitt III; Geri and Ed Rannberg; Marianne Ratcliff; Virginia and Eric Rickman; Don Riepe; Doug Robinson; Carol and Otto Ryssman, Santa Clara Choir; Will Scott; Greg Sharp, NHRA Museum; Cris and Ed Shearer; Sheehan Family; "Prozac" Bob and Judy Sights; Randy Speranza; Joy and Bill Summers; Bill Taylor; Jane and Al Teague; Marguerite Telnak; Danny Thompson; Jim Travis; Gertrude and Mark Tripp; Elice and Bruce Tucker; Jack Underwood; Don Vesco; Rick Vesco; Ralphie Volpi; George "Hairball" Vose; Ken Walkey; Joanne and Dan Warner; Mike Waters; Bob Webb; Stratford Wendelboe; Gordon E. White; Monte Wolfe; Earl Wooden; Jan and John Wright; Helen and Alex Xydias; and Willie Young.

Foreword by Al Teague

This book will give even the inexperienced the feel for the phenomenon we call "salt fever." It is a strange addiction for which the only cure is at least one trip to Bonneville per year. It is an unforgettable experience. Some people have been known to quit jobs if they can't get time off for Speed Week. As we meet back on the salt each year, it is as if no time has passed.

Louise has recounted many personal stories, as well as a history of the salt. It is a detailed, accurate, and entertaining story. It is not a story about monetary gain. Bonneville racing is about being respected by your peers for what can be accomplished by dedication, hard work, and help from good friends. Those who were children when I first started are now the ones setting records. I've been going to Bonneville for over 30 years, but still remember my first trip.

The year was 1967. Recently returned from Vietnam and working for Gene Ohly at Evans Speed Equipment, I traveled to the salt flats in the back of George Bentley's pickup truck with three other guys. Driving more than 700 miles from Los Angeles, going through two tires and a battery, we arrived in Wendover, Utah, in the middle of the night. We slept in sleeping bags on the ground next to the truck outside the A1 Bar and Casino. The next morning I was amazed at how blindingly white, how vast, the salt was. It looked endless.

Our days were spent on the salt trying to set records, and our nights were spent socializing at the State Line with such racing greats as Otto Ryssman, an early drag racing pioneer, and Bill Matthews and Phil Freudiger, who took the time to talk to me, a novice. I was awestruck to be in the presence of such august gentlemen. I was hooked. I wanted to drive, to become a part of a Bonneville team, and a member of the prestigious 200 Mile Per Hour Cub.

In 1968, we entered the No. 76 highboy as Sadd, Teague, and Bentley highboy roadster in the competitive C/Fuel Roadster Class. I drove, Bentley tuned, and Sadd crewed. Suiting up as we neared the starting line for my first run, my heart was racing as we pushed up to the starting line.

Starter Bob Higbee walked up and gave a sharp tug, tightening the seat belt and shoulder harness. After I regained my breath, he said, "You know where you're going, don't you?" Not wanting to appear a novice, I nodded my head "yes," put the car in gear, and was pushed off onto the course! My heart was still pounding, and even though that first run had to be aborted, by the end of the meet we ended up within 3 miles per hour of the A/Fuel Roadster Class record!

As my need for ever-increasing speed became more intense, I built a lakester in my mother's garage, giving the vehicle many hours, lots of money, and total dedication. In 1982, I transformed the car into a streamliner by enclosing the wheels. Always in the back of my mind, though never spoken, was the seed of the idea that maybe one day the land-speed record could be attained with my single-engine streamliner. Every trip to Bonneville was with that one goal in mind.

My friend and competitor, Nolan White, was always just a little ahead of me, and in 1990, he beat me to the 400-mile-per-hour mark. It was a good thing I was already lying on the ground, working under the car with my stepson, Todd, when the announcement of Nolan's speed came over the loud speakers, because my knees surely would have buckled! The next day we also ran over 400 miles per hour, but that did not lessen the realization that Nolan had been the first.

The following year, on August 21, 1991, after years of hard work, sleepless nights, untold hours in the garage, and parties not attended, came the realization of a dream. Just like 1968, my heart was racing as I climbed into the cockpit, and we rushed getting to the line before the meet closed. Bob Higbee approached the car, gave me the customary tug to the belts, and said, "I know you know where you are going." And I did.

I clocked 425 miles per hour in the measured mile, but I had run so far down the course that the car got stuck in the mud. We had less than 1 hour to prepare the car for the return run—change the oil, refuel, and repack the chutes. It was only with the super-human assistance of the crew that we were under way for the return run with 2 minutes to spare. Jim Lattin tugged on the shoulder harness and sent me off. At the other end, Bob Higbee informed me we had our *Fédération Internationale de l'Automobile* (FIA) record!

It is hard to describe the exhilaration of that day. A dream that started so long ago was helped along by so many friends year after year, going to Bonneville with their own money—without them I would have no record. Literally. I had been unable to pay the $1,000 entry fee required for FIA timing, which would qualify us for the official land speed record. Fellow racer Mark Dees had overheard us saying we couldn't run FIA. He walked over and handed the officials $1,000 and said, "Al is running FIA, and I am sponsoring him!"

Again, in 1998, the fine Bonneville competitive spirit emerged when Charley Markley came to help us work on the car. I was trying to regain the C/Fuel Streamliner record held by the Hoffman-Markley car.

I was recently asked by an acquaintance, not a racer, "Don't you wish you had all the money you have spent on the race car now instead of just a race car?" For those who understand Bonneville, the question does not even deserve an answer.

Al Teague

Introduction

The people who go to the Bonneville Salt Flats are a fascinating bunch. Regardless of what they do in their everyday lives, when they are on the salt, they become a family bound together by speed—a powerful force that erases ethnic, economic, political, and religious barriers.

They are time and distance groupies.

They are landspeed racers.

They are speed freaks.

They are people who follow a skinny, black oil line trying to going faster than anyone else has gone before. And they do it again, and again, and again. Some speed wrinkles have been doing it quite well for 50 years.

There may be a way to explain this outlandish behavior, but who's to say what's the best way to decipher a multidimensional dreamscape? Many will tell you it is better than sex, but they have a hard time telling you why. Salt racing invigorates the spirit so thoroughly, energizes the libido so subtly that those immersed in it consider the few definable distillations very intimate, very private.

It's a driver's game, not a ride you take shackled to a computer program. Strapped in the car, hurtling along the salt, it is just you, the machine, and the Almighty. Time slows down and the empirical becomes spatial. Bonneville is the ultimate speed laboratory, where you can spin out at 200 miles per hour and not hit a darn thing. The salt flats have had more land speed records broken on their surface than any other spot on Earth—a revered mecca where drivers flog physics to win velocity crowns.

This is high speed, baby. Not just a few seconds of tromp-your-foot-on-the-throttle and hope you don't get arrested speed, but all-out, flat-out *speed*, a ragged-edge rapture that only the determined few will experience. On the salt you find the limits of your courage, you learn what daring greatly is all about, and understand why a Bonneville speed record is an internationally respected pedigree. Having cubic bundles of money is no guarantee of setting a salt record. Just ask Paul Newman. Salt success comes with salt experience—no substitutions allowed.

Andy Green, the bloke who snagged the land speed racer's ultimate bragging rights by driving a startling 763 miles per hour, past Mach 1, was left unfulfilled.

"You can do great things with a race car anywhere in the world," salt virgin Green told me during tea one day, "But what you do at Bonneville makes a record special. I don't want to be known as the only World Landspeed Record holder who hasn't driven at Bonneville."

Approach this collective history story like a new racing class where the record is open. It's not the whole story by any means—that would require an encyclopedic approach—but I am establishing the minimum with the hope that someone will come along and up the ante, make the story better, richer, fuller. For every story told about Bonneville, there at least three others: getting to Bonneville, going home from Bonneville, and making plans for Bonneville.

Starting in 1896, this is a historical overview of the fastest place on Earth, a chronicle of the determined and the speed that comes in its telling.*

May your courses be long and all your turn-outs be to the right.

*__SPEED NOTE:__ *It is essential to understand that the terminology, like the cars, describing Bonneville racing has continually evolved over the years. Full comprehension requires "tribal knowledge." Not wanting the reader to suffer any undue heartburn trying to keep up with the racer lingo, for the purpose of this book, the terminology used will refer to the period discussed. For example, the 1949 Burke-Francisco belly tank lakester was known as a streamliner.*

Chapter 1

From the Ice Age to the Train Age

The Formative Years

It was inevitable that someone would uncover the vast velocity prospects hiding in plain view on the desolate Bonneville Salt Flats. The earth had taken its sweet time, some 100,000 years, in building the world's biggest race track and then waited, patiently waited, 4,214 feet above sea level, until people with speed needs arrived.

Located immediately east of the Nevada-Utah border town of Wendover, the vast, ancient lake bed is a stark, glistening white plain that was once covered by a body of water 135 miles wide by nearly 325 miles long. Almost 3,000 square miles, it was formed during the last stages of the Ice Age and was as big as the Midwest's Lake Michigan is today.

To get an idea of its scope, think of Wendover as being situated on the western shore and Salt Lake City, 120 miles away, on the eastern shore. In between, the water was 1,000 feet deep. When the water evaporated, the minerals and salts remained behind, settling on the lowest areas. It is these sediments that make Bonneville the world's largest natural "dynamometer," a test track of immense proportions.

Mythomania swirls around which white guy was first to cross the forbidding flats—Kit Carson, John C. Fremont, or Jedediah Smith—but they were all second. The first inhabitants were Native Americans who arrived at the lake shore eons before. Danger Cave, just a mile from the heart of present-day Wendover, has given up artifacts that have been carbon dated to more than 11,000 years

What you can do,
or dream you can, begin it.
Boldness and genius has
power and magic in it.

—Goethe

old. The first inhabitants were making duck decoys about the same time the Israelites were strolling across the parted Red Sea.

Geologically speaking, the block-fault mountains of the Newfoundland Range are the key to how first the ancient lake, and then the salt beds, were formed. A couple of epochs ago, the entire West Coast from California to the Rocky Mountains was submerged, under carboniferous seas. During the Miocene Age, the earth's crust experienced centuries of shrinking, shifting, and upthrusting to form a closed circle, or basin, that trapped the sea water within.

The lake was later fed by numerous little glaciers that flowed down through the mountain peaks. Over time, as the damp and chilly climate warmed up, the glaciers dissolved and the water evaporated. The Great Salt Lake is the only residue of the once-gigantic Lake Bonneville. The story of the expiring inland sea is easily seen in "chapters" along the hillsides—remnants of three distinct shorelines etched into the mountains during periods of stable water levels. Landspeed racers often use the striped hillsides as backdrops when photographing their speed machines.

So straight and long are the "beaches" today, they mimic roads cut into the slopes at various heights, where fossilized sea shells can still be found. The highest, 5,220 feet above mean sea level, is the Bonneville Terrace and was the terminal height for the lake. The Provo Terrace, at 4,840 feet, was formed after a year-long flood caused a rapid erosion through the soil and rocks. Lowest is

Despite the appearance of a hard surface, much of the Bonneville Salt Flats perimeter is a thin, salt crust floating over very soft, wheel-sucking mud that easily breaks under the weight of a vehicle. When the Donner-Reed pioneer wagon train party attempted to cross the salt in 1846, its members lost a critical number of oxen and abandoned many personal articles in a flight for their lives. *Utah State Historical Society*

William "Big Bill" Rishel, 26, was a bombastic yet tireless promoter of the salt flats for auto racing purposes. Pictured here in 1896, he and pal Charlie Emise pedaled across the flats in the middle of the night, scouting a route for a transcontinental bicycle race. Awed by the snow-white surface, the pair cursed the flats when their bicycles became mired down in the gooey mud, stretching their 40-mile crossing to 22 grueling hours. *Utah State Historical Society*

Mineral production started in the Bonneville Salt Flats in the early 1900s, when the Montello Salt Company began extracting halite (rock salt). Except for a 17-year lull after World War I, the flats' geological infrastructure has been continually subjected to mining operations. *California State Automobile Association*

the Stansbury Terrace, located at 4,445 feet. Some have compared the withered lake to a big bathtub without a drain. The terraces are the "rings" left behind.

Originally, the salt ranged in thickness from 6 feet to 1/16 inch, as it graded and meandered into the surrounding mud flats. Subjected to a century of mineral mining and a variety of climatic changes, the once-beefy salt surface has dwindled to an anorexic state.

Mining started around the turn of the century, but when German shipments of potassium salts to the United States were halted during World War I, the Solvay Process Company erected a plant and began production with a vengeance in 1917. The tiny town of Salduro (Spanish for hard salt) popped up nearby. By 1920, it was the nation's largest producer. That same year, a mineral leasing law was enacted that still impacts the flats today. When supplies from Germany resumed, Solvay ceased operations and the 200 workers migrated to nearby Wendover. Mining resumed in 1938; a company called Bonneville Limited began extracting potash, a critical component in fertilizer, from the beds.

Racers of the 1920s learned the hard way about the difficulties of hammering spikes into the salt when trying to erect tents. Even today, it takes a two-handed, half-inch drill to bore through the rock hard, concrete-like surface. Racers know that hardness begets forgiveness during a spin-out. On dirt surfaces, a tire and wheel are more likely to dig in, putting the race car at greater risk of flipping and rolling. The granite-like salt helps to keep the car upright and, hopefully, only make the hapless driver dizzy. For the embarrassed few there is even an unofficial "Spin Out Club," complete with fraternity pins.

Summer temperatures climb above 100 degrees during the day, yet the mercury can drop below 50 degrees—all within a 24-hour period. There have been stories of tumbleweed spontaneously combusting on a hot day and a few smarty pants have even tried frying eggs without a fire. No matter how hot the air gets, the surface is always cool and moist to the touch—another boon for racing tires that build up friction heat at high speeds.

Bonneville will never be a hospitable place for human beings. The sun beats down ferociously, reflecting the rays back up. Skin under your nose, ear lobes, armpits and other unprotected, normally covered body parts burn easily. High grade SPF sun screen and plenty of fluids are essential. Shade is at a premium. Without eye protection, be ready for "salt blindness" because "bright" takes on new meaning here. Photographers are dumbfounded by the exaggerated light meter readouts.

Winter rains can bring up to 6,000 acres of standing water that doesn't evaporate until early summer. This stagnant water is an essential part of nature's annual "salt bed recovery" process, which manicures the surface smooth as the water evaporates. High winds assist with the drying-out process, and have been strong enough to suck off car covers, collapse steel-shade canopies like they were made of straw, and topple well-used portable toilets.

Nothing grows out of the crystalline salt beds except one's imagination and a few mirages—the product of a humongous, reflective pancake. It is so flat that you can observe the actual curvature of the earth with the naked eye. As the temperatures rise, so do the shimmering reflections, making some peaks look as though they are levitating above the barren, silent salt beds.

The mirages have driven men crazy with fear. Pioneer writer Edwin Bryant wrote vivid descriptions of his crossing, calling the

salt "a heaven-condemned waste" after nearly pitching a battle with mythical soldiers he and his companions "saw" on the beds. These deadly optical illusions drastically distorted distances for wagon train pioneers; what looked like 10 miles was sometimes triple the distance. Nothing quite made the point as well as the infamous Hastings' Cutoff, a wagon train shortcut that passed north of Floating Mountain, a mere 10 miles beyond where World Land Speed Records would be set. Developed by Lansford W. Hastings, a frontiersman with political ambitions in California, the cutoff engendered many sad stories, perhaps the saddest of which is that of the Donner Party in 1846. Just as today, where the salt crust was thin, it was easy to break through and get bogged down in the plastic-like mud. Not only did the merciless mud entrap the pioneers, it robbed them of precious time. This delay proved monstrous when a snowstorm marooned the Donner Party in the High Sierras above Reno, Nevada. Survival of the fittest never meant so much, and the 44 who lived through the winter did so only because they resorted to cannibalism. When word got out, travelers happily avoided the salt flats. American journalist Horace Greeley wrote of the salt flats in 1859, "If Uncle Sam should ever sell that tract of land for one cent per acre, he will swindle the purchaser outrageously."

Still, the Bonneville Salt Flats are an awe-inspiring geologic phenomenon. Sunrise and sunset are simply gorgeous, the hillsides burst with color and after a rainstorm, it is not uncommon to see full, 180 degree, vivid rainbows.

The First Racer Arrives

In 1896, the year Utah became a state, newspaper publisher William Randolph Hearst wanted to pump up circulation figures, so he concocted a publicity stunt to send a message from his offices at the *New York Journal* to the *San Francisco Examiner* via a courier in a transcontinental bicycle race. Back then, bicycle racing was big stuff. Horse-drawn buggies far outnumbered cranky, persnickety automobiles. The trendy choice of transport was the bicycle, replaced later by its snorting, motorized cousin, the motorcycle.

Hearst hired two prominent bicyclists, William D. Rishel and Charles A. Emise, to scout a route for the big race. Wanting to avoid the flats during the day, the duo set out at 2 A.M., guided by an old desert prospectors' map. Each carried two army canteens and some sandwiches. Under the glow of a full moon, they rolled northwest to southeast along the iridescent salt, pedaling their long-horned bicycles at speeds up to 20 miles per hour.

Captain Benjamin Louis Eulalie de Bonneville

That Captain Bonneville managed to get the salt flats named in his honor without ever seeing or setting foot on the pristine, crystalline surface tells you the guy wasn't a deadbeat. But who was he and why the honor?

Born in France around 1796, Bonneville and his mother fled to the United States after his father, a deputy in the French Assembly, was killed in the French Revolution. American patriot Thomas Paine was instrumental in assisting mother and child escape during Napoleon's rise to power. Paine was known to be Madam Bonneville's paramour and rumored to be Bonneville's father.

In America, the refugees were taken in by the Marquis de Lafayette, a French hero of the American Revolutionary War. With his help, young Bonneville attended West Point, where he graduated in 1815. He entered military service but remained friendly with Lafayette, who ignited the adventure spark early in the young captain's career.

Bonneville and his mother eventually moved to St. Louis, Missouri, where a large French-speaking population offered an aristocratic, genteel culture. After 15 years of military service on the frontier, Captain Bonneville secured a leave of absence in 1831 to enable him to explore the Oregon country and engage in the fur trade. The expedition lasted a little over three years, and Bonneville's deeds in the West were publicized by his friend, American author Washington Irving, in the 1837 book The Adventures of Captain Bonneville, U. S. A.

Captain Bonneville's hardy, well-seasoned expeditionary force included a band led by his chief lieutenant, Joseph R. Walker. It was Walker, leading a party of 40 men, who ensured his leader's place in history by scouting the territory that included the salt beds and later naming the area in his honor.

Bonneville's expedition was largely a failure, and he returned home to St. Louis in 1836 to resume his military career. He served gallantly during the Mexican War and was promoted to lieutenant colonel. In his mid-60s he took command of a St. Louis army post at the start of the Civil War. He was promoted to brigadier general when he was almost 70 years old and died a civilian in 1878 at the age of 82.

Bonneville served his adopted country long and well. While he may never have laid eyes on the ancient "trapped" lake that now bears his name, the honor was certainly well earned in other ways.

The first, timed racing event on the flats arrived in style courtesy of the Western Pacific Railroad, which transported the race cars, crew, and spectators to the middle of the salt beds. Nearly 200 people were on hand to witness the historic speed trials, touted as "A hair-raising, soul-gripping speed contest." *Utah State Historical Society*

1914. After being unloaded from the Denver and Rio Grande Rail cars, the racers begin to warm up their speedsters. A few of the locals from Wendover and the Salduro Mining Company have congregated to watch. *Utah State Historical Society*

The joy ride turned torturous when they hit the mud flats, and soon they were carrying their bicycles. The sun rose, and the heat along with it. The map proved unreliable, and the deep pool of promised water turned out to be a half-filled hand basin fed by a slow drip from a ledge above. Total time to cross: 22 hours. Because motorcars were little more than a curiosity at the time, Rishel said the idea of a motor speedway "never entered his head."

Rail connections became a priority with Western Pacific Railroad, and it resolved to "conquer" the flats by laying rails directly across the salt beds in 1907. This paved the way for increased access to the flats. Steam trains needed water as they chugged over the land, so a station was established at a sheep herder's stop by tapping into the pioneer water source at Pilot's Peak. The water was gravity-fed through a 26-mile pipeline, and the tiny village of Wendover winked into life. It was little more than a whistle stop back then, but the railroad eventually built a roundhouse and full-service yard for the steam trains.

Rishel, the first man to drive an automobile in Utah, came back in the summer of 1907, this time with two Salt Lake City

Crouching low to slip through the air, David Abbott Jenkins of Salt Lake City gives the Excelsior full throttle and accelerates to 80 miles per hour—bucking a head wind. Jenkins said the ride "gave my spinal cord more chills than any other run I have ever made on the salt flats." *Utah State Historical Society*

businessmen who had plans to promote a roadway and a little racing on the smooth surface. As "Big Bill" Rishel, now 37, peered at the beds through binoculars, he thought he saw a lake, and the trio returned to Salt Lake City. A few weeks later, an amused railroad conductor enlightened Rishel about mirages.

The First Motorcyclist

In 1910, the railroad began offering passenger service from Salt Lake City to San Francisco. Pious Utah state lawmakers deemed unlawful a scheduled prizefight between James Jefferies and Jack Johnson, forcing promoters to move their bout from Salt Lake City to Reno. A young carpenter named David Abbott "Ab" Jenkins was determined to see the pugilists pummel each other, so he hopped on his Yale motorcycle and headed West.

"There wasn't much romance accompanying the occasion," declared Jenkins of his 30-mile jaunt over the wooden railroad ties to avoid knee-deep mud. "Like a bronco-busting cowboy, I approached the salt beds on the railway tracks, riding onto the beds on a bumping, jumping motorcycle." Unless some of the railroad people beat him to it, Jenkins is generally considered to be the first person to "drive" across the Bonneville Salt Flats.

"It was the biggest thrill I ever got on the salt beds," said Jenkins of the 60-mile-per-hour jaunt, "bigger than any I ever had while

driving an automobile." First it was a cow-powered wagon wheel, then a human-powered bicycle tire, and now the first motorized vehicle zipped across the salt.

And Now for the First Car . . .

Convincing Wendover resident Ferg Johnson to take his Packard out on the salt flats, Rishel came back again in 1911. This time, the pair "rode the rails" until they found a way onto the salt and then "let 'er rip," to squeeze 50 miles per hour out of the big car. Both men were astounded; it was like flying on a bullet in those days. From then on, for decades to come, Rishel was unwavering in the promotion of the salt beds as a racing venue.

"We were all alone in the world," wrote Rishel about the salt romp. "The immensity and the solitude were overpowering and the velocity of the car was fantastic. When we reached the horizon it seemed as though we would topple off into nothingness." At the time, neither realized that they had just inked a permanent spot for themselves in the annals of racing history, by being the first motorcar to open a throttle across the salt.

In 1912, Rishel took A. L. Westgard, national pathfinder for the National Trails Association, for a spin on the beds. From his experience, the nationally prominent and well-respected Westgard declared Bonneville "The greatest speedway on the Earth." Sadly,

13

The Blitzen Benz riding mechanic leans against the rear tire as driver "Terrible Teddy" Tetzlaff poses with Utah Governor William Spry after taking the politician for a high-speed jaunt across the salt flats in 1914. Tetzlaff had just "unofficially" bettered Bob Burman's World Landspeed Record of 141.73 miles per hour by 1/5 second. Note the immense chain drive transmission. *Utah State Historical Society*

his remarks fell flatter than the salt beds, and again the saline plain was forgotten.

Jenkins took another bike ride in June 1914, this time with an Excelsior, a bike with "much more vinegar in its system," that accelerated to 80 miles per hour—bucking a head wind. "The force of the wind would not permit me to sit up in the saddle," he told newspaper reporters, "so I grabbed a firm grip on the two handles and spread my body straight out, as though driving on a child's snow sled, stiffened my legs and gave her the works . . . 50 . . . 60 . . . 70 . . . and 80! That was traveling, and the ride gave my spinal cord more chills than any other run I have ever made on the salt flats."

That same year, on June 17, all of Wendover turned out for the "Wedding of the Wires" party when Nevada's Bell Telephone and Mountain States Telephone and Telegraph completed the last link in a coast-to-coast hookup of telephone line. The three-day bash served up roast duck, and on the Nevada side, the champagne flowed like a gusher (Utah was a "dry" state). From that moment on,

the sound of the human voice could be transmitted from the Atlantic to the Pacific at speeds approaching the speed of light. The line was officially dedicated on January 25, 1915, when Alexander Graham Bell in New York called Mr. Watson in San Francisco to reenact their famous first telephone call.

The First Race . . . at World Record Speed

Rishel knew what he knew, and he meant to make others see the speed potential of the salt beds. In 1914, racing promoter Ernie Moross brought a fleet of eight racing machines to Salt Lake City, a motor circus of speed exhibitions touring the West. The jewel of the stable was the mighty 2.5-liter, 300-horsepower record-setting Blitzen Benz, once driven by Barney Oldfield, but now under the command of "Terrible Teddy" Tetzlaff, a noted lead foot of the day. Billie Carlson, Harry Goetz, and Wilbur D'Alene drove a collection of Marmon Wasps and Maxwells.

The Salt Lake City Rotary and Commercial Club solicited the railroad's help in transporting the cars to the salt for some exhibition runs. The deal was simple: If the promoters could sell 100 railway tickets, the railroad company would haul the race cars and crews out to the salt and back. Ads in the local papers announced:

A hair-raising, thrilling, soul-gripping speed contest. This run is not phony—everything is square, honest and above board. Bring your own watches and check up on the official timers. You'll get the kick of a lifetime!

Sales were halted at 150 tickets for the August 11 speed event. Among the ticket holders were Governor William Spry of Utah, who went for a spin on the salt with Tetzlaff. A number of motorcycles from Salt Lake City dealers were also on hand, including a Mr. Ward who rode an Indian through a half-mile in 19 seconds.

Timing was done with a series of stopwatches. As invited, many spectators also brought their own, so nearly two dozen watches were snapped on the cars. Flag men were positioned at each end of the measured mile, with the official timer in the middle at the half-mile mark where they could see both flags. From a rolling start, the first flag dropped as the car passed the starting line. The timer clicked the split-second watch into action, clicking again when he saw the second flag drop.

Promoters were hoping to uncrown emperor of speed "Wild Bob" Burman, who had traveled 141.73 miles per hour in the Blitzen Benz at Daytona Beach in 1911. On his first attempt, Tetzlaff matched Burman's record speed exactly but only needed 25 2/5 seconds to do so. Tetzlaff was 1/5 second quicker than Burman had been, and his half-mile speed was higher—142.8 miles per hour! Spectators reported times from 25 flat to 34 2/5 seconds, but few were as well positioned as the official timer to see the synchronization of the flags.

All in attendance were astonished. The local papers reported, "So fast was the Benz going that it was scarcely possible to distinguish the driver and mechanic. For a mile, it was nothing but a white blur."

A blur? The writer may have been guilty of a little embellishment, but the speed run had nonetheless ushered in an epochal chapter to auto racing. For the first time, a speed trial was recorded on the Bonneville Salt Flats. Sweeter still, Tetzlaff set the salt pace by knocking out a world record speed.

The speed went unrecorded in the record books, then managed by the American Automobile Association (AAA) Contest Board, because despite advance approval for the event, no "official observer" from the Contest Board was on-site to verify the reported speeds. Having the sole authority for sanctioning automobile events of any nature, the Contest Board wielded tremendous power.

This naturally set the stage for power-basing and controversy. According to Southern California Automobile Club archives, its directors became exasperated with the domineering AAA policies and actions, and renounced its AAA affiliation in 1915. "Both the American Automobile Association and the Automobile Club of America gave the record a chilled shoulder," said Rishel. With that, the Salt Flats faded into racing oblivion for another decade.

An admiring group of "flat hats" pose with Wilbur D'Alene, driver of the Marmon racer that had just sped through the half-mile in 19.2 seconds. Marmon had just introduced its honking great 9.3-liter six-cylinder engine, reported to have produced 48 horsepower. *Utah State Historical Society*

The Western Pacific Railroad yard in Wendover, 1907. A roundhouse was erected along with a machine shop and log cabins. Wendover was so named because Nevada and Idaho sheepherders would 'wend' their flocks south 'over' the open range to winter grazing lands. John Cooley's rustic eating place served the traveling ranchers. The Nevada side of the town was originally called Eastlines. *Utah State Historical Society*

Chapter 2

If You Build it, Are they Supposed to Come?

News of "Terrible Teddy" Tetzlaff's world-record-level speeds attained on the salt beds soon spread throughout the racing community, sowing seeds of curiosity about the god-forsaken western wasteland that gobbled up wheel spin and spit out speed. In the August 20, 1914, issue, *Motor Age* magazine called Bonneville Salt Flats "smooth as the proverbial billiard table and hard as a cement highway" and predicted that "soon salt-bed racing will completely displace beach racing."

Ormond Beach in Florida, better known as Daytona, was the current world-record-speed site, having easily displaced all British and French locations with its 25-mile course length. Although tides always demanded negotiating and wind was a constant pest, Daytona had hotels, shops, eateries, indoor plumbing, and, most importantly, good roads!

The Bonneville Salt Flats had nothing of the sort. All the stagecoach roads established the previous century—Hastings, Beckwith, and Overland Stage—had all long been abandoned. Even the wild horses that roamed the area were never seen crossing the salt. It was doubtful that the snowy white, smooth-as-a-ballroom-floor surface had a cheap chance in hell of becoming the cynosure of world speedsters.

Before the turn of the century, when "Big Bill" Rishel first pedaled across the flats, only 500 automobiles were registered

*He who strives never perishes.
I have implicit faith in that promise.
Though, therefore, from my weakness
I fail a thousand times,
I shall not lose faith.*

–Mahatma Gandhi

nationally. By the time Tetzlaff came to Bonneville, that number climbed to 5 million, and in the early 1920s registrations had tripled to 15 million. The United States was rapidly becoming a nation on wheels. Powerful private industrialists, all affiliated with the emerging automotive business, pushed Washington to get the country connected by road.

Rishel was just the man to help. The image of prizefighter Jack Dempsey, he was a big, imposing man with thick features and hair. Already famous for his "Rishel's Routes," he had mapped thousands of miles of motor routes and knew that a roadway was key to bringing the racing world to the salt.

The Lincoln Highway was under construction from the east, but forces were diligently at work to make the cross-country highway turn south at Salt Lake City and route through Ely, Nevada, bypassing the salt beds altogether. The Victory Highway, organized in Kansas to honor those who fought and gave their lives in World War I, favored the route that would cut straight across to Wendover.

Supporters for each highway squared off against each other, and an unholy, bitter battle for approval and funding ensued. For a decade they argued and fought, and the situation escalated into a political war. Everything hinged on Utah's designating the road that would best serve the American motoring

Left to right, dressed in "working whites" of the day, Utah Governor George Dern, Secretary of Agriculture William Jardine, and Nevada Governor J. Schrugham clear away the remaining salt barrier to officially open the Victory Highway, thus ending a 20-year battle to build a road across the salt flats. Motorsports enthusiasts believed the road would attract interest from the racing community—something that would not happen for another decade. *California State Automobile Association*

A unique feature of the Victory Highway construction was found in the all-wood culverts used at intervals in 24-foot-high road embankments. Because the salt quickly eats away iron and steel, engineers used heavy timber box drains, some of which are still in place seven decades later, and can be seen from Interstate 80. *California State Automobile Association*

public as a primary route. More importantly, primary routes got federal funding.

The president of Goodyear Tire & Rubber Company, who favored the Lincoln Highway route, jumped in and donated $100,000 to the cause. On the opposing side was the Salt Lake City Rotary Club, who, together with Rishel, convinced government decision makers that the Victory Highway with its "Wendover Cutoff" should be selected, mainly because it would reduce the road project by 99.4 miles. Rishel's crowd won the fight, and the wild 40-mile stretch over the salt beds would soon be tamed.

The Wendover cutoff section, just like the railway line, was built directly upon the heavy rock salt bed, using the notorious, slimy clay mud excavated immediately next to the roadway. Blair and Ed Lamus, Wendover construction men who won the contract to build the salt section, knew that the gooey mud would produce a thoroughly satisfactory subgrade for the road when dried. Lamus shared the knowledge with highway engineer Lee Wendelboe, and the discovery helped reduce the cost to a mere $9,000 per mile, far below the average of the day. The construction method was considered unique and the Wendorer Cutoff became the fastest stretch anywhere on the Victory Highway route.

As Lamus and his crew were pushing across "The Great White Way" in the summer of 1924, U.S. Army Lieutenant Maughan paid the road crew a visit. Lieutenant Maughan was making his historic "daylight to dark" flight from New York to San Francisco, and he landed on the salt beds in the early evening to refuel.

Victory Highway, Victorious Car

To commemorate the completion of Victory Highway, a ribbon cutting was scrapped in favor of a barrier breakthrough. A

huge arch of glittering salt was erected directly over the roadway at Wendover. Two governors and a member of the president's cabinet were given shovels and told to get busy clearing away a sizable pile of salt blocking the roadway.

A few days before the "shovelfest," at a Salt Lake City Rotary luncheon, Rishel had asked Jenkins to race the special excursion train from Salt Lake City to Wendover, some 125 miles. Jenkins countered with a bet of $250 that he could beat the train. Before dessert was served, the Rotarians had raised the money.

A large crowd gathered downtown at the Denver & Rio Grande Railway Station on June 13, 1925. Dignitaries on the train included Secretary of Agriculture William Jardine, Utah Governor George Dern, and Nevada Governor J. Schrugham. The Salt Lake City mayor, using a whistle and a flag, started the race.

Jenkins took off behind the wheel of a black Studebaker roadster shod with the newly developed balloon tires. Next to him sat Miss McCafferty, secretary to T. W. Naylor, the local Studebaker dealer, who had climbed in by chance just a few moments before the start of the race. In the back seat was native Englishman turned Salt Lake City policeman Tommy Dee.

As Jenkins passed each of the 15 railroad crossings, Dee's job was to toss out a small bag of flour that would splatter onto the ground. If the train riders saw white, they knew the car was in the lead. The term "Victory Highway" must have applied to those who made it to Wendover and still had a car to drive.

Even with 12-inch ground clearance, Jenkins repeatedly scraped the undercarriage. Hanging on for dear life itself was "spindly little" Officer Dee, clinging to the strap in the back. Jenkins noted that "Dee twisted and turned like a circus chimpanzee on a trapeze bar, and twice was thrown into the front seat headfirst."

As it worked out, the train passengers always saw flour when they came to a crossing. Rattling into town under the arch like an untuned brass band, Jenkins and crew arrived in Wendover 2 hours and 40 minutes later—5 minutes before the train puffed into town. Motorists normally took 5 1/2 hours to make the same trip.

Across the salt beds, the railway ran dead straight for more than 10 miles. A large crowd of motorists had gathered in advance, on the western edge, to engage the train in some sport of their own. Driving alongside, at the back of the train, cars on the salt would start, overtake the train, fall back, and then overtake it again and again. All the while, horns honked, the locomotive's bell clanged, and passengers cheered from the windows and from in between cars.

Following the formal dedication ceremonies, Jenkins staged an impromptu race with 10 cars out on the salt. Believe it or not, the winner of the "quickie" race was the governor of Utah. It was this event that made Jenkins perceive the tremendous possibilities of the salt beds.

He investigated and came to understand that the salt crust was like a great lake of frozen ice "suspended" at the bottom of the bowl-shaped basin, atop a fine, but treacherous carbonate mud base. He once misjudged the salt crust during an outing with a roadster, and spent 8 hours extracting the car. That part of the Bonneville experience remains unchanged.

Despite the new highway, no racing came to the salt flats for another seven years. During a 1928 visit to the AAA headquarters in Washington, D.C., Jenkins tried in vain to convince Ted Allen, AAA Contest Board Secretary, of Bonneville's virtues. Allen was not impressed. As a native Utahan, he knew the flats were a goodly long way from civilization. "From all the reports I have heard, the salt course just isn't practical," he said, ending the discussion. The future of the salt flats racing was bleak.

Later that year, Indianapolis Speedway Champion Frank Lockhart died a horrific death at Daytona when a tire exploded on his Stutz Black Hawk race car. The wheel dug into the sand and launched the car into a sickening display of brutal, somersaulting aerobatics. His body was ejected from the car, landing practically at the feet of his petrified watching wife. Long before the days of chrome-molybdenum roll cages, safety harnesses, and helmets, Lockhart made the ultimate sacrifice for his sport. He was the "up-from-poverty" hero that many still believe would have easily stripped Sir Malcolm Campbell of his World Land Speed Crown, had he lived. Had the tire blown at Bonneville, where there was plenty of room to "spin out," he might have survived.

Racing engines were becoming so powerful that speeds in excess of 145 miles per hour would usually induce a centrifugal force that sent the cars flying up and over the edge of shallow-banked board tracks. The tracks were fairly skinny as well—seldom more than 40 feet wide—leaving little safety margin during a spin-out.

Jenkins knew that these serious safety concerns evaporated at the Bonneville Salt Flats; he had determined that the safe racing area measured 10 by 15 miles. If dikes built for the mining of potash could be removed, the racing area could be even larger.

He also knew that even though the moist, concrete-like salt reduced traction slightly, its wonderful cooling effects on tires extended not only their useful life, but allowed for greater speeds than were possible on concrete, dirt, or board tracks of the day. Nobody wanted to listen, until Jenkins hit upon an idea that really attracted attention.

Endearing Enduro—The First 24-Hour Race

In 1931, Pierce-Arrow discovered that its new 12-cylinder car was embarrassingly less powerful than their "regular" eight-cylinder model and turned to Jenkins for help. After coaxing 40 more "horses" out of the car, raising its horsepower from a paltry 130 to 175, Jenkins convinced company big wigs to let him take

Road gangs slowly grade across 40 miles of "The Great White Way," using excavating equipment belonging to Solvay Process Company, a large salt and chemical works at nearby Salduro. Although crude by today's standards, the gravel surface was considered luxurious and became the fastest stretch of road along the transcontinental motor route. *California State Automobile Association*

the car to Bonneville and really prove the twelve's performance.

Next, he contacted the AAA Contest Board for permission to make the runs official. The AAA stalled, still unconvinced that the salt was suitable for racing. When pressed, it gave the terse reply, "Not sufficient time to make arrangements."

Jenkins would not be thwarted; he rounded up a few enthusiastic supporters and headed for the salt. The Utah State Road Commission surveyed and then scraped smooth a 10-mile circular track and marked it off with 4-foot stakes spaced 100 feet apart. Steel wedges were required to drive holes into the rock-hard salt surface, but they would blunt as they were forced into unyielding salt. The course was lit for night driving, using 20 small, evenly spaced oil flares. Dressed in white cotton duck pants and shirt topped with a leather jacket, Jenkins donned a cotton skullcap and two pairs of goggles, and climbed into the hopped-up motorcar, now sans its fenders and windshield.

Driving a black Studebaker, Ab Jenkins races a train from Salt Lake, 125 miles west to Wendover. Clinging to the strap in the back seat was Salt Lake Police Officer Dee who lobbed a small bag of flour over the side at every railroad crossing so the train passengers would know who was ahead. Jenkins and crew beat the train by five minutes. *Jenkins Family Collection*

AAA rules required stopwatches for timing trials of more than 10 miles. Jack Allen, brother of the AAA Contest Board Secretary Ted Allen, Bill Rishel, now with the Utah State Automobile Club, and Gus Backman, Salt Lake City Chamber of Commerce Secretary-Treasurer, timed the runs.

Jenkins stopped for gas 12 times, experienced no mechanical trouble, and never changed a tire or got up from behind the wheel the entire 24 hours, even though the constant roar of the engine made him temporarily deaf. Temperatures soared above 100 degrees and timers took turns resting in an old sheepherder's wagon, but Jenkins' only protection was a thick coating of grease slathered over his hands and face. Hanging onto his sanity under the light of a full moon proved the big hurdle.

"Shadows were cast over the sparkling salt," he noted. "Sometimes they took the form of huge walls. I thought I was steering right into them. I could almost hear the sound of the crash." Other times he would swear the railroad tracks rerouted themselves onto the race course and that a locomotive was crossing directly over his path of travel. "An airline beacon on one of the far hills would mock me by changing position on every lap."

Immediately after the endurance run, Jenkins jumped into a waiting airplane that took him straight to a Salt Lake City Chamber luncheon. He walked in, on time, and Chamber President A. Brown, who had called the attempt "preposterous," was now full of kind, tactful remarks. Unfortunately, Ab was still deaf as a stone statue and never heard a word.

Pierce-Arrow executives laughed when Jenkins told them he was going to log 2,400 miles in 24 hours. Instead, the ideal salt surface yielded 2,710 miles and he averaged 112.935 miles per hour to set a new 24-hour average speed mark on September 18-19, 1932.

The newspapers refused to publish the account for a full week because it considered the feat just a publicity stunt. Worse, the AAA, which had gone on record as saying that racing on a salt expanse was "absurd," sanctioned Jenkins with a $500 fine or a year's suspension for making the run without their "permission." Jenkins paid the fine. When later asked how he was able to complete such a grueling feat, he credited his mother and his abstinence from tobacco and alcohol, forbidden by the Church of Jesus Christ of Latter-day Saints, of which he was a devout member.

The 1932 Jenkins pit area during the first timed runs. The observation plane flies between the Salt Lake City Chamber of Commerce and Pierce Arrow tents. The wooden observation stand is for the KSL radio station broadcaster. To the right can be seen the gravity-feed fuel barrels. Utah State Historical Society

Chapter 3

Daytona's Demise is Bonneville's Sunrise

For anyone to conduct a speed trial without Contest Board approval was either daring or dumb, especially if you entertained any thoughts of running at other AAA accredited events. The sanctioning body was the absolute authority in the United States when it came to blessing all things fast. The board licensed the cars and the drivers and determined venue suitability. Jenkins' boldness paid off; he had proven that the unknown speedway was not only worthy, but tantalizingly fast. Salt racing posterity owes him a debt of gratitude.

Jenkins went back to the salt in 1933 with AAA sanctioning. He snapped up 56 new records in one attempt on the 10-mile circle track. The feat riveted the attention of European racers. Foremost among them was British fur broker and racing driver John Rhodes Cobb, who immediately made plans to personally inspect the salt beds. The Londoner wanted to see firsthand where 14 world, 14 International, and 24 American class records had fallen in one day on the first attempt. Rising speed potential made tracks in Europe woefully inadequate for endurance contests.

Jenkins found that "legitimizing" his 1932 records was not as easy as the 1932 runs. In the early morning hours of August 7, more than halfway through the run, the car's right rear tire blew out at 123 miles per hour. It exploded with such force that the black-and-silver roadster was jerked into a wicked swerve, cannonballing a reverberating echo through the mountain slopes.

One day we shall endow chariots with incredible speed without the aid of any animal.

—Roger Bacon,
a 13th monk who narrowly escaped heresy charges for tinkering in things scientific

Spectators were paralyzed with fear. Still 3 miles from the pits, the 54-year-old driver never lifted his foot and won the fight to bring the car back on course. He pitted without further excitement. Mechanics changed the wheel, added fuel and oil, and let him go 3 minutes later. The official stopwatches were ticking, always ticking. No time to lose! Gotta, go. Bye, bye!

The run was not all such high drama. When Jenkins got bored, he would dash off a quick note from the tablet secured to the center of the steering wheel and send it flying as he passed the pit area. One of the crew would retrieve the slip of paper to see what the boss wanted.

Once he directed the crew to send a telegram to a friend in New York. Another asked for a pint of ice cream. Considering the desert heat, a crew member beat it back to town for the frozen "Mormon heroin." The note also bade a crewman to run alongside the car and hand off the bag as he passed the pit—at over 100 miles per hour. When Jenkins reached for the bag, his hand smashed it to smithereens, numbing his arm for hours.

Then there was the mouse note. No one could find the alleged varmint out on the course, but Jenkins insisted, specifying at precisely which barrel the little rascal was trying to shade itself from the blazing sun. Sure enough, the delirious mouse was rescued, but it was too far gone. The crew held a little burial ceremony for its furry comrade with full racing honors. That's some eyesight

Ab Jenkins never left the pits without a fresh supply of note paper tucked under the elastic band in the center of his steering wheel. He would scribble notes while traveling at speeds in excess of 100 miles per hour and toss them out when he passed the pit area. Crew members were always on the lookout for a flying Ab notation. *Jenkins Family Collection*

Knight of the Realm Sir Malcolm Campbell streaks across the flats on his way to a new World Land Speed Record of 301.13 miles per hour on September 3, 1935. The first flying mile record attempted and set on the salt, it elevated Bonneville to leadership position as the world's fastest speedway. *Utah State Historical Society/Robin Richardson*

at 125 miles per hour. Ab's wife, Evelyn, his sister Mae, and daughter Ruth saw that Ab received his liquid vitality, milk and orange juice, the only nourishment he would take while at the wheel!

With 2 hours left to go on the 24-hour record, lightning flashed and angry clouds unloaded a gale-force storm onto the salt beds. The winds sent tents whirling across the flats like autumn leaves, flags were torn from their poles, and the timer's stand was rocking in the spitting, sideways rain. Jenkins struggled to keep the car away from the 4-foot wooden stake course markers, held in place by steel wedges.

"We better stop him," concluded AAA officials Ted Allen, Art Pillsbury, and Gordon Betz, who had taken to their cars for shelter. The timers were huddled under a piece of canvas. Jenkins, who already had nailed more world and international records than any two drivers combined, would not stop. The officials sat in grim

silence . . . if Jenkins would not stop, they were obliged to remain at their posts. One cannot help but wonder if Jenkins took any amusement in the fact that it was now he who was making the AAA Contest Board wait.

"Dad didn't have to drive the entire 10-mile circle in the rain, only when he was running near the pit area," recalled Jenkin's son Marvin, a lad of 13 at the time. "Only a portion of the course near the pits and timers was deluged, and the salt was a lot harder back then."

As Jenkins was nearing the end of his speed trial, with practically a box-stock car, the sun came out. Finishing 2,710 miles, the distance of his entire 1932 run, in 23 hours and 2 minutes, he was a full hour ahead of the previous year's schedule, despite the blowout and drenching.

Spectators made their way to the finish line, but iron-butt Jenkins ignored the "last lap" signal. Had the poor guy cracked?

Was he in a dizzy stupor? Why wouldn't he stop? A few laps later, Jenkins signaled the timers with a raised hand that pointed straight ahead—an inimitable gesture for which he became well known.

The mechanics understood and sat down to relax. Puzzled, the score keepers eventually figured out that Jenkins was after another record; the 3,000-mile mark could be toppled if he could hang tough for 90 minutes more. Even then, when it was over, with 60 new world-speed records in tow, Jenkins added on one more lap for safety.

The bag of tricks wasn't empty yet. During the last pit stop, Marvin had slipped Pops a safety razor and a tube of shaving cream. As Ab unlatched the door and stepped out, the crowd was dumbfounded, because the mighty driving man was sporting a clean-shaven grin!

Many simply refused to believe one man could have driven throughout. After all, the records set on the Montlhery track, near Paris, had required as many as five drivers. The French, the biggest skeptics, would have gone cuckoo had they also known Jenkins' age and, even more outrageous, that he had never drank alcohol, smoked, nor sipped tea or coffee. If there was a testament to clean living, the Welsh Mormon was it.

Collecting the Kudos

Captain George E. T. Eyston, in his book, *Speed on Salt*, declared, "Not only did this record prove that Jenkins was a man of exceptional endurance, but that his native salt flats offered advantages which were not to be found either at Brooklands or Montlhery." Later that year, Harry Hartz and Wilbur Shaw, two highly regarded drivers of the day, wasted no time and tested the mettle of the new speedway themselves. Driving the newly introduced Chrysler Airflow Type-CU, fitted with an eight-cylinder 298-cubic inch displacement engine, the duo shattered a total of 72 Class B records. Over the 24-hour period, the stock car averaged 84 miles per hour, traveling 2,205 miles. It was the smallest of the Airflows, but the new, aerodynamic shape, featuring integrated headlamps and a concealed luggage compartment in the rear, helped make up for the lack of horsepower. Hartz, a national champion, commented on Bonneville's superior racing surface: "Its freedom from dust—hard, solid, and smooth; the salt base, which retains moisture and thereby exercises a cooling influence on the tires; its outstanding safety factor in having so much room, all go to make this the greatest racing track in the world."

Building the *Ab Jenkins Special*, a 235-horsepower Pierce-Arrow 12 that had "more blueprints than a house," Jenkins was back at the salt in August 1934 and improved his 24-hour marks. He averaged 127 miles per hour and covered 3,053 miles—226 more than in 1933.

Off to Detroit for a voice-over session at Metropolitan Studios, Jenkins put the final touches on his first "salt talkie," a film about the record runs. While in town, he met celebrated race car designer Reid Railton. The Englishman was the architect of both Campbell's and Cobb's cars. So impressed with Jenkins was Railton that he agreed to come to the salt the following year.

Jenkins next approached Malcolm Campbell, the most celebrated racing driver of the time, whose hobby had already brought him eight World Land Speed Records. The speed king, son of a wealthy diamond merchant, dreamed of setting a five-mile-per-minute pace. Campbell's latest car was powered by a 7-foot-long, 1,630-pound Rolls Royce V-12 engine that produced 2,500 horsepower. The driveshaft was geared off to the side to allow Campbell to sit lower in the 13-foot 8-inch wheelbase car. Measuring 28 feet 3 inches in length, it weighed close to 11,000 pounds. Mechanical brakes were supplemented with air-brake flaps behind the rear wheels to help stop the behemoth.

Campbell fitted a lever in the enclosed cockpit that actuated a sliding metal curtain closing the nose slit in the ram air feed to the radiator. The idea was to temporarily streamline the front of the car while in the flying mile. This little gadget was used only once.

Named after a play written by Maeterlinck entitled *The Bluebird*, this was the best of Campbell's racing squadron. However, Daytona's soft, undulating sand was robbing the car of precious speed by inducing gobs of wheel spin. Think of a tiger trying to catch a rabbit on a highly polished surface and you get the idea.

Jenkins arrived in the middle of Campbell's Daytona problems and then spent three weeks in Florida proselytizing on behalf of the salt beds. After viewing the salt beds film, Campbell was impressed, but in typical, reticent British fashion, he remained uncommitted. It wasn't until Jenkins paid another visit, bringing

On the left is the tire-mounting equipment for the Firestone Balloons, and in back are two of the gasoline barrels Jenkins had shipped from the East Coast with his special blend. Mechanics needed energy to work all day in the blazing sun. Note the Milky Way candy bar box under the bench on the right. *Jenkins Family Collection*

"I took a wild ride in one of those things," were Ab Jenkins last words when he passed away in 1956. Here in 1935, he fuels the Allis-Chalmers farm tractor that he drove to a world-class record of 68 miles per hour in the summer of 1935, one of most thrill-packed experiences of his life. Son Marvin, with puckered lips, far right, helps Dad with the fueling procedure. *Jenkins Family Collection*

along Cord Corporation President Roy Faulkner, that Campbell promised to bring *Bluebird* to the salt later that year. The salt would, at long last, have its chance!

Word of Britain's racing knight coming to Utah caused quite a stir. On September 2, 1935, despite the remote location, an enormous crowd (for tiny Wendover) had assembled to witness as history got a hard, deep mark etched into it.

At the edge of the salt, hundreds had slept in their cars or tents overnight. Others had motored through the night and kept arriving all morning. Native Americans came in from the wilderness, ranchers and farmers left their daily chores undone, and city dwellers from three states poured in to watch. Though no official tally was made, several reports estimated 2,000 people watched Campbell's first runs.

The town of Wendover, population 400, with its white line painted on Wendover Boulevard marking the state line, was besieged. Anna and Bill Smith's Cobble Stone Café and Service Station (later the State Line) ran out of food. This was a spot that was always open, where the light was always on for the traveler, and

which usually operated just fine with a single station attendant, waitress, and cook.

Campbell and crowd changed that in a hurry. Smith's wife started cooking and serving; she pushed a mop so hard it broke in two pieces. The Western Service down the street had a café with a counter and a half-dozen tables. The lone "tourist attraction" was on nearby Three Mile Hill. Ira Eugene Wines, the son of a Pony Express rider, had carved his initials "EW" 20 feet high onto the eastern face nearly a century before. Only the E remained, but few understood its origin.

The dusty streets were jammed with spectators. Hordes of radio broadcasters, reporters, and photographers arrived. Movie cameras rolled, hoping to capture exciting newsreel footage for the folks back home. Airplanes droned overhead surveying the spectacle below. The whole affair had a circus-like air to it.

Out on the salt, wood-framed, canvas-covered tents made great sleeping quarters and refuges from the sun. Huge iceboxes held an array of fresh food to rival fine restaurants. Marv Jenkins chuckled about the racers' camp, "It sure was luxury camping back then."

In a way, when the racing crowd flocked to the town, little Wendover experienced much the same metamorphosis the tiny town of Gerlach, Nevada, would go through some 60 years later, when the world-speed battle would leave Bonneville for the Black Rock Desert. But for now, the hubbub was a-boilin', the air crackled with anticipation, and the collective imagination of the sidelines craned its neck waiting to see *Bluebird* fly.

Although he was wearing dark glasses, the glare off the surface made Campbell squint as he came out to inspect the course on Monday, September 2. He marveled at what little preparation was required to scrape the salt surface perfectly smooth. Campbell had requested that an 8-inch-wide line of diesel oil be sprayed the length of the course—the first time the salt was marked in this fashion. He would run in the morning, when the air was cool and crisp, maximizing the acceleration potential. The champion expected some power loss in the thinner, high-elevation air, but oh, what a place, what space upon which to race! Mechanics Leo Villa, Harry Leach, W. Hicks, and A. E. Poyser, fearful of a spin-out, warned Campbell to stay below 180 miles per hour.

As the cacophonous roar of the Rolls-Royce engine bled into the silence of the flats, a cheer went up from the onlookers. Campbell was feeling his oats, spectators were safely ensconced almost a half-mile away, the car was right, and the course was so inviting that the mechanics' warnings seemed silly. At 90 miles per hour, he shifted into second and then at 200 miles per hour, he moved into high gear. *Bluebird* responded by easily scampering up to 240 miles per hour.

At the far end, positioned opposite the center of the timing traps, sat British racing driver Capt. George Eyston, who would take to salt with his giant lizard of a car dubbed *Speed of the Wind* once Campbell was finished. Eyston described the test run this way:

A great cloud of salt blew in the wake of *Bluebird*. It was the first intimation I had of the car's arrival. . . . As the car roared by it seemed to swish past and glide into the distance in a seemingly effortless spurt, the engine emitting a smooth crackle.

Marvin Jenkins remembers *Bluebird's* song:

It was an awesome thing and made quite a racket when it started. The British didn't have any experience running on the salt. There was a lot of black smoke pouring out the exhaust, because the mechanics hadn't compensated for the altitude and the engine was running too rich.

The run was so impressive that Campbell scheduled a record attempt for the following morning after removing parts of the wheel fairings to prevent a salt buildup. Campbell himself learned a tender lesson about the salt beds, emerging from the car with a cherry red face, burnt by the reflecting sunshine. Tomorrow's checklist would include a protective grease job for the driver's face and hands.

Ab Jenkins—Our Father, who art of the salt...

Without a doubt, David Abbott Jenkins (1883-1956) was the father of salt racing. It was his dogged determination that put the Bonneville Salt Flats on the international racing map, not to mention the hundreds of speed marks he set there proving the salt's worth. Considering his limited resources, Jenkins enjoyed remarkable achievements. What distinguished him from his contemporaries was his precise use of local, "tribal" salt knowledge and unlimited guts. He was a deeply religious man who put his faith in God, and by God, he went far.

Born January 25, 1883, in Spanish Forks, Utah, Jenkins was often oxymoronically called "The World's Safest Speedster." As holder and breaker of more world records than any other driver, past or present, he was prouder of his million-mile "no accident" street driving record than all his speed and endurance records combined. His watchwords were simple: "Safety First." Still good advice today.

His circle of friends was a testament to his congenial, outgoing nature. Harvey Firestone was an avid admirer. He became pals with Metropolitan Opera Singer Richard Bonelli when they were working as mechanics before Bonelli discovered he could sing. Bonelli would attend many of Jenkins' speed runs, and invariably a music fest would ensue, with everyone joining Bonelli in singing. Imagine that, a salt opera!

Decades later, no one has toppled Jenkins' exhausting, 48-hour endurance record. As for the marks that have fallen, it required the efforts of several drivers compared to Jenkins' one-man driving shows.

Once considered Utah's "one-man public relations machine," Jenkins' racing fame got him elected mayor of Salt Lake City in 1940 without ever giving a speech or spending a nickel on a campaign. He served until 1944.

Ab Jenkins was certainly the first person to catch "salt fever," and luckily he passed it on to succeeding generations with a need for speed. When Jenkins died at age 73, on August 9, 1956, the world was a little slower for his having left it.

Daytona was finished as a World Record site; compared to Bonneville, it was a stubby sliver. From this moment on, all eyes would be on the salt when World Land Speed Records were sought. Here, Bonneville's brightest shining moment was about to unfold, but where was the man most responsible for making it so?

Ab Jenkins was conspicuous by his absence, but the plain truth of it was he had to make a living, and his schedule had him racing tractors at state fairs back East when Campbell showed up. Jenkins had already set some records on the salt that year, first in a stock Auburn before driving the jumping bejeebers out of, of all things, an Allis-Chalmers tractor, which he took to a new world mark of 68 miles per hour. "It was like riding on a frightened bison," confessed Jenkins, "one of the most thrill-packed experiences of my life." Thrilling? Bet on it. Still, it was a shame he couldn't be there to witness the new era blast into being.

At 7:00 A.M. Tuesday, September 3, 1935, Sir Malcolm Campbell, the man with the tan from the day before, set off down the oily black line—his constant companion and only reference point for the next 13 miles. He steadily passed the mile-marker boards looking for the red numerals of the flying mile . . . the money mile . . . the record mile. The personal threshold he had set for himself years ago was now only seconds away.

Reaching for the lever to close fresh air feed to the radiator, *Bluebird* surged faster . . . the tachometer needle climbed steadily, arcing up, and over the instrument's hash marks and then . . . Slam! The shutters closed. The engine howled, and the body panels were in a state of vibratory ecstasy. Campbell wrinkled his brow, as oil spray began to cover the windshield before he noticed the foul stink of exhaust fumes filling the cockpit. Entering the flying mile, he was on the verge of asphyxiation. His temples began to throb and the feeling of prickly needles radiated down his head as the car flew across those all-important 5,281 feet. By now the oil had seriously obscured his vision; he had lost sight of the line, his only port in this awful storm, and veered off course at 300 miles per hour.

Lifting his foot off the throttle, he felt *Bluebird* begin to swerve. The gas was affecting Campbell's ability to control the hurtling hellion. Back and forth the thundering tonnage swerved; the violent lateral movement was too much for a front Dunlop tire rotating 2,400 rpm—it burst. With good driving and good luck, now down around 200 miles per hour, Campbell demonstrated how champions are made. He applied the wind flaps and brought *Bluebird* to a stop a couple thousand feet from his waiting crew.

A cyclist appeared with the happy news that the car had been clocked at 304.33 miles per hour, or 11.83 seconds for the timed mile. Imagine the emotion: Campbell, the fastest man on Earth, now a wee bit faster. Campbell cried, "The Utah salt flats are the speed laboratory of the future!"

Two-way runs had been established for World Records in 1922, to ensure that a driver could not gain a single direction advantage using a sloped course or following wind. At double-time Campbell's crew worked; the car had to be turned and run back through the mile within 1 hour to have a chance at the world record. All six tires (twins in the rear) changed, goggles and windshield cleaned, fluids replenished, Campbell climbed aboard; he wouldn't bother with the shutter this time.

Engine started, he awaited the timer's signal to leave. Instead, word came that a timing wire had failed; would he please wait until it is replaced? The "all clear" came 5 minutes before the end of the unextendable hour, and the engine refused to start; the plugs were oil-fouled. Anxiety attack? The next press of the starter brought the stubborn Rolls Royce back to life.

The run went smoothly, and the car galloped through the mile flat out. Rapidly approaching a highway embankment, Campbell backed out of the throttle a bit too quick and *Bluebird* began a mile-long, four-wheel skidding slide. Tromping on the binders, he held the wheel straight, bringing the car to a stop 250 feet from the embankment. The wheels were littered with white salt clumps. Smoke and fire poured out from the broiling tires and brakes.

How fast had he gone? Backing off the throttle early certainly placed something in the minus column. Or did it? The word came that the average was 299.874 miles per hour: a new world's record, but a personal disappointment for Campbell. The time-keepers said he needed another 0.126 miles per hour to clinch a treble milestone. Or did he?

Malcolm Campbell causes a stir on Wendover Boulevard, when he arrives in front of the Cobble Stone Café and Service Station towing his world-famous *Bluebird* race car. *Utah State Historical Society*

More than 2 hours later AAA official Art Pillsbury approached Campbell and admitted that an arithmetic error had been made. Instead of a 12.18-second run, the actual elapsed time was 12.08, and so Campbell's flying mile was officially 301.1292 miles per hour! Campbell was purple with anger! He immediately wanted to run again, to remove any hint of doubt.

The idea that such a big mistake could be made by men who were otherwise so precise struck an odd note with many on the scene, including the reporters. Marvin Jenkins remembers that the whole messy math business aroused suspicion about a less-than-honorable special deal cut with the Contest Board and some of Campbell's entourage. Was something done to prevent the great man from running the car again? Campbell had taken exhausting, back-to-back wild rides. Did they fear for his safety?

Sir Malcolm did retire from racing after that day and rarely spoke of race cars afterward, turning instead to gardening and dog breeding. An examination of AAA, Contest Board, and California State Automobile Association (CSAA) private correspondence between officials reveals a serious concern about the conduct of an AAA Contest Board representative, even though the documents are cloudy and ripe for conjecture. Another official, Ted Allen, the AAA Contest Board Secretary, was admitted to a Salt Lake City hospital for extreme exhaustion and immediate stomach surgery following his timing of Campbell's runs. For a time his condition was critical. Was Allen's condition brought on by a moral dilemma, or was it purely coincidental?

Marvin Jenkins said his father distanced himself from the whole affair—easy to do since he never witnessed the runs. "For all Dad's 24-hour runs, there was never a bobble. We could ask the timers for all kinds of information, the last lap completed, or the average to that time, and it was never a problem. Knowing this made the Campbell situation seem so ridiculous to all of us," recalled Jenkins.

Earlier that year, Campbell's American manager, William Sturm, had tried to extract $10,000 from the Salt Lake City Chamber of Commerce, stating the money would be necessary before Campbell would make the trip. Campbell was in Africa and knew nothing of the money drive. Ab Jenkins got wind of the deal and told Chamber Secretary Gus Backman that Campbell had already agreed to come. Sturm was sent packing.

Is Campbell's record tainted? Or is it just sour grapes, the taste of which is caused by the world's finest racing prize being held by someone other than an American? In his book, *Speed on Salt*, George Eyston spends three pages carefully explaining the whole affair. So detailed is the explanation that it is reminiscent of Shakespeare's well-worn phrase, "Me thinks thou doth protest too much." His attempt to be comprehensive may have been just that, if the other red flags are not considered.

Had the AAA Contest Board tried to bully the Britons into some side deal? The runs were electronically timed, and paper tape strips were generated. Those who would know the truth, the timekeepers, have all passed on. Where the paper tape strips have gone is anyone's guess, but it would not be the last time Pillsbury's name would be associated with questionable proceedings.

For those people who thrive on grease and iron and numbers and nerve, setting records is rarely an easy victory. Indeed, the hardest won are the most sweetly savored. The more thrilling the competition, the better the contest. Fortune can frown one moment and then smile the next on one or another racing hopeful. This ever revolving wheel of fate is tempered by preparedness, moxie, and, many times, a prayer.

This much is certain, the racing career of a valiant racing knight ended that day, and he couldn't have picked a better place to say farewell. No one before or since has earned the title "Fastest on Earth" more times than Sir Malcolm Campbell.

Lighting the 10-mile Endurance Track in 1932 was accomplished by setting up burning smudge pots at regular intervals on the perimeter. Drivers reported seeing "midnight mirages" while keeping pace through the night. Ab Jenkins once thought a train had jumped the rails and was heading straight for him. *Jenkins Family Collection*

Chapter 4

The Monster Car Era

Yes, indeedy, it was daring do and a mighty big year for the salt in 1935. Sir Malcolm Campbell's high-speed spurts kicked off a Bonneville showbill chock full of big name acts. In less than one season, the voluptuous velocity salt feast added more tasty endurance records than Daytona, or its European counterparts, could manage in a decade. The exquisite straight-line acceleration track and dandy circular course was better than anyone imagined. Montlhery, supposedly Europe's fastest speedway, could only claim three successful 24-hour records in nine years. In contrast, by 1935, Bonneville gave up five new marks in two years.

This is not to say the job was easy. Few understood that because the circle track was not banked, it put considerable stress upon driver and car. The vehicle was always "rounding a curve," inducing whopping steady amounts of the centrifugal force determined to push the car into an outward skid.

Trying to collect any World's Hour Record at Bonneville, although safer, was considered the toughest because the car and driver could never relax. In 1935, a 12.5-mile circle was used, but afterward the salt expanse began to degrade, squeezing down the available hard surface to a 10-mile course.

Extreme care was taken staking out the course. Stakes would be driven into the salt at various points along the course to determine the salt bed thickness. For a good traction grip, at least 2 inches of hard salt were needed. Lath sticks with reflective cat eyes for night drives were put in 100 feet apart as course markers. Driving on the

To miss being a part of the history makes your heart sink.

–Bob Webb,
SCTA/BNI Assistant Timer

salt for more than an hour dissolves the perspective of speed because there are no visual aids except the pits to gauge the rate of travel, or determine a speed relationship for a pit stop. To signal the approach to the pits, drivers used the timer's stand as a 1-mile marker. When the car passed that point the driver would depress the clutch pedal, clean out the motor, and start to brake. "Without the markers," explained Marv Jenkins, on the scene for all his father's record attempts, "it would have been easy to overshoot the pit area, or disastrous if a car came in too fast."

Hard salt years meant drivers had an easier time of it setting records. When the salt was soft, avoiding potholes at 150 miles per hour was a frightening affair. Making a driving correction, however slight, had to be done slowly, carefully, and well in advance of trouble.

When Jenkins came to the salt in June 1935, he brought three machines: an Auburn Speedster, the Mormon Meteor powered by a supercharged Duesenberg J, and an Allis-Chalmers tractor. There was something wacky about trying to race a machine that was designed to perform at its best by going slow, but manufacturers needed some sort of record—speed, endurance, hill climbing—to capture the attention of the fickle buying public.

More British Are Coming!

Jenkins got word that John Cobb would be ready to run by July, and he graciously vacated the salt to let the Englishman see what he could make out of the chance. Jenkins left the entire

Thunderbolt, the massive, eight-wheeled landspeed car of George Eyston, is prepared for its "invisible" run in 1938. The photoelectric timing eyes could not see the car due to a combination of blinding white salt and reflectivity of the silver body. After painting the sides matte black, Eyston got the job done on August 27, setting a 345 miles per hour new World Land Speed Record. *Utah State Historical Society*

JOHN COBB
on the
Railton Mobil Special
gained the
World's Land Speed Record
394·7 mph
on
Mobiloil
as sold by
HUBERT DEES Ltd

The *Railton Special* on display in a British service station. It held the World Land Speed Record for 16 years. John Rhodes Cobb was the first man to drive over 400 miles per hour. He reportedly invested more than $100,000 in the Reid Railton design. American racers wondered why Cobb spent so much money to perfect the fluid teardrop shape, only to ruin the aerodynamics with hundreds of bulging rivets. *Robin Richardson Collection*

infrastructure in place for Cobb's convenience—tents, towers, trucks, everything, even his son Marvin.

"I thought it was the greatest thing that ever happened," mused the now-septuagenarian Marv Jenkins. "In the moonlight, the salt was a big crystal. With a cot for my bed, I slept in the open watching the skies . . . there were so many shooting stars, everywhere you looked."

Cobb came looking for both endurance and straight-line acceleration marks. Shipping over his 450-horsepower Napier-Railton, a car that had twice failed to achieve any records in Europe, including at Montlhery, Cobb nailed 21 world records within a week. Foreign convert number one, thank you very much. Unlike "Just Me" Jenkins, Cobb needed the help of co-drivers Tim Rose-Richards and Charlie Dodson to boost the 24-hour average to 134.85 miles per hour. Cobb hurried home to collect kudos and cash for his job well done, missing Campbell's later feat.

Attempting to regain the lost records, Jenkins, for the first time and at the insistence of his sponsors, shared the driving chores with Indianapolis driver Tony Gulotta. August "Augie" Duesenberg was also on the scene, personally supervising the operation and maintenance of Jenkins' new supercharged steed, a Duesey with beefed-up connecting rods.

Soft-spoken Duesenberg had retired from racing after his brother, Fred, had been killed in an auto accident. Returning to help his friend, Jenkins, Augie displayed a peculiar method of working out engineering problems. While the car tooled around the 10-mile, Duesenberg walked a circle of his own; the crew called it his "trouble track," where he would pace trying to work out a problem or devise driving strategies.

The trio brought the records back to America after three attempts, despite a fire, electrical system failure, and "struggle for life" when a tire blew out. What made the triumph sweeter? Their engine was a 7,108-cc engine compared to the 23,953-cc brute of Cobb's. Driving 3,251 miles, they had certainly made more out of less in 24 hours.

Eyston's Zippy Lizard

Once Campbell returned home, Captain Eyston trotted out his giant metal lizard, *Speed Of The Wind*. Eyston also relied on co-drivers Albert Denly and Chris Staniland. By sharing the driving chores, each stayed a bit fresher to bump up the average speed to 140.52 miles per hour in late September. A versatile endurance and straight-line racer, Eyston observed of the salt beds, "There is no place in the world offering so many favorable conditions for scientific testing of a car."

Through it all, the British were well looked after, from the desert mavens, Blair and Ed Lamus, who knew the salt better than anyone (one of the mountain peaks is named in their honor), to Horatio the black cook, who kept the 40 men happily fed from his specially built trailer home. Townspeople milling around the Western Service garage watching the British were perplexed by their odd terminology. Once everyone understood that a dangling lead was a drop light; that a bonnet was a hood, not a hat; and that spanners were wrenches, not some reference to distance, everyone got along together quite well.

The British racers were all aristocrats. Unlike most of the American racers, they were quite wealthy and inhabited highbrow social circles. Marv Jenkins confessed that they made him realize how very special a place Bonneville was after listening to their stories of other racing experiences. "Setting a record on the salt has a special flavor," he said. "The British understood better than any of us that a record set at Bonneville had a greater meaning than if you did the same thing anywhere else."

An updated *Speed Of the Wind* helped Eyston grab 60 new records in 1936 and hiked up the 24-hour record to 149 miles per hour, before he slapped a new 48-hour record into place at 136 miles per hour. Eyston also established diesel-powered records with *The Flying Spray* at 158 miles per hour through the mile: another salt beds first.

Air Screws and Spins

If Ab Jenkins were to snatch back any more speed records on the salt, he would have to switch to aircraft engines used by the British. The only thing available was the 700-horsepower Curtis Conqueror, to which he added a flywheel, clutch, and bell housing before having it shipped to Auburn, where son Marvin helped Augie install it into a Duesenberg chassis. Christened *Mormon Meteor II*, the result of a 1935 Salt Lake City newspaper contest, the car was turned loose on the salt—literally—when the 1936 season got under way.

Screaming along at 159 miles per hour, Jenkins' tires hit a soft spot and the car went into a 400-foot wingding, wahoo, or just plain skid to you. To avoid tipping over, he deliberately cranked the

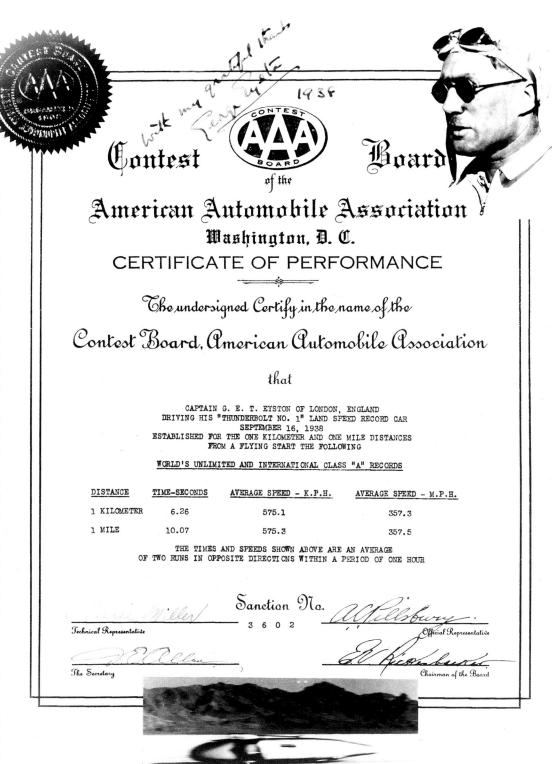

Certificate of Performance provided by the now-defunct AAA Contest Board, at one time a monopolistic sanctioning body for racing in the United States. This one piously confirms Captain George Eyston's 1938 World Landspeed Record. It is signed by Chairman Eddie Rickenbacker, Secretary Ted Allen, Technical Representative Eddie Miller, and Official Representative Art Pillsbury. *Jim Miller Collection*

The Big Money Runs

For 1937, once the rains let up, Jenkins took a romp in September, but marathon running receded in favor of the mile record. Sporting a new blue, cream, and orange paint scheme, *Mormon Meteor II* showed its nasty side. Jenkins was slightly injured when two rear tires tore off and a piece of metal penetrated his arm 2 inches after he ran through a patch of rough salt. The mishap temporarily paralyzed Jenkins' arm.

Taking over was three-time Indianapolis champion Louis Meyer, who filled in as Jenkins' relief driver. Meyer later confessed, "I used to think the Indianapolis 500 took a long time to drive. I don't see how that Ab does it for so many hours. It's easy for the first 3 or 4 hours. It's not bad, but when you drive 10, 12, 15 hours . . . ."

Eyston brought his monster *Thunderbolt* to the salt, but twice clutch problems would rob him of return runs and the prized measured mile record. Leo Goossen, the legendary, self-taught draftsman and engineer for the inimitable Harry Miller, redesigned *Thunderbolt's* discombobulating clutch. Eyston then easily set a new absolute landspeed record. During a live radio interview immediately following the runs, Eyston declared that Goossen had saved the day. On November 19, 1937, Eyston's five-gallon-a-minute, fuel-gulping, eight-wheeled *Thunderbolt* eclipsed Campbell's World Landspeed Record by turning in a two-way average of 311.42 miles per hour. England had a new hero.

Bonneville sizzled with speed during the 1938 season after Jenkins' runs were rained out and the rivalry shifted between Cobb and Eyston. Under the monopolistic eye of AAA's Art Pillsbury, they battled for domination of the flying mile crown, driving cars that were as different as "chalk and cheese." In less than a month the boys had whomped-up the World Landspeed Record 46 rungs, from 311 to 357 miles per hour. They managed to swap two world titles in just two days. The rolling wrestling match for speed crowns went like this:

August 27, Eyston popped out 345 miles per hour;
September 15, Cobb spit out 350 miles per hour;
September 16, Eyston cut a 357 miles per hour year-end closer.

Jenkins, then the holder of 146 speed titles, cabled Eyston at Bonneville and stated:

Congratulation Captain on a marvelous record you just set. If you and John Cobb don't make your minds up it will be necessary for me to build a new car as your records will be beyond the speed of the one I am now building, but go to it, I wish you both lots of luck.

The eyebrow raiser of the year belonged to Eyston. While driving his 7 1/2-ton *Thunderbolt* at 270 miles per hour, he put on a spectacular skid show in front of 6,000 spectators. Thankfully, the onboard breathing system functioned perfectly when he literally smoked the brakes. Eyston was unhurt, except perhaps for a bit of

In light fit for owls, averaging 179.434 miles per hour, Marvin Jenkins drives the *Novi Special* to eight new national and international records in the 5- and 10-kilometers distances, improving on the existing record set seven years previous. Inset, left to right: Marv Jenkins, co-driver; Ab Jenkins, co-driver; Lewis Welch, owner; Bud Winfield, builder of *Novi Special;* Radio Gardner; Frank Lehew, Champion Spark Plugs. *LandSpeed Productions Composite*

steering wheel to the left and nailed the accelerator, sending the car spinning for 2 1/2 miles. "During the spin we darted by telephone poles, between parked automobiles, tents, and spectators," remembered Jenkins. And he brought a witness! Indianapolis driver Babe Stapp was riding shotgun and immediately dove under the cowling. Nothing was damaged, and Jenkins continued until a burned-out front universal joint parked the car.

Cobb promptly took to the salt and improved on Eyston's 24-hour record, driving an average of 150 miles per hour. Jenkins and Stapp finished the year by regaining every record from 50 miles to 48 hours inclusive—72 records all together.

The speed curtain closed with the Americans pumping the 1-hour record to 170 miles per hour, the 24-hour record to 153 miles per hour, and the 48-hour record to 148 miles per hour. That year all three teams probably had as much fun as you can have standing up exchanging records.

wounded pride. Eyston's deluded philosophy toward land speed records had been, up to that point, "Big Speed. Big Car." One might wonder if he eyed Cobb's little silver fish with envious longing after the trouser-loading slide across the salt.

On September 30, 1938, AAA Contest Board Official Representative Art Pillsbury filed a report with AAA Secretary Ted Allen in Washington, D.C., about Eyston's runs. Included in the report were Technical Representative Eddie Miller's certifications of Eyston's and Cobb's engines. In another letter to Allen, dated the same day, Pillsbury referred to confidential, technical information about Eyston's August 27 and September 16 record runs:

Captain Eyston was particularly desirous and insistant(sic)that the Technical Reports dealing with the conditions of his tires be not made part of the report filed with Paris. Further more he has at all times been extremely

careful and cautious to see that no pictures were ever taken of his tires after a run and has resorted to every means at his disposal, to even mis-state the facts to the press to protect the Dunlop Company and to be assured that no adverse publicity of any kind that they might consider detrimental leaked out. . . . Mr. Cobb has made no request for such secrecy. . . .

The only "cc:" was to G.E.T. Eyston.

Examination of Miller's original Technical Reports reveals Eyston needed all eight wheels—the tires were not up to the job. Despite all tires being changed after each of the August runs, tread came off on four tires, and the right rear inside tire went flat! It's a wonder Eyston made it back for the September record runs. Miller's notes for that day include the remark, "Air in all tires for first time on any Eyston run." In all fairness to Dunlop, land speed racing was then, and still is, experimental racing.

Captain George E. T. Eyston's *Speed Of the Wind* endurance car [upper left] that traveled the 10-mile circle track. Some racers referred to it as a giant lizard. When *Thunderbolt*, the landspeed car, arrived in Wendover, people were shocked by its immense size. *LandSpeed Productions*

In addition to World Unlimited records, Ab Jenkins held practically all speed marks in other AAA Contest Board classifications. During his 1940 record attempts, he turned in a lap of 189 miles per hour—the fastest ever at the time for a circular course. *Jenkins Family Collection*

Augie Duesenberg holds up the piano-hinged hood as Ab Jenkins tries the new racer on for size. Harvey Firestone, a big fan, admirer, and supporter of Jenkins stands with his hands on his hips while Firestone President John W. Thomas poses as if distracted by something going on behind the photographer at Firestone Headquarters in Akron, Ohio. *Jenkins Family Collection*

Cobb's Halibut

On August 23, 1939, John Cobb began what would later be a 34-year hold on the land speed record. Cobb drove his *Railton*, shaped like a 5,000-pound halibut (named in honor of designer Reid Railton), to a 367.910-mile-per-hour World Record. Cobb's attempt was paid for by American oil giant Earl P. Gilmore, president of Gilmore Oil company. Gilmore personally met the team at the airport when it landed in Salt Lake. Jenkins, who believed that keeping a race car connected to the ground was better achieved by air pressure than by weight, telegraphed Cobb,

"Congratulations, John, you did a wonderful job and I am glad. The Captain and you are making it plenty tough for the rest of us, more power to you."

Powered by dual 1,250-horsepower Napier aircraft engines, the British equivalent of an Allison engine, the car had a total of 2,921 cubic inches of displacement—half that of Eyston's 4,925-cid Thunderbolt. Both supercharged bullets were mounted at an angle in an S-shaped backbone chassis. The fresh design drastically streamlined the body. One engine drove the front wheels, the other powered the back wheels. In first gear, the car accelerated from 0 to 60 miles per hour in 10 seconds. The second gear change-up came at 150 miles per hour and top gear was engaged at 250 miles per hour.

Had this car any keys, Cobb could have left them in the ignition all the time, because the starting procedure and gear change process was so convoluted that it would deter the best

of thieves. Any deviation, and the engines would stall. It was the car's biggest flaw.

Under the forward cockpit bubble, which looked like a bulging fisheye, the instrument panel featured dual controls. A unique ice water cooling system was replenished by lifting off the entire lightweight body. Cobb's car weighed half as much as Eyston's massive six-axle, eight-wheeled *Thunderbolt*.

Time Out for War

As the 1930s drew to a close, racing was enjoying great grassroots participation nationwide. In southern California, young adults started to modify automobile bodies and tinker with engines

A Utah State Road Commission worker adjusts the drag behind the state truck that scrapes the salt surface smooth and clean for safe, high-speed runs in 1937. This part of land speed racing has changed very little over the decades. The trucks are newer, but the number of slow, tedious hours required to prepare a racing course can total well over one hundred! *Jenkins Family Collection*

By 1935, Jenkins was racing boat tail speedsters for Auburn. Here, the two men in white hold a thermometer indicating over 100 degrees. They are standing in front of an old sheepherder's wagon-turned-Bonneville bunkhouse. At the far left is a wooden barrel water truck owned by the Utah State Highway Commission that was also used as a shower facility. *Jenkins Family Collection*

State Line Hotel and Casino proprietor Bill Smith painted a line down the middle of the cafe explaining that customers could eat in Utah, but had to go to the Nevada side of his business (indicated by a painted line down the middle) to gamble and drink. Where the true lines were, no one knew, but it sure made for lively conversation. *Utah State Historical Society*

as a form of personal expression. They became known as "Hot Rodders," and they tested their machines on dry lakes such as Muroc, Harper, El Mirage, and Rosamond.

The first speed trials were conducted under the auspices of the Muroc Timing Association before the Southern California Timing Association (SCTA) was formed on November 19, 1937. Ironically, this was the same day Eyston in his *Thunderbolt* ripped past Malcolm Campbell's record—a good omen for an emerging racing organization.

The first organized speed event took place May 15, 1938, and it opened not only a training but also a proving ground for the ingenious hot rodders. Nurtured in their own speed fish bowl, they acquired the skills to develop the equipment necessary for bigger and better speed thrills at Bonneville. Comprising local car clubs, SCTA had seven charter member clubs. They included the 90MPH Club, Idlers, Knight Riders, Ramblers, Road Runners, Sidewinders, and the Throttlers.

Racing was on quite a roll until Hitler's scummy Nazis invaded Poland in 1939 and hijacked the world into war. Then, the German flying pestilence, the Luftwaffe, bombed the daylights out of England, and the British forgot all about speed records. Americans were next to abandon racing when the sneaky Japanese bombed Pearl Harbor in 1941.

Before the European continent dissolved into heartbreaking chaos, the *Mormon Meteor III* debuted on the salt in July 1939, dressed in a striking new blue-and-orange paint job. The car was the last of Jenkins' purpose-built race cars, assembled by Augie Duesenberg and 17-year-old Marvin Jenkins back in an Indianapolis shop that was once a horse and buggy trash-hauling business.

At 56, Jenkins persisted in astonishing the racing community with his driving prowess by taking another crack at Eyston's 12-hour record. A little more than 3 hours and 638 miles into the run, the universal joint on the whizzing driveshaft began to howl like a banshee. When he pitted to check the problem, the superheated, failing part caught fire. Flames roared up into the right side of the closed cockpit, eagerly licking at Jenkins' cotton clothing. Son Marv and crewman Bill Oliver saw that Ab was trapped, ripped off the canopy, and extracted the blazing Jenkins from the car. Moments later, fear in stasis, the cool, blonde-haired Evelyn was at her husband's side with the first aid kit. The rapid teamwork saved Ab and the car from serious injury and damage.

At the hospital, doctors treated second- and third-degree burns on Jenkins' right arm, shoulder, leg, and foot. After only a week in the hospital, Jenkins went back to the salt and nabbed the 12-hour record, but the foolish stunt put him back in the hospital with blood poisoning for three tense weeks. However, his injuries sparked a political campaign that resulted in his election as mayor of Salt Lake City the following year.

Rough salt in 1940 caused the *Meteor's* fuel economy to deteriorate badly, but Jenkins and codriver Cliff Bergere packed in 21 records. Bergere, whose hands were badly blistered after 10 hours at the wheel, was dumbfounded by senior citizen Jenkins' fortitude. In a July 24 *Salt Lake Tribune* article he confessed:

I've race at Indianapolis ever since 1927 and seen some of the greatest racers in the game, but I'll take my hat off to Jenkins. Any man who can drive a car six solid hours on this course at the speed that Ab got out of the machine is a marvel. The car purred just as smoothly at the finish of the test as it did at the start!

A chilling, historical footnote directly linked to ending World War II began in Wendover. Unbeknownst to the local populace, when the United States built the one-million acre Wendover Field Air Base, it was for the single purpose of training the *Enola Gay's* flight crews. In its heyday, Wendover Field was the largest on Earth.

Cartoonist Tom Medley, creator of the "Stroker McGurk" series, recalled when a neighbor, Jim Garris, received orders to report to Wendover AFB. "When Garris arrived, there wasn't any air base," said Medley. "A few hours later a lieutenant came along who didn't know anything more than Jim. Eventually trucks and buses showed up and they *built* the air base."

Well known to the community were the B-29 Superfortress pilots, Colonel Paul Tibbets and William Parsons, who would drop the bomb on Hiroshima, Japan, on August 6, 1945. For reasons known only to the military, the atomic bombs were given cute nicknames of "Little Boy" and "Fat Boy."

Let's Race Again, Shall We?

Having been denied high-speed rides until the global vermin could be brought under control and the world returned to peace, gentleman driver John Cobb came back for his last race on the salt, in 1947. He was eager to drill past the 400-mile-per-hour barrier. For Cobb's latest landspeed bid, Reid Railton had engineered a new auxiliary drive and hiked the top gear ratios, while Dunlop developed new tires. Still, it was an old warhorse, based on Railton's 1935 design and powered by vintage 1929 engines. The bulky, studious Cobb proved that good design and engineering do stand the test of time, when on September 16 he upped his own mile record to 394 miles per hour.

Cobb was not alone on the salt. At the same time, Bud Winfield was running the *Novi Special* car for owner Lewis Welch. Drivers Ab and Marv Jenkins had the job of trying to wrest the Class C record (three-liter engine) away from the Germans. At twilight, averaging 179.434 miles per hour, Marvin Jenkins drove the *Novi* to eight new national and international records in the 5- and 10-kilometer distances, improving on the existing record set seven years before at 155 miles per hour.

Southern California racing enthusiasts Kong Jackson, 28, and Chuck Abbott, 26, had come to watch Winfield make horsepower come alive in the petite race car. The duo went up in Abbott's 1929 V-8 roadster, and spent their nights in the sleeping bag motel. "The salt was wet that year," recalled Abbott. "By the afternoon, it was like running in mud because the sun brought the moisture up to the surface and made the course sloppy and wet."

Also on the mushy straight line was Ed Balch running an Offy-powered midget driven by "Dapper" Danny Oakes. Abbott remembers they couldn't get the car to go faster than 139 miles per hour for three days, and when he casually mentioned it might be the tires, the Firestone rep drilled through him with a killing look.

"Cobb's one-way run of 403 miles per hour impressed me with how straight it went," said Jackson. "We talked to him afterward and he told us the car needed very little correction and was easy to handle." The straight-arrow characteristic was no doubt due to the opposing direction rotation of the two Napier crankshafts.

Winfield jibed Railton about the rivets screwing up an otherwise perfect aerodynamic flow. "There was lots of kidding," said Abbott. "Ab and Marvin were full of good humor." Over dinner the next day, Jackson and Winfield met Railton, a stimulating but sometimes caustic conversationalist. The talk was total tech. Jackson, far from being a shy boy, jumped right into the debate with the two experts discussing cork-float carburetion at altitude and high-speed streamliner design.

Jackson, a short and cocky type with an eye for cars and women (always in that order), enlisted the help of the elder Jenkins in securing some salt time for his hot rodder buddies back home. When Jackson reported his good luck to SCTA officials, no time was lost. The sanctioning body, desperate to find better racing sites for its rapidly developing association, quickly sent representatives to Salt Lake City to cut a deal—one that would bring the Bonneville Salt Flats the most devoted, loyal, and protective host of racers the world would ever know.

This was Wendover's residential area in 1940. Today, many of these houses still exist but the streets are paved and a few street lights have popped up. Progress has come to the sleepy burg and you'll no doubt see some rollerblades and skateboarders as well as bicyclists. *Utah State Historical Society*

The Tristate Mercantile was a traveler's best bet for 100 miles in either direction of the Flats in 1940. That's the "Pastime Club" next door and right around the corner is the bakery. *Utah State Historical Society*

Chapter 5

Boys, Toys and Noise

Before the 1940s closed out, a new type of salt racing would arrive, one with more vibrancy, depth, and scope. The people that would come would stay and become the best friends Bonneville had, next to Ab Jenkins. They would be young, adventurous spirits. They would be strong, heaving with intestinal fortitude and exploding with enthusiasm and impatient creativity. What's more, even they did not know they were coming yet.

The racing conditions at the dry lakes in southern California had deteriorated to the point that something had to be done if the sport was to survive. Poor course surfaces combined with faster racing vehicles led to an increase in crashes, injuries, and deaths. The resulting bad publicity was exactly what responsible amateur speedsters had tried to avoid by banding together their car clubs to form the SCTA back in 1937. Bigger, safer sites were needed if the speed trials were to continue.

A polite appeal for help had beeen sent to Art Pillsbury at the powerful AAA Contest Board asking for assistance to stage an event on the Bonneville Salt Flats. Pillsbury's terse reply: "The Class C record is 203 miles per hour, and it is doubtful that any hot rod will ever reach that speed."

It was clear Pillsbury thought hot rods were little more than a screwball diversion for a bunch of reckless kids. SCTA battled against this image constantly. Adopting the slogan, "Sponsors of

A Vision to seek, a beckoning peak,
With a courage in your soul,
that mocks at a goal,
there lies the land beyond.

—Robert Service

the World's Safest Automotive Speed Trials," brought them little credit. The group had a commendable record of staging safe meets that reduced dangerous, impromptu street racing contests. They also participated in community service activities, but it wasn't enough to fight the national "bad boy" street heathen image.

Ignoring the AAA snub, SCTA decided to find another way onto the salt, believing the ancient Utah lake bed held the key to the organization's survival. Investigation revealed that the AAA had no authority when it came to who used the salt. For years, when Jenkins wanted to race, he had simply enlisted the aid of Wendover resident Blair Lamus, who would prepare the course. It was that simple. As more and more racing came to the salt, the federal government appointed Utah the custodian of the land for tourist and recreational activities.

State officials realized that some control measures and a governing body should be established. Up stepped the Salt Lake City Chamber of Commerce, basically the same group of people who had privately thrown in together to help Jenkins make his first endurance runs in 1932. The feds were all too glad to have private citizens take up the day-to-day operations responsibility, reserving their authority and involvement as public land stewards only when necessary. So it was that anyone wanting to use the salt flats for racing purposes had to gain permission from the Bonneville Speedway Association, a committee within the chamber. However,

Not just the dawn of a new day, but of a new era. Admirers gather around Ak Miller's lakester at dawn. This meant a 4 A.M. wake-up call for many, even if they had been up late working on their cars, gambling at the State Line Casino, or visiting some nice girls in Wells. *Tom Medley Photo*

Left to right (seated) are board member Ak Miller, manager Wally Parks, and *HOT ROD* publisher Bob Petersen, conducting an early Southern California Timing Association (SCTA) board planning meeting for the first Bonneville Speed Week. The 1949 event cost $2,000 or $3,000—no one really remembers which. *Ak Miller Collection*

Lining up the eager in 1949, an SCTA official, sporting a pith helmet, walks between a belly tank and the lakester of Fred Carillo and Stan Betz from Monrovia, California. The white roadster was George Scully's from Las Vegas, Nevada. Directly behind Ak Miller's lakester on the far right is Bill Kenz's *Odd Rod* from Denver, Colorado. McAlister & Walker's *Daffe Jaffe* sprint car is behind No. 346. *SCTA Archives*

since most speed attempts were privately sponsored, professional affairs, this knowledge was not widely known.

This was the situation when hot rodders Kong Jackson and Chuck Abbott went up to the salt to watch Novi builder Bud Winfield and machinist Gene Marcenac run the Indianapolis car. While there, Jackson made a good impression on racing legend Jenkins and gained his support for an amateur speed trial event. Circle track racer Ernie McAfee had also been up to the salt and told the SCTA board, "The salt is so hard, when you drive a nail in, it would bend over." Salt racing pioneer Alex Xydias distinctly remembers McAfee's comment, and confesses, "It really hit a nerve with me."

The SCTA had, in 1947, sent inquiry letters to Salt Lake City about using the salt that year, but withdrew from the idea when Cobb announced his landspeed bid. After Jackson reported his experience, SCTA decided the time was right to send a contingent to negotiate directly with the Speedway Committee. Wally Parks was tapped to represent SCTA. He asked Lee Ryan, a manager at Petersen Publishing, and *HOT ROD* Publisher Bob Petersen to join him: Petersen because he was the only one who had a car that could be relied upon to make the round trip (a 1939 Mercury Club Coupe), and Ryan because, being in his 40s, he would imbue a sense of maturity.

Today, it's hard to imagine the SCTA needing someone older to engender respect. Celebrating Bonneville's Golden Anniversary 1998, a great many of the racers who attended the first event came back, and some had never stopped racing. One '49er cracked, "We should change the name of this group to the Senior Citizens Timing Association."

Things were very different in 1948, when Parks, Ryan, and Petersen went to Salt Lake City to meet soft-spoken, Robert D. "Gus" Backman. As secretary of the Salt Lake City Chamber of Commerce,

The best guess for the first driver on the first day of the first SCTA Speed Week is Carl McAlister, driving the McAlister and Walker race car, shown here getting a push-off from the patrol truck. The man in the pickup bed holds onto his hat while steadying himself around a barrel of water. More than 20 people who attended the 1949 event were consulted, yet no one could remember who really went first. *SCTA Archives*

Backman was one of the city's three most influential and powerful men. Whatever the three did, they did right, and local authorities agreed the hot rodder rated a chance—but only one chance. In an April 4, 1949, letter, Backman announced to SCTA manager Parks, "We will be pleased to allocate the salt beds to your organization at some time during the month of August, for the purpose of conducting time trials." If the group didn't screw up and if the racers conducted themselves in a civil manner, then the Speedway Association would consider allowing the group back for another year. After a few more letters, the contract was signed to officially schedule the First Annual Bonneville Speed Trials for August 22-27, 1949. As part of the contract, SCTA agreed to refer to the salt beds as the "Bonneville Salt Flats" (BSF) in all press releases.

Now What Do We Do?

OK, the pressure might be off about finding a new place to race, and the proverbial foot was full in the door. Now the question was: How do we do it, and how the *hell* do we pay for it? A hatful of hard cash was needed if the big idea was going to become a big reality. The first event was estimated to cost a couple thousand dollars. (A half century later, according to Bonneville Nationals Chairman Mike Waters, that figure was easily $50,000 for the 1998 event.)

SCTA was, and always would be, an all-volunteer group. At the time, staging a speed trial at the BSF was about as daring a thing to do as wearing a bikini in public. But if girls were starting to walk around in two-piece bathing suits, certainly a few boys could manage a national event.

A "Board of Management" was formed. Its members included SCTA President George Prusell, SCTA Secretary-Treasurer George Radnich, SCTA General Manager Wally Parks, Marvin Lee, Lee Ryan, and Robert "Pete" Petersen. The Contest Board comprised SCTA Vice President Boswell "Bozzy" Willis and Directors Akton "Ak" Miller, Doug Hartelt, Fred Woodward, and Alex Xydias, as well as Radnich and Prusell. Ernie McAfee also assisted. Ab Jenkins turned down an invitation to serve as technical advisor due to his AAA affiliations.

According to handwritten board meeting notes, the next few months of controlled chaos were spent hooking sponsors, working out logistics, and planning a publicity strategy. American Power Boat Association Chief Timer Otto Crocker was hired for a week of timing services at $455. Union Oil Company, *HOT ROD* magazine, Grant Piston Rings, and Service Sales of Texas signed on as sponsors.

Lee Ryan was hired as a $75 per week publicist. He crowed to Firestone racing director John Moore, "You can put down in your book that this meet will grow into the biggest thing in the country in the way of time trials." Queen of Tooele County Marilyn Barrus agreed to present a trophy for the Best Designed Car from her county. Western Service and the Lion's Club of Wendover agreed to handle concessions, parking, and crowd control. For a $500 flat fee, Tooele County Chamber of Commerce agreed to provide an ambulance equipped with a mobile phone and offered air transport if required. In comparison, the ambulance charges for the 1998 Speed Week were $90 per hour, adding up to $6,300.

Alex Xydias was deeply concerned about being overshadowed by professional racers who might enter, but the board invited "name" drivers, owners, and foreign car clubs anyway. Mr. Xydias' fears later proved pointless when he and Dean Batchelor recorded the fastest time of the meet.

Entries arrived from Texas, Colorado, Nevada, Tennessee, Florida, Iowa, Utah, Arizona, Minnesota, Illinois, and Nebraska. Although sedans and motorcycles would not be allowed, by mid-August an SCTA press release boasted that 200 roadsters, lakesters, streamliners, coupes, and sports and racing cars had committed by paying the $7.50 per car entry fee. The same press release then wildly predicted that 350 cars would compete, although only 60 actually showed up. (In 1998, a single entry fee was $260.)

The operations crew consisted of three technical inspectors, a starter, and patrol chief, two at the signal post and three each for the starting stand, finish line, and setup. (In 1998, the volunteer staff is 10 times that number with the inspection area alone needing a minimum of 16 people to "tech" all the vehicles.) Interestingly enough, the name at the top of personnel list was San Diego race enthusiast Bob Higbee. Decades later, it is clear his name must have been written down with indelible ink. For the next 50 years, "perfect attendance" Higbee arrived to set up every Bonneville, and he never left for home before the tear-down work detail was finished.

Bozzy Willis was another behind-the-scenes backbone of the SCTA organization. He not only hauled the course equipment from San Diego all the way up to Utah the first few years, but maintained it in first-class condition and provided the communications system to boot. His only payment was being part of the scene. Without all the unpaid work he and so many others like him performed, the Bonneville Nationals would have been only a dream.

Enough With the Paperwork, Let's Go Race!

Whew! A lot of work just to go fast! Would it be worth all the trouble? None knew they were in for the shock of their little, amateur racer boy lives.

The hot cars to beat were all from Southern California. They included the belly tank streamliner of Bill Burke and Don Francisco, the lakesters of Don Waite and Johnny Hartman, and the roadsters of John Browning and Don Olsen.

Great hope was placed in Marvin Lee's *City of Pasadena* Chevy 6 streamliner, and because it had averaged 153 miles per hour, the fastest ever for a lakes racer, the car was selected to grace the cover of the first program. Its construction was considered outstanding for the day, using 3-inch steel tubing for the frame and roll bar, the latter being a giant step forward in driver protection. Powered by a 248-CID 1942 Chevy block, it used GMC rods; Wayne head, manifold, and pistons; Bill Spalding cam; and Tom Spalding ignition. Carburetion was interchangeable for a three or six body setup by Hilborn and Travers. This "mixed bag" was typical of the serious hot rodder who employed the best modified parts that money could buy.

Chief Timer Otto Crocker, "the clocker," far left, has a commanding view of the race course as Bob Higbee records the time. Phyllis Lindsley and Wally Parks check out the starting line action. Notice Mrs. Lindsley's footwear. The man with his eyes glued to the binoculars is Jim Lindsley. The tubular steel, shaded timing stand was built by SCTA volunteers. *SCTA Archives*

The salt "grandstand" in 1949 was just a lumpy line of upturned mud. No crowds, just pure racing for a trophy and a timing slip. This was the scene around high noon, when the speed trials were in full swing. *Don Ellis, Courtesy of Richard Dixon's Bonneville Speedway Museum/ LandSpeed Composite*

Also running a Chevy 6 engine with a Wayne head were brothers Bill and Tom Spalding. They ran a very respectable 142 miles per hour, to lead their class, but pulled their car from record runs so that competitor and friend Marvin Lee could use the Wayne after his had cracked. This behavior is one of the sport's most distinguishing characteristics, constantly repeated among strangers as well as friends. The goal is speed; whether you get it, or someone else does, the point is to get there. If a car had reached its peak but some of its parts could assist another to further push up the speed, the parts usually changed cars.

Competition began daily at 6 A.M., with qualifying runs made daily throughout the week and record runs conducted first thing the following morning. The racers took aim down the 5-mile straightaway with measured quarter-mile and full-mile timing traps. Safety belts and crash helmets were required but hard to find, so the SCTA brought a pile of bright red- and- white brain buckets for the drivers who needed to borrow head protection.

From Denver, Colorado, came Bill Kenz, who unpacked the surprise of the meet, *Odd Rod* (a nickname given it by *HOT ROD* magazine editors), an aptly named yet amazing twin-flathead-powered 1931 machine with a big box Model A pickup body. According to George Hill's diary, Kenz was first on the line that year, and his car was first every year thereafter until 1956. "His run was a kind of unofficial opening of the meet," stated Hill. Although the "Odd Rod" was rather goofy looking as a racer car amidst the little roadsters, lakesters, and sprints, the snickers ceased when Kenz buzzed though the traps at almost 141 miles

There was plenty of help when Art Tremaine needed a push to start his 126-mile-per-hour run through the course. Paying a $7.50 entry fee bought five days of competition with no limit on how many runs a car could make. *SCTA Archives*

When Bill Kenz appeared on the salt in 1949 with *Odd Rod*, a dual-engined Model A pickup fitted with swing axles and torsion bars, the snickers and ribbing went into high gear. Kenz had the last chuckle when he won his class with a record-setting 140-mile-per-hour average—10 miles per hour faster than the roadsters. *Ron Leslie Collection*

Union Oil President Earl Cooper shakes driver Dean Batchelor's hand, as co-owner Alex Xydias looks on in 1949. The duo had the fastest car of the meet, clocking 193 miles per hour, more than 25 miles per hour faster than any hot rod had ever gone before. *SCTA Archives*

per hour. He made it plain that discounting his vehicles in the future would be a big mistake. Kenz had named the truck *Angel* because there was a drawing of the celestial being on the cowling when he bought the body from a junkyard.

"The pick-up truck was actually the result of lengthy arguments I'd had with many local (Denver) enthusiasts," wrote the genial and much admired Kenz in an editorial for the SCTA. "I had claimed that two engines coupled together to drive one car would give the machine double pulling power. Their arguments against the feasibility and practicability of such a machine were challenge enough."

On the other end of the competition scale was kindly Multy Aldrich's *Bardahl Special*, a 1922 Model T Ford with a Rajo engine. Not only did he race the car, but it was his daily driving machine as well. All the way from Mentone, California, Aldrich was one of the sport's friendliest ambassadors.

SCTA Manager Wally Parks, driving the Burke-Francisco tank, earned the honor of being the very first driver to spin out on the salt course. While busy with an engine fire, he applied the newly relined brakes a bit too hard and went twirling into the history books.

The twin-tank experiment from Howard Johansen was a brilliant idea that performed atrociously. Its lackluster performance was a direct result of a last-minute, cobble-together construction job. Running with the engine in one compartment and the driver in another, it made an initial run of 147 miles per hour, but then scared the stink out of on-lookers every time thereafter when, spinning out of control and unbalanced, it dug into the salt surface. Johansen discovered he had serious front end suspension problems, and officials withdrew the car from running for the safety of all concerned.

Safety rules were gradually added as the experiences revealed deficiencies, hopefully before someone got killed or hurt, but not always. When the Dietrich Special sprint car caught fire, the driver learned the hard way that pyrene-type extinguishers are useless against burning alcohol.

Instant Hot Rod Heroes

The pivotal point for the event centered around the new streamliner of Alex Xydias and Dean Batchelor. Inspired by the prewar body style of the German Auto Union Grand Prix car, the pair decided to convert the SO-Cal Speed Shop's belly tank into a fully streamlined race car. Xydias owned the speed shop, Batchelor had the art background, and with the help of Valley Custom shop and many friends, the striking new body style was fashioned.

Xydias went to pal Vic Edelbrock, Sr., to find a more potent engine. The Class A V-8 60 Ford Flathead from the belly tank didn't quite seem enough for what Bonneville promised. Edelbrock agreed, and provided not only a stouter Mercury engine, but also sent motor ace Bobby Meeks along to work on it.

Months of daily work behind them, a team of six left for Bonneville with two cars, two trailers, two engines, and a gleaming white race car trimmed in gold leaf numbers. However, the race car trailer had personality disorder; it thought it was the pendulum

of a grandfather clock. Just as Xydias started to climb the final ridge line outside of Ely, the trailer finally got a good swing in and jackknifed the rig, smashing the left front of the streamliner into the rear fender of the tow car.

The boys spent several downtrodden hours with borrowed body tools banging the body back into shape at an Ely body shop. Thankfully, pretty doesn't have "jack" to do with fast, and the car ran 156 miles per hour with the V-8 60 engine—20 miles an hour faster than it had run with the belly tank body.

The team anxiously changed out the engine to the big Merc and in doing so, also changed the course of landspeed racing. They ran fast. Real fast. So fast, that driver Dean Batchelor unzipped the treads right off the ribbed front racing tires, yet the car never wavered off course. The carcasses stayed intact, but sharing the tire information improved safety regulations; it meant others would be able to learn from the experience. Street tires were no longer feasible. Future rubber would be Indy-type racing tires rated for high speed.

Batchelor's first run was 185.95 miles per hour backed up with a 187.89 miles per hour. The collective racing jaw dropped; the speeds were 20 miles per hour faster than top dog Bill Burke's tank had run on the lakes. Saturday's record runs of 193.54 miles per hour and 185.95 for a Bonneville average of 189.745 miles per hour got the pits buzzing again.

"When we ran on Friday, our time slip was delayed when Crocker had to figure it out by hand, because the speed went off his prepared chart," said Xydias, recalling how they discovered their good fortune. "We asked what speed the chart went up to, and Crocker said, '180.' We were stunned because on the lakes we had been crawling along, gaining a mile per hour, or two, with each run . . . and here at Bonneville we went more than 30 miles more than anyone ever had; it was a hell of a thing." The hundreds of press clippings generated by that single event, focusing on the amazing speed, by a hot rodder no less, changed not only their lives, but changed everything for everybody.

"When we left for home we were on top of the world," said Xydias in 1998. "I look back and shudder to think what would have happened if I had totaled the streamliner going up that hill. Would Bill Kenz had been so motivated to come back the next year with his incredible streamliner?"

Everyone appreciated how clean the salt was in comparison to the dusty dry lakes. By the end of the week, the salt had proven itself countless times. Competitors remarked that they had learned more in one week at Bonneville than in a whole year of competition on the lake beds. There was so much potential, how could they not? Of the 60 entries, the record setters for the first Bonneville Speed Week shook out his way:

Vehicle	Vehicle Number	Entrant	Average
Class A			
Streamliners	5A	Xydias & Batchelor	156.39
Class B			
Roadsters	60	Lean & Harrison	132.075
Lakesters	20	Starr & Alger	134.730
Lakesters*	54	Spaulding Brothers	141.765
Streamliners	24	Jim Lindsley	117.915
Class C			
Roadsters	100	John D. Browning	129.690
Lakesters	122	Don Waite	151.900
Streamliners	5C	Xydias & Batchelor	189.745
Class D			
Roadsters	74	Jot Horne	127.565
Streamliners	302	Kenz & Leslie	140.950
Competition Coupes	200	Bill Phy	92.870
Sports Cars	326	Kurtis-Kraft	142.515
Race Cars	87	McAlister & Walker	144.350

Body style was a modified roadster configuration, but no specific class had been developed at that time.

Union 76 freely distributed decals to Bonneville racers in 1949. Long before the days of "peel n' stick," these were applied to hard surfaces after being soaked in water and then carefully lifted from the paper backing. Many of the decals were affixed to the white pith helmets the oil company gave out that year. *LandSpeed Productions*

76 BONNEVILLE SPEED TRIALS

For more than 20 years the racer's best friend during Speed Week was Bell Auto Parts. The company would bring a wide variety of modestly priced parts and accessories onto the salt, erect a tent, and offer free technical help. Cases of oil flowed out of the truck as the week progressed. After the introduction of its Bell-brand helmet, the retailer would loan, free-of-charge, a helmet to any racer who needed one. Bell left the salt when the State of Utah demanded it start collecting sales tax. *Alan Welch Photo/LandSpeed Productions*

Report Card Time

Aside from the racing, the normally rambunctious gang of guys were, for the most part, on their best behavior. Wendover responded by making available every possible housing facility, including the barracks at the abandoned air base. Everywhere you went that week, you'd find racers working on their cars. Ab Jenkins attended and was also pleased with what he saw. So numerous were the "good report cards" received by Backman, that before SCTA left the salt in 1949, it had already earned the right to return in 1950.

Hot rod hero Mickey Thompson, in his book *Challenger*, written with Griffith Borgeson, said of the first event, "The whole show was the dream of a life time come true, of pinch-penny kids turned loose on the world's greatest race course. . . . It told a lot of us that we hot rodders were becoming big on the national scene, that our big meet someday could rival Indianapolis as the last word in American speed."

Thompson didn't make it the first year, but when he heard about the Xydias-Batchelor success, he was crazy with envy. He promptly went to his boss and put in for next year's vacation—the last week in August. Destination: the salt.

Lest you get the idea the racers were all choir boys, the recollections of never-shy Holly Hedrich and some Wendover residents add perspective. "For a few nights each year, the representative for a parts manufacturer rented brothels in nearby

Only two roadsters are on the starting line as the starter indicates that the salt now belongs to the car on the right. Forget about the world for now, there is only the speed deed at the moment, nothing else matters, nothing. *Kay Kimes Collection*

WHAT'S IN A CLASS

The classes have changed dramatically, changed often, and grown significantly throughout the past half-century. Today you can find everything from itty-bitty minibikes to splendiferous streamliners, or honking humongous diesel tractors alongside Mom's grocery-getter. Electrically powered vehicles are pushing 250 miles per hour right along with the piston motors. Fuels are utterly exotic, far more than just gas and "white lightning" alcohol. Those who can recite all the current classes and respective engine sizes probably do not have a life.

Originally, there were three main divisions: roadsters, lakesters, and streamliners. Only cars and trucks competed; sedans and motorcycles were not allowed to run until later years. Although the three divisions remain today, only the roadster maintained its basic, original definition.

Roadster class is American-made, 1928 and later convertible bodies unaltered in height, width, or contour. They are equipped with production-type radiator grilles.

Lakesters were originally modified roadsters but today are special construction cars with uncovered wheels. They may also be called "belly tanks" because the body shell came from an aircraft wing-tip fuel tank. Others look like 1/4-mile dragsters.

Streamliners were originally any type of fireproof constructed body not allowed in roadster or lakester classes. Today, these are the slippery-styled vehicles with all wheels and driver enclosed. They are the fastest salt racers.

Classes were further divided by engine size. "A" was the smallest and "D" was the biggest. In 1949, the SCTA classed the powerplants in direct conflict with international class distinctions. By 1960, the classes were changed to match the rest of the racing world.

At one time, engines with superchargers or added double overhead camshafts were automatically advanced to the next higher engine size class. Today, they have their own class designation. Originally, all engines were of American automotive production manufacture, but now they include a variety of automotive and motorcycle powerplants.

A pretty miss poses with the #28 entry Breene & Haller C Class roadster entry from Long Beach, California. Today, this car would run in the lakester class, but in 1949, the class designations were not that sophisticated. The belly tank body covers a 1940 258 CID flathead Mercury engine. Notice the cardboard over the intake stacks to prevent foreign ingestion. In the background is the number 734 C Class roadster of James M. Nugent from Bakersfield, California. He ran a 1942 296-CID Mercury flathead. *Hugh Coltharp Collection*

Dave Ratliff helps break in the Mercury engine in the Kimes and Gilchrist "streamliner" on the way to the first Bonneville speed meet. The boys had no time to run the engine before they left for the first salt meet, so they unhitched the car and drove the racer on the open highways. When they encountered a town along the way, they shut it down and pushed the car through so as to not raise any undue suspicion. They covered 300 miles in this fashion. The '41 Dodge pickup-made-tow vehicle did not have the horsepower to pull the race car over mountain passes. *Kay Kimes Photo/LandSpeed Productions*

Wells," chuckled Hedrich, explaining how some racers coped with the lack of housing. "In the morning, the girls would make breakfast for their johns. A lot of guys used the free services. A couple of girls set up shop at the A-1 Motel in Wendover and did a brisk trade. We were kids, 700 miles from home, having a hell of a time. "Gene Jones, former general manager of the State Line Hotel and Casino, had just started working for the business in 1949. He recalled, "In the early days, anyone who could put a car together would show up, they would bring their own beer, work on their engines all day and night, and left salt everywhere. Very few racers ever had money, or time, to gamble"

Life-long Wendover resident Gert Tripp remembers that if you didn't hide your car when the racers were in town, parts might disappear off them in the night, only to be returned at the end of the week. "They overwhelmed us and made a big commotion for a week," she said, "but were basically a good crowd."

Energetic cartoonist Tim Medley recalled, "The guys worked on their cars wherever they could, day and night. When Bob Tattersfield needed to warm up his engine one evening, he fired it up and roared right down Wendover Boulevard."

Not all the racers were overjoyed. Virgil Gardner of Salt Lake City wrote long letters of complaint, but his tone revealed he was mostly overwhelmed by the vast number of California cars. Parks' reply mollified Gardner, who then revealed that the city's biggest newspaper killed the final day story for fear it would promote hot rodding. Gardner, who had suffered from polio as a child, built and drove his car using only one arm. He revealed that car racing was the only sport that he had been able to qualify for, and ended his letter by offering help in the future.

The much trumpeted Bonneville meet was a resounding success from the racer's perspective, but a financial disaster for the SCTA, which came out the back end $300 in the red. Part of the reason was the SCTA had waited too long to fix a firm date. As late as June of 1949, the Board was still pussy-footing around. That was just too late for many people, especially from the Midwest and East Coast, to participate. "I didn't go up the first year because I didn't think it would catch on," confessed Tom Eiden, President of the Sidewinders Car Club. "That was too far to go."

On the other end of the spectrum were guys like Bob Higbee, who said, "I didn't have a car to race, but I would have taken the Greyhound bus if I had to."

"The people who went, loved it," recalled Ak Miller, now 78, who still tries to smoke cars off the line. "We could race flat-out and the cars would disappear over the horizon, taking their exhaust note with them, on this beautiful hard, smooth surface. We saw right away the salt was a rolling dynamometer; you just followed the black line up and over the peak power curve."

Regardless of the financial disaster, the SCTA recognized that Bonneville was nothing less than speed nirvana. Only here could the full potential of hopped-up Ford flatheads, Olds, Studebakers, Cadillacs, Chevrolets, Buicks, Nashes, Hudsons, and even Duesenbergs be explored and exploited.

Once the racers learned to adjust for the elevation, to lean out the fuel mixture, and to control the urge to over-correct the steering on the slipperier surface, a whole new racing adventure was theirs—straight ahead toward Floating Mountain, the detached peak of the Silver Range that seems to levitate above the surface like a mirage.

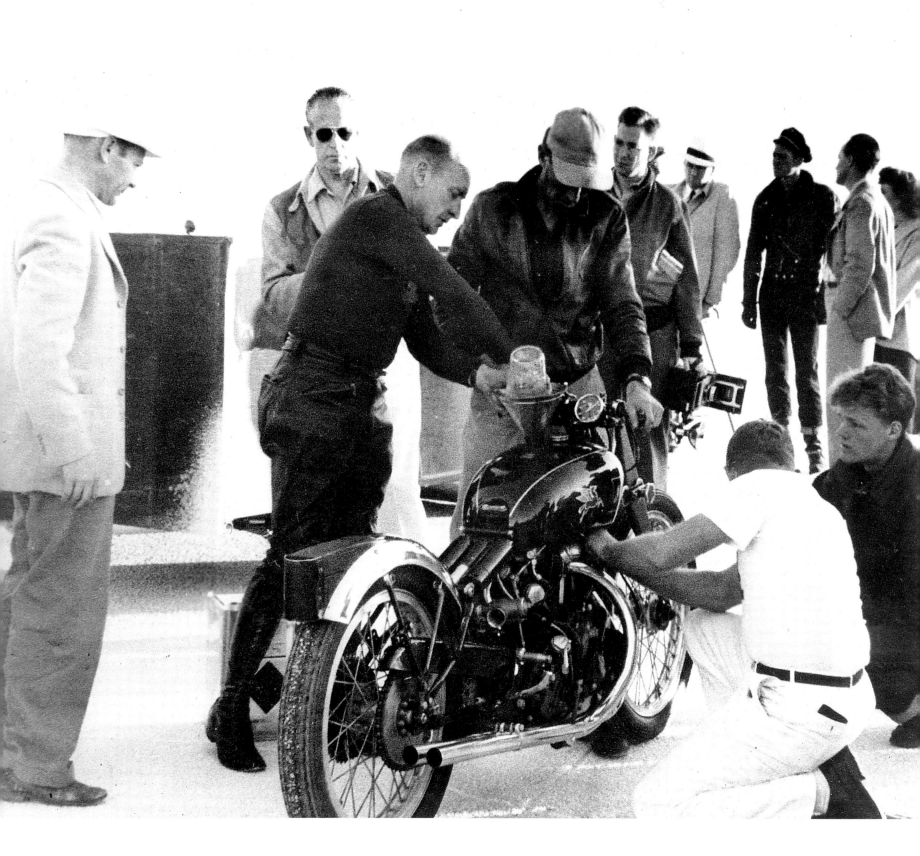

Chapter 6

Got the Fever, Beaver Cleaver?

Sapiens nihil affirmat quod non probat (Don't swear to anything you don't know firsthand)

—Anonymous Roman Charioteer

Cars weren't the only ones having fun on the salt. A year prior to the SCTA event, a World Record attempt was conducted surreptitiously, for fear an unmanageable crowd might adversely impact the streaking speck of a man on a snorting, black two-wheeler.

On September 13, 1948, riding in his best "superman-in-flight" prone position, Roland "Rollie" E. Free set a World Motorcycle Record of 150 miles per hour aboard a Vincent H.R.D. Black Shadow. He was wearing only a bathing suit, light shoes, and goggles. Not an erotic circus act, he was after the Harley Davidson-held U.S. national motorcycle speed record.

The private salt time for the record attempts was arranged by the bike owner, John Edgar, from Glendale, California. Described as a "wealthy sportsman who gathers motorcycles as some people do fine horses," he invited a few journalists, friends, and Ab Jenkins, the first man to ride a motorcycle across the salt.

As the bike was shipped over from the English factory in modified tune, the desired alcohol carburetors were already in place, but the saddle was swapped out for a special rear fender to support the rider's extended legs. Other special features included the first-ever Vincent use of a rear hydraulic damper and Mk II racing cams. "The bike was consistently running faster than the record," said Free after the Sunday morning test run, "but we made a gearing change and waited for the AMA officials to arrive that night."

AMA timing officials Frank Christian and Blacky Bullock set up using the same equipment that was used at the Indianapolis Motor Speedway. For a record, Free would have to run twice, within a 20-minute window. AMA referee Jack Williams arrived the 13th (what a day for record runs!). Free made a number of runs, and then accidentally ripped a seam in his leathers. The bike was ready for a return run before any stitching could be repaired, so Free stripped down to his swim trunks and took off. That single act, combined with the record speeds, chiseled Free into celebrity on the "bathing suit bike."

"I tach shifted all the way, first at 90 miles per hour, then quickly into third at 110, and hit top gear at 130," explained Free. "I didn't lay out on the bike until I hit top gear and then no longer looked ahead, but used the back corner of the gas tank as a sight to keep the bike on the painted line."

Once the naturally aspirated 998-cc V-twin engine was measured, the new record was certified at 150.313 in 23:95 seconds, to eclipse Joe Petrali's 136-mile-per-hour record. Danger behind him, he later cavalierly joked, "The engine was so smooth, I could have gone to sleep on the job."

Word of how good racing was on the salt beds spread through the ranks, and more hot rodders appeared in 1950. This time, with voracious appetite, they made 1,307 runs over the seven-day event. Bill Phy took a whack at the track 40 times, and when SCTA President Ak Miller saw what Phy had done, Miller gave his car 41.

Roland "Rollie" Free fuels the John Edgar owned Vincent HRD Black Shadow in preparation for his 150-mile-per-hour World Record run in 1948. That's Ab Jenkins with dark glasses. It was shortly after this picture was taken that Free ripped the seam in his riding leathers and removed them and the boots to make the famous "bathing suit" run. Crew member Mel Held holds the handlebars steady as mechanic Bill DeMott (kneeling in white) makes final adjustments to the carburetors. Held's son, Albert, looks on. *Deseret News* photographer Mr. Cody (holding the Speed Graphic camera), has his eye on Jenkins. In the background, Los Angeles Vincent agent Vincent Martin (in fedora) converses with AMA Timer's Assistant Blackie Bullock (hands in pockets). *Herb Harris Collection*

More than 90 cars preentered in 1950—30 more than the first year. In 1950, the expanded competition classes included roadsters, modified roadsters, lakesters, streamliners, coupes, modified coupes, and foreign cars. The new, B modified roadster of brothers Tommy and Jim Dahm from Pasadena was picked as "Most Typical Hot Rod" of the week.

A few racers pushed up over 200 miles per hour, but for one contestant it was disastrous. The *City of Pasadena II*, now a streamliner, was driven by "Puffy" Puffer. While in the timing traps and traveling in excess of 200 miles per hour, the car lifted off the ground, flew 150 feet, landed upside down, and while spinning like a top, scattered plastic body parts all over the course. Puffer, an experienced racer, was out of the car and on his feet long before rescue crews got to the wreckage. His only injury was a skinned ear, owing mainly to the car's outstanding safety construction. The accident made a lasting impression on others as to the merits of quality construction and sound aerodynamic design.

The sparkling new streamliner of Bill Kenz and Roy Leslie, driven by 28-year-old Willie Young, screamed into hot rod history cutting the first-ever 200-mile-per-hour run, at 206.504 miles per hour. On his return run, Young lost the treads off both front Indy-type tires, leaving room for speculation that his vehicle could have clearly outperformed the Xydias & Batchelor car, had the tires held up. "I knew it was a good run, but I didn't think it was 200," explained Young. "As I reached down and pulled it out of gear, the horizon line blurred out and my hands were forced wide open on the steering wheel. The vibration was so bad I thought the engine had blown."

Worse, the diamond-studded Longines watch, a gift from his mother, had disintegrated. "The band, case, and crystal were still on my wrist, but the hands were lying at the bottom of the dial face and the gears were sticking out through the face," added Young, noting how violently the steering wheel danced. He stopped without incident, but the car was through. Inspection of the car revealed the normally round tie-rod ends were now scrap metal, the radius rod ends had shaken oval, and the steering gear was so out of whack that it took three-quarters of a turn before the front wheels would respond.

Another engine battle was raging in the Class C roadster category. Early in the week, Don Waite had set the bar at 159 miles per hour. This left LeRoy Titus, Don Blair, and Ak Miller to scrap it out for days, each struggling to eke out another mile-an-hour from their machines. Blair's crew hit upon the winning idea of rigging-up some cardboard streamlining effects; they cut out discs from Sta-Lube boxes and, using yards of masking tape, covered the wheels and shaped a conical nose. Comical as it looked, all that mattered was that it worked. When the salt spray cleared, Blair was on top of the heap with a 161-mile-per-hour average. You can bet there was later discussion with the rules committee about the perpetrated genius.

More common among the speedsters was using one car, but swapping engines to compete in multiple classes, a practice that continues to modern times. Proving the point was the stylish 1934 modified coupe of the Pierson Brothers, who calmly set new top speed marks in both B and C classes at 150 miles per hour. All through the seven-day speed fest, engines went in and engines came out, parts went on and parts blew off, wheels were trued and tires got chewed, and the smell of greasy oil perfumed the air.

Home Sweet Wendover

Bing Crosby said the town reminded him of the end of Tobacco Road, and Bob Hope told a city official they ought to consider changing its name to Leftover. The racing crowd might have agreed that it was a sparse outpost, where pious Utah met frontier-spirited Nevada, but they were grateful for what little there was.

Each night, most racers headed for Wendover to work on their cars. When the sun went down the hot rodders pulled out flashlights, turned on headlights, or relocated to well-lit motel rooms to reassemble their engines. Fred Bannister, who had come all the way from Wilmington, Delaware, was tired of driving. Remaining instead on the salt, he engaged in vigorous heave and huff exercises, swapping engines by using two-by-fours and a length of chain.

Spicing up the entry list to give the event a national flavor were John Greytak, Jr., who brought a coupe from Great Falls, Montana, and Jack Heitzler from St. Louis, Missouri, who coaxed 113 miles per hour out of his big, five-window coupe. Other cars came from Pennsylvania, North Carolina, Wisconsin, Ohio, Indiana, Alabama, Michigan, and Arizona. What can you say about Tad Campbell and Bill Niendorf who drove all the way from Seattle, Washington, at 35 miles per hour? The puttering pair were so late, that by the time they arrived there was only time enough left to make two high-speed runs. You gotta wonder. Many people were

Willie Young, of Colorado, was the first hot rodder to exceed 200 miles per hour, driving the Kenz and Leslie streamliner in 1950. Pictured here in 1952, the crew works feverishly on the twin flathead engines in preparation of what would be the first 250-mile-per-hour run. *Ron Leslie*

Under construction in 1950, at the Denver, Colorado, shop of Bill Kenz and Roy Leslie is the pair's new streamliner. Fitted with the same dual flathead engines Kenz had used to run 140 miles per hour with "*Angel,*" the Model A truck body, during the inaugural SCTA Bonneville Nationals in 1949, the driver's compartment has an unpadded bucket seat, single lap safety belt, and hand-operated brake and clutch controls. The car could run with either one, or both engines operating. *Ron Leslie Collection*

curious about the potential of Lee Chapel's Tornado overhead-valve engine conversion, featuring his own brand of rocker arms, dual Riley side-draft carbs, and a 180 degree crankshaft atop a 3/8 by 3/8 295 bored and stroked CID Mercury.

The Big Switcheroo

Although there was no award for heroics, it no doubt belonged to Barney Navarro of Glendale, California. Near the close of the week, something possessed Navarro to convert his B modified roadster into an O streamliner. Yes, you read that right. Off came the blower and one V-8 head before his crew cut off the four respective connecting rods. Next, the appropriate intake manifold passages were blocked. Pictures of the day show Navarro's pit area swarming with more than 20 people thrashing to ready the car. Engine done, a rough, stinger-style tail was grafted onto the car's posterior before they changed the gears,

Bill Burke's first streamliner, *HOT ROD Magazine Special*, was powered by a stock 80-CID Harley Davidson motorcycle engine. With a fiberglass body, the car weighed 740 pounds and set the Class O record at 136.90 miles per hour, which stood for 10 years. A colorful sight, the helmet was royal purple, with orange motorcycle goggles to filter out the glare. Burke competed at all 50 speed trials since 1949, and served as SCTA president and starter. *Bill Burke Collection*

Bud Hare sits astride his record-breaking 30.5-CID Triumph during the 1951 Bonneville Nationals, the first year motorcycles were invited to compete with the hot rodders. Hare improved the rider's comfort (?!) level and lowered wind resistance by fabricating the "ironing board" plate. The lowered riding position was made possible by tipping the engine on its side and fitting it with a two-barrel Stromberg downdraft carburetor. *Leslie Long*

Depicted here early in the week, Norm Lean and Doug Harrison have a casual chat with friends around their pretty red roadster. Lean used his 1934 convertible to pull the racer 700 miles to the salt, from Whittier, California. In the background, the SCTA volunteer crew can be seen setting up the timer's stand. *Leslie Long*

tires, and wheels and pushed the buzzing, 180 degree crankshaft creation, with all of 88 cubic inches, off the line.

Actually, it was a symbiotic speed run as the push truck stayed with the car until just before the traps to garner Navarro a 78-mile-per-hour timing slip. Humble as the numbers were, it was the first run chalked up for the new O Class and gave Navarro the record and a trophy. Only a die-hard hobbyist would exert that level of effort.

Competitors established nine new Bonneville records and improved on seven old ones. The Kenz and Leslie streamliner was presented with the "Best Designed Car," but Xydias and Batchelor lugged off the new, immense 4-foot high *HOT ROD* magazine National Championship Trophy for fastest one-way time of the meet.

One thing was certain, the sport of land speed racing was on the upside of the power curve. As long as the sport was done for fun and recreation, not money and fame, it would thrive. Content with bragging rights, a timing slip, and an occasional trophy, racers put little value in the "certifications" available from AAA or similar organizations.

Part of the speed chase was the design and fabrication of the new, improved performance parts, developed by the racers themselves. Kong Jackson's popular "Roto-faze" two-coil ignition design for the flathead germinated from need. "Engines would pop and miss, so I developed precision ignitions that would not wobble," Jackson explained.

Innovators Bill and Tom Spalding were fascinated with ignition systems. Tom claims to have built the first dual-coil, dual-point ignition system while a sophomore in the high school machine shop. Bill liked to work with camshafts.

Ed Winfield was legendary for his carburetors, cams, and cylinder heads. He even taught Stu Hilborn a few things about fuel injection, and Chevrolet picked up a Winfield design in 1956 when his patent ran out. So protective was he of his creativity that Winfield allowed precious few into his shop, his sanctuary. When you came to visit, conversations took place through a tiny, 6-inch gap in the door.

Lee Chapel made a big noise on the salt when he showed up with this blue-and-white streamliner that could double as an early version of the *"Batmobile."* Fellow racers were fascinated with Chapel's fuel injection and overhead valve conversion. *Leslie Long*

Eddie Miller, Jr.'s, aluminum-bodied lakester won Best Engineered Vehicle at the 1952 speed trials. A half century later, few cars can rival its outstanding attention to detail. Miller cast ALL his own parts from patterns of his own making, except the wheels. A particular work of art was the quick-change rear end. The car ran 150 miles per hour with the 1949 Pontiac six-cylinder engine. *Jim Miller Collection*

An Ed of a different sort was an Armenian named Ed Isk-enderian, another student of Winfield's whom the racers dubbed, "The Camfather." Possibly connected at birth to an unlit cigar, the hefty "Isky" had a knack for developing cam profiles just before the racers knew they needed them.

Everyone knew that if anyone could make power with a super-charger, it was Tom Beatty. He built and drove a damn fast lakester, but could destroy parts as fast as he set records. Tom Beatty and his uncanny knack with superchargers complemented Barney Navarro's genius for intake manifolds. Navarro also served up a design lesson to Vic Edelbrock, demonstrating the importance of large intake passageways and the merits of precisely matching the intake runners. Navarro's preaching triggered a shift away from a 90 degree matching angle to a more effective 45 degree angle.

The competition among the performance parts makers was congenial and good-natured, and they engaged in a friendly banter about whose stuff was the best. There was little malice or litigious behavior. If some new widget appeared, the only thing that mattered was if it made the car go faster.

Speed Wrinkle Rides Again!

Ab Jenkins, now 67, started at dawn on Labor Day, 1950, and chalked up 26 World and American records, including a new 1-hour record of 195 miles per hour. He drove the big, blue-and-orange *Mormon Meteor III*, which had been "unmoth-balled" from its state capitol shrine after seven years. Taking the checkered flag, he remarked, "I'm a little tired, because I'm not used to getting up so early in the morning anymore."

Have Youthful Exuberance; Will Go Faster

When 151 racers pre-entered for another "Mardi Gras" of speed in 1951, Bill Burke was SCTA president. This year, all record-breaking vehicles would be inspected and engines measured before the times would be certified as legal. For the first time, two black oil guide lines were laid the length of the track after Ab Jenkins suggested it would help the racers stay on course.

Hot rodders fumed hither and yon, gapping plugs, adjusting carburetors, and mixing wild fuel concoctions in the early morning darkness. This year they were joined by the nervous roar of 10 motorcycle entries. The "invitation only" riders were:

1. Marty Dickerson   60 CID 1948 Vincent
2. Jim Witham   40 CID Triumph
3. Bud Parriott   40 CID 1949 Triumph
4. Eugene Thiessen   B.S.A.
5. Chet Herbert   80 CID 1947 Harley
6. Bud Hare   30.5 CID Triumph
7. Bus Schaller   61 CID Harley
8. Jack Dale   45 CID Harley
9. Joe Simpson   61 CID 1948 Vincent
10. Lloyd Bulmer   21 CID 1948KSS Velocette

BONNEVILLE NATIONAL SPEED TRIALS

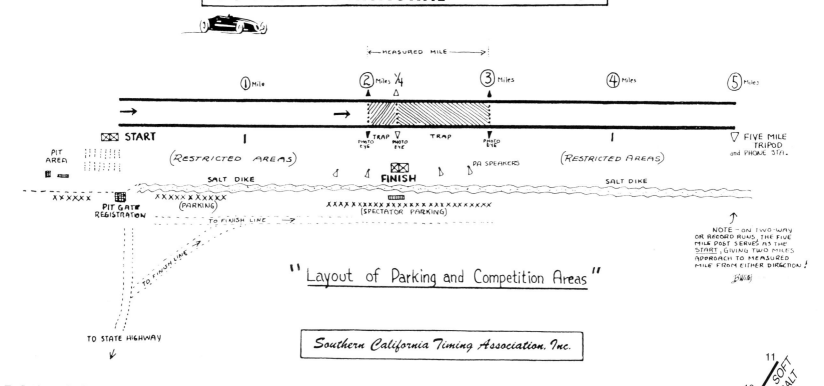

"Layout of Parking and Competition Areas"

Southern California Timing Association, Inc.

NOTE – ON TWO-WAY OR RECORD RUNS, THE FIVE MILE POST SERVES AS THE START, GIVING TWO MILES APPROACH TO MEASURED MILE FROM EITHER DIRECTION!

The first international course required drivers to negotiate a gentle curve, before it was relocated further west. The circular endurance track locations changed with the salt hardness from year to year. The access road was constructed in 1970, along with Interstate 80. Until then the racers simply turned off the highway and parked just past the mud dike. Most early hot rod racing took place along a 5-mile course with the pits located at the starting line. *Walt Metcalf*

Women Tried but Were Denied

At age 20, Doris Stinson of Bell, California, was already so technically savvy that she bought her first 1932 roadster by herself from racer Don Lutes. Smitten with Doris' hot rod know-how, he offered to help make the car a competitive lakes and drag strip car. She accepted first his help and then later his marriage proposal. For Bonneville, Doris handled all the car's mechanical work: re-jetting, plug reading, tire changing, etc., and ran consistent 136-mile-per-hour runs in Class C. Although Stinson was the car owner, the car had to be driven by her husband.

The SCTA was still in the Neanderthal stage of its existence when it came to women drivers, and forbade them competing. Ak Miller explained the reason for this prejudice: "If a woman was ever killed, or maimed in a car, it could spell disaster for the entire sport. In those days, the men were terrified that if a woman was hurt, or worse, killed, and left behind children, the sport might never recover from the bad publicity."

Naturally, no one mentioned how seriously bunched up the hot rodder's BVDs would have been had they been beaten by a girl. Over time, women were issued competition licenses, but only after a protracted, puddin-head battle.

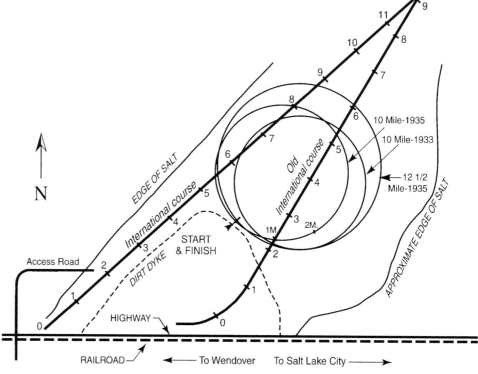

With all these eager beavers working on the Blue-and-Gold modified roadster, the team of Osborn and Garrett certainly need the unique "flip-top" body mechanism. In the background can be seen the mountain peaks named for early salt racers: Tetzlaff and Rishel to the left and Jenkins and Campbell to the right. *Leslie Long*

Jim Lindsley's wife, Phyllis, was a stalwart and much-admired volunteer for the SCTA in the early days, but her involvement was limited to traditional clerical and administration tasks. Once, though only because of her tremendous volunteerism, the men allowed her to make one run, probably the first by a woman. It was the same story for Marge Francisco, Fran Cagle, and Doris Ellenberg.

Making nearly 2,000 runs, 200 entrants from 15 states set a total of 16 new class records in 1951. A little rain loosened the track, but Willie Young was unfazed and perpetuated the ground-pounding ecstasy as he drove the *K&L Streamliner* to another all-time, one-way run of 230 miles per hour.

Several thousand spectators came to watch the salt spectacle wind up between two very long oil lines. So safe were the trials, only Ak Miller's onboard fire at 172 miles per hour gave any cause for nail-biting all week. His 1927 Model T was powered by a rear-engine flathead and dubbed *Miller's Missile* because of its aerodynamic styling, designed by Art Ford of P-51 Mustang fame.

A Troop of Coupes

This year the big battle raged in the C Modified Coupe division that held 18 closely matched entries. Dawson Hadley pitted against Doug Hartelt and Paul Leon. Both cars were chopped and channeled 1934 coupes. The two teams spent the whole meet out-running each other until they ran out of horsepower and then switched classes and started the whole battle anew.

Spirited rivals on the salt, both teams hung out together even when the racing was done for the day. Yup, it was Bonneville

Speed Week again, that sociological wonder that mixes competition with a technical psychology for a marvelous blend of Americana, pure and loud.

Stink, Stinkers, and The Stink

Stinkers Clem Tebow and Dan Clark stuck an Ardun (so named for engineer Zora Arkus-Duntov, who also heavily influenced the Corvette) OHV Merc engine in a 1932 roadster to run a 164 miles per hour. That blew the lid off the once-cozy 152-mile-per-hour lead enjoyed by the Lean and Harrison team.

The only malodorous stink of the meet came when a few competitors protested Fred Carillo and Robert Betz's sleek, modified roadster, which had nailed a 178-mile-per-hour run. Funny thing, the second-place man, the one with the most to gain, wasn't interested in the beef. According to the rules, Carillo's slippery body was a fraction-of-an-inch too skinny. Carillo got sacked, but came back with body additions of cardboard-and-tape that hilariously appeased the technical committee.

You could tell when the liquid dynamite was uncorked; there was no mistaking the acrid, nose-wrinkling, eye-watering smell of nitromethane. Sometimes called "nitro," or "the poor man's supercharger," it is a volatile, colorless chemical used with methanol and other additives to blend exotic fuel charges for the hot rodder's engine. The explosive chemical helps produce more oxygen in the combustion chamber, which can boost the potency of a given fuel charge, but misuse could destroy an engine. Closer tolerances in the heads, proper jetting of the carburetors, and precise percentages of additives were mandatory before loading up a hefty charge.

Long-Range Roadsters

Roadsters, the car of choice all over the nation, were plentiful at Bonneville. Bob Hamke, from Indianapolis, Indiana, had the best recorded time for a non-California car at 149 miles per hour. Bill Waddill drove from Flint, Michigan. Chuck Adams from Dallas, Texas, managed 136 miles per hour. But the big show was the entire Cheyenne, Wyoming, roadster club turning out to compete at Bonneville.

Blowers began to show promise when Tom Beatty rolled in with his new girder-type tube frame wing tank chassis that sported a swing axle rear suspension. His 296-CID Mercury engine was topped with Navarro heads and Roots-type blower. The combination clocked a staggering 188 miles per hour through the quarter-mile.

Were the Flatheads Through in '52?

The much-loved and thoroughly exploited Ford flathead was in the sunset of its distinguished service career by 1952. Chrysler had debuted its new overhead valve "Hemi" the year before, selling more than a million in Dodge, DeSoto, and Chrysler models. Of the 10 OHVs that showed up at Bonneville, five were Hemis, four were V-8 Cadillacs, and Oldsmobile had a Rocket for your pocket. What the Chryslers didn't do, the amazing Chevrolet small-block would, when it was unveiled three years later.

HOT ROD magazine claimed a circulation of 300,000 in 1952, and the fledgling speed parts industry had just rung up gross sales of a million dollars annually, testament to the auto enthusiast's insatiable desire to rework Detroit iron. Wendover was growing as well. The State Line built a new two-story hotel and erected the world's tallest moving sign to attract customers in 1952. Wendover Will, the world's tallest, arm-waving cowboy, instantly became the town mascot. As a prelude to the 1952 Nationals, Goldie Gardner brought a streamlined MG based on the EX-135 chassis designed by George Eyston to capture five new international records in Classes F and G, plus 66 more national records.

The Speed Week race for horsepower expanded into 41 separate divisions for 1952, with many of the new overhead valve powerplants immediately being adapted for salt racing. The 10 "invited" motorcycles from the 1951 event had trampled so many AMA records, some decades old, that it prompted SCTA officials to double the invitation list for 1952.

Establishment automotive engineers often informed the enthusiasts their modification ideas were impossible, yet every year more impossible things were done and engineers' work improved upon. A prime example of this was Eddie Miller's Pontiac-powered lakester, one of only two Pontiacs entered. Both were considered as powerful as boat anchors by the speed set. Miller's bronze-painted creation was superb, built from the ground-up over a three-year period. He had painstakingly cast all his own parts from patterns and designs of his own making, right down to the cast rear-end gearbox. All the cast parts bore his name. Writer and tech head Don Francisco drove the car 156 more-than-respectable miles per hour.

The Kenz and Leslie streamliner, now called the *Floyd Clymer Motorbook Special*, gained top speed of the meet, again, at 250 miles per hour. Tom Cobbs and Bud Fox got two records with their modified coupe built to compete in Class B and C, using Cobb's GMC 3-71 blower setup. Bill Burke nailed the O Class record with a 740-pound fiberglass *HOT ROD Magazine Special* streamliner.

Streamliner designs and performance potential for 1952 were so astonishing that the SCTA was compelled to lengthen the course to 6 miles. *The Beast III* was the creation of Chet Herbert and Ed Johnson, who poured themselves into the project. Herbert, confined to a wheelchair, did much of the mechanical work. His design called for umpteen blueprints, wind tunnel tests, and engineering services to achieve as near "neutral" lift as was possible for the new car. It was a radical departure from traditional hot rodding, but necessary, as the pair was looking ahead for a 300-mile-per-hour run. The all-aluminum 300-CID Franklin engine, once used in Tuckers, returned an effortless 236-mile-per-hour run, the second-fastest of the meet.

Harold Post of Orange, California, and Doug Hartelt trotted out the tube-chassis *Post Special* with the first-ever quick change fuel tanks, and Lee Chapel's *Tornado* was an all-aluminum body. Willie Davis and George Hill turned up with the *City of Burbank* (designed by Dean Batchelor) to collect Chicago-based Maremont Automotive Products' newly commissioned Maremont Cup, given to the car that had not only the best engineering idea, but that also

No doubt one of the most industrious racers on the salt in 1951 was Barney Navarro of Glendale, California, who converted his B modified roadster into an O streamliner in less than a day. To the amusement of all, the push truck didn't peel off until just before the traps to help the metal creature scrape up a 78-mile-per-hour timing slip—good enough for a trophy and O Class record. *Leslie Long*

proved itself in the traps. Also included was a $1,000 scholarship to any university or accredited college.

After the Nationals, Hill and Davis came back to the salt two weeks later and George Hill set new international Class C records for the flying start kilometer and mile, taking the record away from the Auto Union. With that one act, the hot rodder achieved a legitimacy heretofore unknown. It would be the first of many.

The speeds were up but spirits were down after so many Firestone Indy tires threw their treads, prompting serious concern for the future of unbridled enthusiasm for a sport where dependable, high-speed tires were essential to safety. The "Stones" were rated only to 175, but many cars were exceeding that speed. Higher-speed Dunlops from England were too costly for a hot rodder budget.

What would become Bonneville's biggest threat for continued vitality arrived that year. The newly formed National Hot Rod Association (NHRA), although in its infancy, a decade later would be the single biggest reason salt racers steadily defected to the hard-surfaced quarter-mile tracks. Why run a few times a year when you could run several times a week?

But, just like the Little Mermaid, the newly baptized drag racers would pay a dear price for racing more often. They would leave behind the alluring song that echoed for many a mile, and their car's thunderous, haunting voice would be exchanged for the wham-quick, slam-squawk burst of a measly quarter-mile.

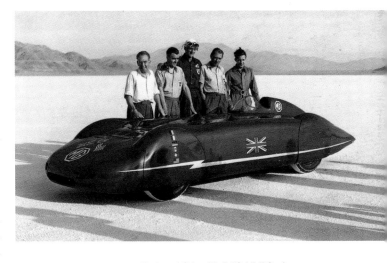

Lieutenant Colonel A. T. "Goldie" Gardner (center) stands with his able and delighted crew in August of 1952. Just prior to the SCTA Bonneville Nationals getting under way, Goldie drove the streamlined MG to five new international records in Classes F and G, plus 66 more national records. *Bill Shipler/Utah State Historical Society*

Chapter 7

Learning to
Fly, or Not

The single most important development in the early days of Bonneville racing changed the course of amateur racing forever. Firestone Tire and Rubber heard the salt racer's cry for help, and responded with a new brand of high-speed tires, reliable up to 300 miles per hour.

Firestone's critical contribution marked the first time that a mainstream company had designed and built a product specifically for use at the Bonneville Salt Flats. The new, eight-ply tires were appropriately named "Bonneville" and featured a new method of tread adhesion. To Firestone's further credit, the specialty tires were priced well within the reach of hot rodders. The new tires allowed many to aspire to loftier goals and lifted the entire sport to a new level of motorized creativity.

Unlike modern record-setting, this was the era where vehicles were obliged to make three runs before an existing record would fall, so it was plain that tires played a major part in any speed attempt. The procedure started by making a "qualifying run" with a speed that exceeded the existing record. On the following morning, those "qualifying" vehicles would make two more runs up and down the course, and if the average was over the existing record and the car's engine passed a subsequent inspection, a new record was declared.

Life magazine in 1953 ran a cover feature on hot rodding acknowledging the sport's explosive growth. Had the modified vehicle crowd finally achieved some respect? Hardly. The National Automobile

Against the ruin of the world There is only one defense— the creative act!

—Unknown

Dealers Association (NADA) viewed the hot rodder as a national threat and voted at its national convention "not to sell, or give service to hot rodders."

Joining the dealers in their ignorance was *New York Times* columnist Bert Pierce, who equated anyone who wanted a "souped car" to someone who had "flagrant disregard for commonsense driving regulations," and accused the hot rodder for all increases in traffic accidents and fatalities.

It was clear that if recognition were to come for hot rodder achievements, it would have to come from within the ranks, and it did. Over lunch one day, Lou Kimzey, managing editor of *Hop Up* magazine, and Dean Batchelor dreamed up the 200MPH Club. With the help of *Hop Up* publisher Bill Quinn, the club was established. The 200MPH Club was created as a way to recognize the remarkable speed achievements of hot rodders (see the accompanying sidebar for details). The sole requirement for lifetime membership, and the *only* way to get in, was to drive a car two ways over a measured mile at a clocked speed of 200 miles an hour or better. It was not necessary to set a record to qualify, but the time had to be certified by either the AAA or SCTA.

Captain George Eyston was elected its first president. Ask anyone on the salt; it is a goal of Olympian proportions, one that requires a concerted, synergistic effort of mind, body, and machine coupled to a cooperative weather pattern.

During the 1953 Fifth Annual Bonneville Nationals, out of almost 300 entries clocked on 1,171 runs down a 9-mile course,

An advocate of high compression ratios and high boost pressures, Tom Beatty and his tenacious tanks were always guaranteed to "blow" or "go!" Beatty blew up more motors in one week of salt racing than any other racer might trash in a year. He qualified for the 200 Mile Per Hour Club in 1955 at 211 miles per hour. *Bob D'Olivo*

Trigger got a vacation in September of 1953, when Roy Rogers swapped horsepower to drive this Chrysler Town & Country station wagon at a comfortable 106 miles per hour. He later hightailed it down the course on a motorcycle. *Utah State Historical Society*

If ever there was a motorized version of the great American cowboy, Johnny Allen would be it. Riding Stormy Mangham's Triumph-powered *Texas "Cee-gar"*, these backyard speed surgeons cut down every record the well-financed NSU German motorcycle company team had set only a few days earlier. The bike featured a spring-loaded parachute, one of the earliest examples of its kind. *Bob D'Olivo*

only five qualified for membership in the new, go-fast fraternity. The regular entry fee for Bonneville had risen to $15. A scant 16 motorcycles were preentered.

A fellow who literally swapped horsepower was America's singing cowboy, Roy Rogers. He had parked Trigger to hightail it down the course in a station wagon and on a motorcycle. The conservative Chrysler station wagon may have putzed along at only 106 miles per hour, but it was a mighty special ride, pardner. Rogers was a real

speed fanatic and owned bikes up until the day he went to find his happy trails in the sky.

Tom Beatty was awesome, but when he ran bad, you'd better duck for cover because parts would be flying. In 1953, he blew up a week's worth of engines, one for every seven days of the meet, but tickled 200 with a 198 run. Quite possibly, over the course of his racing career Beatty blew up more engines than 20 salt racers combined. As die-hard a racer as they come, one year he even yanked the engine out of the push truck, blew it up, and had to call his wife back in Southern California to bring spare parts before he could leave for home.

Others made a name for themselves right on the salt. The *Northern Washington Special* from Tacoma got plenty of double-takes in O Class with its "Hey, let's go fish" 60-cc Evinrude outboard. It made folks wonder if those guys were nippin' on the nightcrawlers to come up with this entry.

Through the years, the high degree of safety at Bonneville could be traced back to Roy "Multy" Aldrich's stringent technical inspection process for the SCTA. Aldrich, a service station owner, had an uncanny sense of mechanical right and wrong; he could easily see flaws and dangerous conditions that eluded some of the most dedicated inspectors and knowledgeable racers. It is safe to say many a young life was protected because Aldrich chose to volunteer his time.

SCTA's safety and technical regulations constantly tried to stay at least one run ahead of the salt racer, especially the streamliner bunch. At this point in time, racers were beginning to realize that streamlining was certainly the fast track to high speed, but it could also be a slippery path to disaster as well. Such was the lesson that Sonny Rogers learned driving Lee Chapel's *Tornado* during the fifth Bonneville Nationals. While under power in the last quarter-mile of the timing traps, the car fishtailed, flipped, and skidded right

through the lights, to record a speed of 215 miles per hour, upside down. The driver's compartment was virtually undamaged and the driver, remarkably, unshaken.

Because the early Bonneville streamliner designs were usually copies of other vehicles from other segments of motorsports, rather than original designs rooted in science and engineering, most experiments were carried out in the seat-of-the-pants laboratory while traveling quickly down the black line. The streamliner classes were responsible for more advancements in safety protocol than any other class. When the design was right and horsepower applied properly, oh, what a sight they were! What speed potential they unlocked!

Not so lucky was Fred Carillo, driving the 1,300-pound (mostly engine) streamliner built by himself and brother-in-law Bob Betz. The brutish Firepower engine was the creation of Chuck Potvin and Doug Hartelt. Early test runs had proven that their wind tunnel testing predictions for stability were on target. Carillo approached the Firestone racing representative and explained he was going for a 300-mile-per-hour run. The tire man tried to discourage him, but Carillo was adamant. The Firestone guy told Carillo to pump an additional 30 psi into each tire—for a total of 90 psi! Unfortunately, Carillo was using new, experimental, magnesium wheels that were later discovered to have had a high degree of porosity. The extra air pressure split the weak, alloy wheels at 270 miles per hour.

"At that point, I knew I was just along for the ride," Carillo said, recalling that when the car began to tumble, "Oh shit, here we go," was all he could find time to say. For more than a mile he bounced and banged in every possible direction. "The four-part body broke away as designed," he added, "but I wished I had taken the time to install the rest of the driver compartment shielding." Those floor pans would have prevented his legs from moving outside the framework, but as it was, the driveshaft chewed out 4 inches of his leg just above the ankle. Doctors tried to save the foot with an experimental procedure, but failed.

Even though the accident occurred after the regular SCTA speed week, during a special session devoted to setting International Records, HOT ROD editor Wally Parks must have been terrified the accident might put a safety blemish on the Bonneville Nationals. Parks' report in HOT ROD painted a more rosy, benign picture of the tragic wreck: "Carillo emerged from the wreckage with lacerated hands and a broken leg . . . he climbed out of the car by himself . . ."

Those who knew the truth saw Parks' remarks as an anemic attempt to preserve a no-longer spotless safety record of the salt. "We all understood the inherent dangers of speed attempts," said Carillo. "Sometimes accidents can't be avoided."

Surprisingly unexpected, actions by the AAA Contest Board staff immediately following the Carillo's accident prompted racers to reevaluate their negative opinion of the organization. "Art Pillsbury was the only one of the whole group who came to see me in the hospital," said a grateful Carillo, whose family moved to Salt Lake City during the medical procedure. "He came by several times, making sure everything that could be done was being done."

By 1953, the pits swarmed with Detroit's new overhead valve engines. Of the 17 records set in 32 classes, 12 were with the overheads. Counted among the rocker-arm brigade were Chrysler Hemis, Cadillac V-8's, Studebakers, and Olds Rockets.

The Vesco-Dinkins lakester was a 3-foot-high, open-wheeled car that sported a mere 36-inch tread, front and rear, and was powered by a Model B engine that stormed to a 156-mile-per-hour average equipped with a Riley four-port head and custom-built fuel injection. The team was voted "Best Appearing" in 1957 for their efforts.

Drag racing great Art Chrisman came to the salt, arriving with a stunning rear-engined Ardun competition coupe trading ogles with Texan Gus Maybee's Streetliner, a roadster-style open sports car with the Chrysler V-8 that sailed to a 203-mile-per-hour average. Among the other entrants was the San Diego drag racing contingent led by Joaquin Arnet. His Bean Bandits were plagued by problems, but had a gas of time anyway. Arnet, a diminutive man with a beguiling smile and unvarnished wit, was fond of saying he raced just to prove that a Mexican could be as fast as the gringos.

Navy pilot Lt. Harvey Haller brought his high-quality lakester (built for only $691 on the air base) all the way from Oahu, Hawaii, and snapped at 200's door, turning in a 199-mile-per-hour run. Don Waite, finished with his Army stint, pushed his pointy-nosed modified roadster up to a very fast 191 miles per hour.

When Mike Waters made his very first run down the salt, it was so long that he feared he might not get to the other end. In 1955, Waters and partner Dean Murray believed their spunky 318-cubic inch Chevrolet was the first successful small-bock used in salt racing—the same year General Motors introduced the tasty engine in passenger cars. Because no speed parts were available for the new engine, they made their own. *Mike Waters Collection*

Unlike "big business" racing, amateur racing offers rewards that are much more valuable than money, fame, and celebrity. In exchange for thousands of hours of work and money that no one keeps track of for fear they might learn how much they have spent, the humble timing tag and the trophy bring a lifetime benefit of bragging rights and the respect of their peers. *Mike Waters Collection*

Bonneville from the push truck perspective. Ever so gently does the truck bumper connect with the push bar on the tail of Ak Miller's modified roadster in 1955. Together they sprint down the course until the Oldsmobile engine fires and the truck veers off to the right. Averaging 225 miles per hour, Miller joined the 200 MPH Club at age 71 in 1991, driving a Crosley-powered car built by speed elf Ron Benham. *Bob D'Olivo*

Mohammed Comes to the Salt

Of course, the big news of the 1953 Speed Week was when Mohammed came to the mountain, or AAA came to the salt. Immediately following the SCTA event, five of the hottest hot rod streamliners in the country took aim on World, International, and National records. When it was through, a total of 22 records from three cars belonged to hot rodders. It was big plus for the sport. Wally Parks summed it best when he later wrote in a *HOT ROD* magazine editorial, "Back yard boys have accomplished what it took industry to do in other countries—and improved versions of this country's industry, American production automobile engines."

In addition to the six international and six national records for the Shadoff Special, Chet Herbert and 22-year-old driver LeRoy Neumayer set two international and two national Class B records, some of which were Ab Jenkins' old Duesenberg records. Dana Fuller, Jr.'s, red-and-yellow "Big Mamoo" diesel (the ex-Herbert *Beast III*) streamliner powered by two superchargers; a GMC centrifugal feeding through a standard side-mounted Roots-type blower, thundered into two International, two World, and two American records bounding past the clocks at 170 miles per hour. Captain George Eyston climbed into an Austin-Healey, newly introduced to the American market, and grabbed a number of American-held stock records. Then, creator Donald Healey took the wheel and set a 3,100-mile endurance record.

THE 200 MILE PER HOUR CLUB

A Glimpse of the Formative Years . . .

Thinking of a way to recognize the remarkable accomplishments, Lou Kimzey, managing editor of *Hop Up* magazine, and Dean Batchelor dreamed up the Bonneville 200 Mile Per Hour Club (sometimes called the "2 Club") at lunch one day. They approached publisher Bill Quinn, who liked the idea and agreed to furnish decals, T-shirts, and membership cards, and announce the club's formation in the June 1953 issue of *Hop Up*. Batchelor wrote the article, which became the speed club's constitution. It said, in part:

It's about time our small group of record holders are given the recognition they deserve. . . . It is just my opinion that the achievements of men who can take a production engine, hop it up, and build a body around the chassis and then turn the fabulous speeds these men do have long been underrated.

Hop Up magazine takes pleasure in announcing our 200MPH Club. The sole requirement for membership, and the *only* way to get in, is to drive a car two ways over a measured mile at a clocked speed of 200 miles an hour or better. It is not necessary to set a record to qualify, and the time has to be certified by either the AAA or SCTA. Once a member has qualified, he is in for life.

Speeds in excess of 200 miles per hour, especially two-way averages, were rare in 1953. The first five charter members all drove streamliners. Some debate persists about whether George Hill or Willie Young was the *first* "2 Club" member, but on page six of the 1955 SCTA program, it clearly states, "Senior American member of the club is Willie Young." Art Chrisman, John "Sonny" Rogers, and Otto Ryssman were all original inductees.

Ironically, Batchelor never got in the club because he quit driving. Neither did either of the other SO-Cal streamliner drivers, Bill Dailey and Ray Charbonneau. Both had exceeded 200 miles per hour dozens of times, but they took turns at the wheel, and neither ever completed the required two-way run.

The first official meeting of the 200 MPH Club was held September 2, 1953, at the Bonneville Nationals, and the five charter members voted to include living foreign drivers who met the requirements. This added three more names to the roster: Capt. G.T.E. Eyston of England, Rudolph Caracciola of Germany, and Col. Goldie Gardner of England. Eyston was elected the 2 Club's first president, and he predicted that if the World Landspeed Record was to be broken by an American, it would fall to a hot rodder who gained his experience at the Bonneville Nationals.

During the 1953 Nationals, Leroy Holmes drove the Scotty's Muffler Service Ardun-powered belly tank lakester, in which he became the first nonstreamliner driver to qualify for membership. Texan Joe Mabee became the first to qualify in a sports car. Malcolm Hooper, in his beautiful *Shadoff Special*, became the first hot rodder to qualify for membership under FIA-AAA timing, setting six National and six International Class C records.

SCTA President Jim Lindsley, using two Chryslers on methanol, met the requirements for membership at 202 to become the first to join driving a roadster. At the end of the 1955 Nationals, 12 of 15 new records had been set with engines using hemispherical combustion chambers. George Bentley blasted his way in with the NieKamp-Petersen knife-nosed, Chrysler-powered, rear-engined 1927 Model T roadster. Supercharging pioneer Tom Beatty endeared himself to flathead lovers everywhere using a 258-cubic inch blown flathead Mercury in his belly tank lakester to turn the tremendous average of 211 miles per hour.

By mid-1955, *Hop Up* was now *Motor Life* and was sold to Petersen Publishing Company. According to "2 Club" member and president Gordon Hoyt, publisher Bob Petersen offered the opportunity of sponsorship to *Hot Rod* magazine's largest advertiser that year. Ed Elliott, working in advertising and promotion for Grant Piston Rings, urged the company to take over sponsorship responsibilities. Under the direction of Grant's John Bartlett, the Grant 200 MPH Club was ordained anew. Although never a member, Ed Elliott was a good friend to the club. He was so devoted to the club and Bonneville that he once sold his car to pay the printing bill on that year's programs.

Wilhelm Hertz of Germany became the first motorcyclist to top 200 miles per hour. Days later, Texan Johnny Allen rode "Stormy" Mangham's home-built, streamlined Triumph motorcycle nicknamed *Texas Cigar* 214 miles per hour, thus bringing the motorcycle LSR to the United States and becoming the first American motorcyclist to qualify for membership.

In its eighth, and what was to be its last, appearance at Bonneville, the celebrated Kenz and Leslie streamliner reached a two-way average of 266 miles per hour. Roy Leslie was at the wheel of the vehicle, which was powered by three flathead Fords.

When charter member Otto Ryssman was elected president, he instituted the "Most Valuable Man of the Year" award to honor those who make sure that every competitor on the salt has every chance for success. Roy Richter, longtime president of Bell Auto Parts, was the first recipient.

The 10th Annual Bonneville Nationals was Mickey Thompson's year, qualifying once and then improving his pedigree with a two-way run at 266 miles per hour. The most indelible qualification had to be the Summers Brothers, when Bob drove their modified roadster 23 different times during the meet at speeds of more than 200 miles per hour!

Bob Bequette and Phil Freudiger both drove Phil's front-engined modified roadster, powered by a 258-inch blown Chevy of Tom Cobb. The record stood for 20 years, until it was finally broken by Willie Freudiger, Phil's son, in 1979!

Ted Worobieff and George Calloway's Crosley Competition Coupe powered by a 331-inch blown Chrysler was one of the most dramatic entries. On their first run they qualified over 200 but burnt a piston. While they were scrambling to replace the toasted hole, another racer, Don Rackeman, halted the action for a while when he crashed. This gave Worobieff and Calloway time to complete their repairs. In precisely the nick of time, the little Crosley returned at 203 (while burning another piston, same hole), thus putting Worobieff in the club as well as adding the first competition coupe. Whew!

In 1959, American road racer Phil Hill nailed an astounding 254.91 miles per hour for the International Class "E" record, driving British Motors Corporation's tiny EX-181 streamliner. Early members came from all walks of life. Included were Navy pilot Harvey Haller, Navy Chief Petty Officer Fred Larsen, policeman Gary Cagle, fireman Bob Bequette, and house painter Freudiger. Joe Mabee was a Texas oil baron, but Tony Waters worked in the oilfields in Bakersfield, California. Bentley and Ryssman drove trucks for a living, while Phil Hill drove grand prix cars. Losinski was a plastering contractor and Lindsley an electrician. Bob Bowen was a missile technician and Mickey Thompson a pressman for the *Los Angeles Times*. Lloyd Scott, Summers, and Charlie Markley were machinists.

Today, the youngest member is 18-year-old Jess Thomas, and the oldest is 74-year-old Jim Frederick. The "slowest" is Jerry Hathaway at 200.002 with only one pass over 200, and the fastest is Squadron Leader Andy Green at 763, the speed of sound.

In 1978, dirt bike champ and stunt woman Marcia Holley did all the ladies proud when she climbed onto a streamlined, turbocharged Kawasaki motorcycle and nailed an average of 229 miles per hour to brilliantly pierce the all-male membership. "It took me all week just to learn to balance the bike," Holley said. "You don't know how fast you are going until the chute hits. I learned my lesson about peeking over the fairing at speed because I almost got my head ripped off."

Holley came back in 1985 and drove the Vescos' famous streamlined car 272 miles per hour and qualified again for club membership with a car. "The car was a cakewalk compared to how difficult it was to drive the bike," she added. "I almost fell asleep waiting in line for my runs."

In 1987, stylish Tanis Hammond and hard-working Sylvia Hathaway put another couple of wrinkles in the once all-male bastion. Friendly Judie Burkdoll joined in 1990, followed by Pat Zimmerman in 1992. At Bonneville's golden anniversary event, perky and professional Sue Christopherson of Michigan brought the total to six women in the "2 Club."

"Driving a race car requires a clear mind," explained Christopherson. "You have to be prepared to make some serious decisions at critical moments. I sat in the car practicing my run, start to finish. The mental preparation allowed me to concentrate on driving."

Ron Benham and Les Leggitt will never qualify for membership, but both are directly responsible for nearly three dozen people gaining entry: Benham for his remarkable ground-up race-car design, and Leggitt for his growling, snorting engines. Seth Hammond's lakester was responsible for getting more members—10 people—than any other vehicle. As qualifying speeds rose, a 300 Miles Per Hour Club chapter was established.

Somewhere along the way the original charter evolved from merely exceeding 200 miles per hour, to setting a record as well. How this actually happened, or whether it's right, is fodder for long-winded, bench racing debate. Little, if any, documentation exists. The management of the club moved out of private industry control in the early 1970s and is now operated by an elected board of directors supported by membership, events, and selected sponsorships. Without exception, "2 Club" membership remains a most distinguished accomplishment because each time a record is broken, the speeds go up and become harder to break. The vast majority of early 200 Mile Per Hour Club history was compiled by NHRA Museum Curator Greg Sharp, and the salt speedsters are grateful that he did.

Opening the meet in 1956, the Cagle-SanChez Studebaker 1953 coupe is moments away from recording a 160-mile-per-hour run in the timing traps that qualifies the car for a record run. *HOT ROD* photographer Bob D'Olivo used his personal gear (15-inch Wollensack barrel mount lens on a Speed Graphic 4x5 camera) to capture this sharp shot. *Bob D'Olivo*

By 1954, the sixth consecutive gathering of Bonneville speed devotees had gained a modicum of national attention and respect as America's newest automotive proving ground. Although the top speed of the meet was not increased from the previous year's, 18 new records were set out of 209 car and 21 motorcycle entries.

The meet was interrupted by rain twice, and officials closed down the mushy track until it dried up. Racers discovered it is wise to avoid the salt surface when it is covered by water, because the brine solution is highly corrosive and will short out vehicle electrical systems. It was the first time weather had been a problem for the racers. The Great Salt Bear (equivalent to naughty pixies and grouchy gremlins) lowered the potential of all the cars that year. "Salt Bears are an old tradition that came into being somewhat like the Boogie Man who will get you if you don't behave," explained former *HOT ROD* photographer Eric Rickman. "It was used to keep kids from wandering off and getting lost. The term has since evolved into an affectionate label for old timers, like me."

Another "first" came from Stormy Mangham of Smithfield, Texas, who ran his fully streamlined Triumph *Texas "Cee-gar"*. Unless other documentation can be found, he should be credited with being the first to use a braking parachute on a motorcycle. Stored in the tail section, it was spring-loaded for quick deployment.

George Smith, from tranquil and pleasant Blue Island, Illinois, had built a stripped-down and hopped-up Harley-Davidson Knucklehead drag bike that incorporated his own ideas on engine design. Smith's Bonneville appearance tripped the clocks at 158 miles per hour.

The "beauty queen" of the event arrived with the Chrisman Brothers and Duncan as a rear-engined Competition Coupe. Art

Chrisman drove the radically chopped Model A body with an elegant streamlined nose mounted on a tube chassis. Competitors were wowed by the heavily doctored 275-CID DeSoto V-8 that drank a potent fuel mixture of 60 percent methanol and 40 percent nitromethane. Conversely, Bruce Crower's Hudson sedan, which also doubled as his daily driver, averaged a whopping 151 miles per hour with only a supercharged Chrysler overhead V-8.

Driver Otto Ryssman received minor injuries when the Potvin-Hartelt streamliner, running on a 50/50 fuel mixture of nitro and methanol, blew a right rear tire after the traps. The solid frame did its job in preserving Ryssman's life, as the car rolled at 224 miles per hour, crinkling up the aluminum body like a paper sack.

Jim Lindsley joined the 200MPH Club when his *Harold Raymond Special* roadster inched over the 200-mile mark with a 201. It was the first roadster to do so, but it required the power of two Chrysler V-8s. The only other "2 Club" qualifier was Bob Bowen.

Bombastic "Big Bill" Edwards, who always came to Bonneville via Wells, planted a blown V-8 Cadillac engine topped with a six-pack of Stromberg carburetors in his 1953 Ford pickup, only to have a persnickety Hydramatic transmission end his running.

A factory-built entry from Cooper Racing Cars of England run by U.S. dealer John Fox only attracted attention when motorcyclist C. B. Clausen convinced Fox to use his fire-breathing Harley engine. Fox "feather-footed" the car on the first run before lead-foot Bud Hood exploded the fragile Norton gearbox on the second run.

Chevrolet unveiled its new V-8 small-block in 1955, and racers were hot to put it to the salt test, but too much rain made for crummy course conditions. The Utah State Highway crew made several valiant attempts to regrade and repack the salt, but it wasn't enough to prevent two sorrowful events at the seventh annual meet.

First, Glen Pengry at the controls of the LeBlanc twin-Chrysler, four-wheel-drive streamliner lost an arm after the car flipped in the lights at an estimated 177 miles per hour. Worse, and a first the Bonneville Nationals could have done without forever, was the death of John Donaldson, driving the Reed Brothers' lakester—in a car that had many times gone more than 200 miles per hour without a hint of trouble. Donaldson's luck ran out when his 6-foot 4-inch frame prevented him from ducking for cover when the car rolled. From that moment on, the SCTA Bonneville Board ruled it mandatory that all cars have adequate driver protection in the event of a roll-over. Those discovered lacking were withdrawn for running for the rest of the event.

Motorcyclist Marty Dickerson zipped through traps and into the record books at 180 miles per hour riding Joe Simpson's unstreamlined, blown Vincent HRD. Ensuring snarling horsepower engine output was a reworked Mercedes Roots–type blower pushing an additional 15 psi into the cylinders. Topping the two-wheel feats of speed and mirth was the *Texas "Cee-gar"* streamlined Triumph that made a single pass of 191 miles per hour. Much as people were in awe of the bike's capability, its starting operation was comical to watch. Rare was the time when the bike wobbled up to speed without running over one of the push crew.

In the sports car division, the 1955 program shows a Cadillac-powered entry by Peggy Hart, the wife of C. J. Hart, who was the organizer of the famed Santa Ana Dragstrip, the first in the Los Angeles area. The car placed third in the class, with a speed of 119.68 miles per hour. Hart may have been the first woman timed at Bonneville, but poor record-keeping prevents confirmation.

Let's All Take a Moment . . .

Ab Jenkins was 73 years of age in 1956, when Pontiac had a new coupe ready for market and thought a couple of endurance records might boost sales. No longer the one-man show of his youth, patriarch Jenkins shared the driving chores on the 10-mile circle track with 36-year-old son Marvin. On the salt before the hot rodders that year, the pair steered a 1956-series 860 powered by a 285-horsepower Strato-Streak V-8 engine and shattered every record American mark up to 24 hours, averaging 118 miles per

hour over 2,841 miles. Although the 9.5-hour stretch at the wheel would be grueling for most, when elder Jenkins emerged from the car, onlookers were astonished at his fluidic, effortless body movements. He was as graceful as a swan gliding through the water. Later that year, on August 9, Jenkins suffered a heart attack and died within minutes. That day the Bonneville Salt Flats lost the best friend it ever had.

Also on the salt prior to the eighth running of the Speed Week shindig was the German NSU motorcycle factory team going after the American mark of 190 miles per hour. Rider Wilhelm Hertz climbed under the paint of the *Delphin III* streamliner to become the first motorcyclist to top 200 miles per hour, with his 211-mile-per-hour average. Little known was that the NSU team used an experimental, three-lobe Wankel supercharger rotary device during its record runs. The device worked so well that engineers later added a spark plug and the Wankel engine was born.

There's a Cadillac engine stuffed into the belly tank lakester entry of Bob Brissette, Howard Eichenhofer, and Quincy Automotive. Both men joined the "2 Club" in 1958 with the "wrenchful" help of young Jim Brissette. Close pal Jean Perry remembered, "We were young and perfect and had all the time in the world for everything. Sigh." *Bob Brissette*

came from Illinois, Michigan, Arizona, Texas, and California.

SCTA began to "name the days" in 1956; every day of Speed Week was known for the sponsor that supported the Bonneville racing efforts. One day belonged to Iskenderian Racing Cams, another to the Grant Piston Rings folks, then Champion Spark Plugs got the nod, or Firestone. The companies were very generous in providing free technical assistance and product and trophy underwriting.

The roadsters were holding their own nicely, especially from the efforts of Bob Bequette driving the C Class Freudiger Special to 184 miles per hour, and the Perry Boys ripping off 168 miles per hour in Class B for a shiny new roadster record. Fred Lavell of Birmingham, Michigan, brought his racy J2 Allard chassis fitted with a DeSoto engine and Powerflyte push-button transmission, running the car up to 150 miles per hour.

When the hot rodders left, the British used a couple of sports cars to grab a total of 91 records. American Ken Miles and Brit John Lockett drove a streamlined four-banger MG to nab 63 records. Meanwhile, Carroll Shelby and Roy Jackson-Moore did the hot laps with an Austin-Healey, establishing 28—every possible one for its class.

By 1957, the SCTA entry fee had risen to $20 at the Ninth Annual Bonneville Nationals, and more sports car classes were created that year. Even though salt conditions were poor at the start of the week, the average speed for record runs was 193 miles per hour. Entries had risen from 142 to 174, despite NHRA's national event running the same week.

Dr. J. E. Teverbaugh thought it was time to try a parachute on a car and tied one to the back of his Bonneville racer. Today an essential stopping and safety device, this was its first known use on a car at Bonneville.

Deflating the puffy pronouncement that no car with exposed wheels could attain a speed higher than 200, the Eichenhofer and Brissette lakester, a Plexiglas window tank that fully enclosed the driver, scampered up to 231 miles per hour. The Kenz and Leslie group elevated the high-speed mark to 270 miles per hour—one-way—yet averaging 266 miles per hour. Driver Roy Leslie broke the four-year-old record set by another group driver, Willie Young, in 1953.

Teamwork paid off for the quartet of Waters, Sughue, Edwards, and Smith from Bakersfield, California, when their stock-height

Why are these fellows smiling? No doubt because they are all members of the 200 MPH Club, sponsored by Grant Piston rings. Pictured here at there annual banquet at the State Line Hotel in Wendover, in the front row, left to right, are George Hill, Bob Bowen, Tom Ruddy (?), Bill Perry, Ted Frye, and Bob Bequette. Back row: Leroy Holmes (?), Malcolm Hooper, Ermie Immerso, Bob Summers, Gary Cagle, Tom Beatty, Howard Eichenhofer, Dave Ryder, and Bob Brissette. *Bob Brissette*

Before the group got back home to Germany, their records got clobbered by the amateur group of Texans with their *Texas "Cee-gar"* streamliner. Unlike the well-financed factory squad, the Lone Star State residents were shade tree mechanics. Powered by a naturally aspirated, 650-cc Triumph Thunderbird engine, rider Johnny Allen recorded a 214.40 miles per hour average—good for entry to the 200MPH Club—the first American motorcyclist to do so. It was also the first time America had held the record since 1921.

Both the AMA and Fédération Internationale Motorcycliste (FIM) officiated at the events, but a raucous scandal erupted when the FIM refused to make the runs official, even though the FIA was perfectly satisfied that the Texans had whomped the Germans. Not wanting his team to be smeared by the arrogant stink, the NSU company director penned a capitulating letter, stating his team had been beaten fairly. Moreover, the dependable and accurate timing equipment used by Otto Crocker for the runs had been certified by the U.S. Bureau of Standards as well above the requirements of the FIM and FIA.

By the time the Eighth Annual Bonneville Nationals finished in 1956, another 15 records were broken over the 9-mile course. The average speed for all 132 entries was 151 miles per hour, 1 mile per hour faster than the top speed of the first event in 1949. Heavily populated were the new competition classes for cars running straight pump gas. Truly a national event, the record setters

PARTICIPANT

SIXTH ANNUAL

BONNEVILLE NATIONAL SPEED TRIALS

Sponsored By
Southern California Timing Assn.

and Hot Rod Magazine
AUG. 29 to SEPT. 5

1954

1954
BONNEVILLE
NATIONAL SPEED TRIALS

With the issuance of this sticker the occupants of this car hereby agree to abide by the regulations and requests of the Control Committee in regard to the safe conduct of these events.

● 20 mph. Speed Limit on Salt Beds.

● Stay out of restricted areas.

● Drive carefully at all times.

Every entrant was given one of these 3.5-inch circle decals at registration to affix to his race vehicle. The colors were red and white in 1954, but changed from year to year, thus indicating how many years the vehicle had been racing on the salt. A separate safety sticker was added after the vehicle had passed inspection. The starter would check for both stickers before allowing the car out onto the course. *LandSpeed Productions*

For the Vesco clan, it's always been a family affair at the salt. Here in front of the 444 streamliner in 1961 (left to right) are Don and Norma Vesco, mother Betty, father John, and young Rick Vesco. Built in 1957, 444 continues to race to the present day with the same number. *Vesco Family Collection*

Ak Miller's red and white modified roadster depended on 320 cubic inches from a 1950 Oldsmobile engine to nab the 1953 Class D record at 174 miles per hour—24 miles per hour faster than the second place car. Miller was one of the first to break away from the flathead and experiment with the new-fangled, "rocker-arm" engines. *Tom Medley*

1932 roadster flew like a brick with a vengeance to clip the D Class record, with a 191-mile-per-hour average, running a 292-CID blown DeSoto engine. That was very fast for the era. John Vesco and Jim Dinkins entered what had to be the world's thinnest streamliner. The radical car did not meet the general formula set down by SCTA for safe wheelbase and tracking width, but its stupendous detail, sound theory, and quality workmanship earned the car a waiver to run in an experimental class. Dinkins pushed the 182-CID four-cylinder 1932 Ford engine with a Riley overhead conversion to 166 miles per hour.

John Vesco's 17-year-old son, Don, had been coming up to the salt with his father since he was 12. A newly licensed driver, Don rode his Triumph T 100 R, a bike he would put together by drop light out in the front lawn. Regarded today as one of America's brightest racing sparks, back then young Vesco had just begun his racing education. "To break in the bike, I rode it from Nellis Air Force Base outside of Vegas, and almost made it to Wendover," recalled Vesco of

the long ride that made his hands swell from the constant vibration of the engine. "I stopped when the sun went down because the bike didn't have a headlight. My teenage brain finally engaged—I had no money, hadn't eaten since breakfast, and had only worn a T-shirt. The temperature fell to 50 degrees Fahrenheit. I shivered along the side of the road until Dad finally came along." It was the only car Vesco saw in more than 4 hours.

The late 1950s saw the gas coupe sedan classes pregnant with entries. In 1958, during the 10th Annual Speed Week, the Chrysler-powered Studebaker entered by SanChez and Cagle was the first to crack the 200-mile-per- hour mark using a deadly 100 percent nitro fuel load for a one-way speed of 210 miles per hour. Not bothering with anything other than plain old pump gas, Karol Miller from Houston, Texas, turned up again with his 1956 Ford Victoria, now fitted with a Latham axial-flow blower, and set a new record in Class C of 150 miles per hour.

Mickey Gets His Kicks

Flexing horsepower muscles in a big way at the speed meet were Marion Lee "Mickey" Thompson and Fritz Voigt. The pair appeared with *Challenger*, a reconditioned slingshot drag chassis over which they slapped a drag-reducing aluminum body. Their original plan was to attend the NHRA National Drag Meet in Oklahoma City, but they headed up to Bonneville to see if their creation might benefit from a bit more super tuning on the flat, white salt dyno. Using plain 'ole pump gas, with everything except the gearing set for the 1/4 mile, Thompson spit out a 242-mile-per-hour run off the trailer. Eyebrows went to the sky. They switched the front engine to alcohol splashing in 30 percent nitro, but left the rear engine on gas.

Wham! Thompson clocks a 272-mile-per-hour run, faster than any hot rod and driver have ever been clocked. Scratch one entry from the NHRA meet. Even faster the next day, both engines gulped down the alky/nitro tonic, and the timing slip said 286 miles per hour. On Sunday morning Thompson popped out a 294-mile-per-

hour pass, but on the return run the front engine broke, ending the dream of a 300-plus hot rod romp. In the years that followed Thompson would own more than 265 speed records.

Fifties Finale

Thompson and Voigt showed up in 1959 with quadruple Pontiac V-8s jam-packed into a brand-new and improved *Challenger*. Only 19 feet long and 59 inches wide, two engines powered each axle. Everything was set in an unsprung chassis and connected to a rigid suspension. Thompson and sponsors were on a mission. Locked in their sights was the World's Unlimited Land Speed Record held by Englishman John Cobb.

Goodyear developed a radical, new treadless landspeed tire that would mount onto Ted Halibrand's new 28-pound magnesium wheel. The rubber compound was blended from a high proportion of carbon black and pure, natural rubber in a painstaking three-stage process. Both wheel and tire were developed to keep tire growth in check at speed.

Many a run was made with last-minute "tidy-ups" such as the ones seen here on drag racer Art Chrisman's way-cool coupe. He picked up the Maremont Trophy in 1953 for this car's high degree of design, performance, appearance, and safety. Note the sealing of the door and windshield and streamlining additions to the front axle area with masking tape. The tube frame coupe's nose was made from two 1940 Ford hoods. In the rear was a snorting 258 CID Mercury with an Ardun conversion done by Harry Duncan. The brakes were only on the rear wheels and applied via a hand lever. *Tom Medley*

The first few runs in late August were spent sorting out hellish parachute problems that sent the car into oscillating, 1/4-mile slides. Thompson finally fired the engineers who designed them in favor of a twin, a 5-foot ribbon hot rodder setup. It worked beautifully, and the car ran 362 miles per hour.

Beyond Mickey

Of course there were others at the 11th Annual event: 124 additional ones, to be precise. This year, SCTA had adjusted its class designations to align with those of the international racing world, so "A" Class was now populated by the biggest engines with smaller cubic inch displacements slotting in as the alphabet progressed.

Heavy summer rains had made the salt mushy in places. The push trucks took the brunt of the wet salt, getting so plastered in the sticky, white spray that it looked as though they had been in a cottage cheese factory explosion. Safety at Bonneville got a boost with the development of the Bell 500TX helmet. During Speed Week, Bell Auto Parts would lend, free-of-charge, a helmet to anyone who needed one.

The meet officially opened as the Vesco-Dinkins streamliner pushed off the line, its ancient engine coughing. The car, now competing in the D Gas Class, would before week's end record a remarkable high speed of 172 miles per hour.

Bill and Bob Summers, after Bob experienced a seven-revolution spin and flip at over 200 miles per hour, glued their modified roadster back together in time to set a record of 225 miles per hour on the last day of the meet.

Bill Martin, with sons Dale and Lonnie from Burbank, California, brought their tiny, single-cylinder 12-cubic-inch Triumph-powered belly tank streamliner and wowed the crowd when Dad steered 149

SCTA official Jim Lindsley and his snappy-appearing crew begin to pull together for another run. The twin Chrysler-powered roadster was beset with synchronization problems and only managed to clock a run of 158 miles per hour. Lindsley got things sorted out in 1954 and ran a 202-mile-per-hour average. This was the first roadster to do so, giving him entry into the "2" Club. Sadly, on the way home, the trailered car and tow vehicle were demolished when the driver fell asleep at the wheel. *Tom Medley*

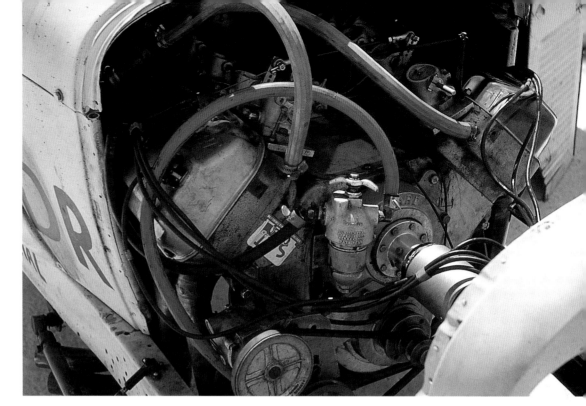

This Chrysler V-8 with a primitive fuel injection system may not be pretty, but it was fast enough to bring home first place, Class D roadster honors for the Howard's Cams Chopsticks Special at 166 miles per hour. 1953 lit the beacon of decline for the flathead when the Bonneville program listed 23 Chrysler Hemi engines. These better-breathing, cooler-running engines were as easy to beef-up as the flatheads, but yielded much better performance for the time and investment. *Tom Medley*

miles per hour in a one-way run and then averaged 139 miles per hour to set an AMA Class formula SC record. Built from catalog parts and enjoying some port relief, Martin ran his streamliner on pump gas. Few could think of anyone else who got so much out of so little.

Although engines must be measured to verify correct displacement, fuel use verification is much easier. The vehicle's tank is drained prior to the run, filled by an official, and then sealed. A broken seal immediately disqualifies the entry.

L. W. "Knot" Farrington ambled in from New Orleans with a sleek T-Bird fitted with a 452-inch Chrysler V-8 and clocked 173 miles per hour in the A sports racing class. Farrington was convinced that merely switching to Firestone "Bonneville" tires gave him a 16-mile-per-hour speed increase. Studebakers were hot stuff this year, and the 402-inch Cadillac-powered Bennett-Rochlitzer B gas coupe zipped up a class win at 165 miles per hour and recorded a two-way record average of 164 miles per hour.

On Tuesday it looked as though a washout was imminent as rain poured down all around, but not on the course. The course was shut down when the wind blew up and drivers couldn't keep the cars going straight. By Wednesday, the course was dry enough for 29 cars to qualify for record runs.

A battle had raged all year between hot rodders and the United States Auto Club (USAC) after the Bonneville Nationals Contest Board had appealed to the FIA for official recognition of their speed runs. USAC objected for no other reason than it would be deprived of timing fees (very expensive for the average racer) that it charged the racers. Money. Ugh! Again the almighty dollar had shown itself to be a boil on the butt of amateur racing. At the 200MPH Club banquet, a petition of request for recognition was circulated, signed and sent to the FIA in Paris, France.

On Thursday, Joe Locasto, driving the SanChez-Kamboor-Ansen Automotive Studebaker coupe, screamed through the traps averaging an eye-popping 213 miles per hour and became the first to qualify for "2 Club" membership for the 1959 season. A few minutes later, Fred Larsen broke a record that had stood since 1954 with his modified roadster; he averaged 206 miles per hour and also joined the "2 Club."

The last run of the day on Saturday was as close to disaster as a driver could come yet emerge unscathed. On his second run, after nailing a 191-mile-per-hour pass, Joe Carboni, driving a hand-crafted fiberglass-bodied sports car, watched his left front tire split in two just after clearing the traps at 190 miles per hour. The debris flew through the top of the fender and ripped the hood loose, which flew back and smacked his helmet before it tore off the headrest

Another soldier that help pound the flathead into obsolescence was General Motors Oldsmobile and Cadillac overhead valve engines. The V-8 Olds pictured here is fitted with a Italmeccanica supercharger and a pair of Stromberg carburetors. The shared, Siamese central exhaust port might fool some to think this was a six-cylinder bullet, but the four pairs of rocker arms reveal the truth. *Tom Medley*

Before all his 1959 high-speed Bonneville runs, Mickey Thompson would walk the entire length of the course at night—up and back—sometimes 12 miles, with his wife, Judy, following in the Pontiac Bonneville station wagon. He would look for slight, but important, surface changes thrown into sharp, shadow-defined focus by moonlight or by the light of headlights. *Bob Brissette*

and fairing. Carboni hung on and safely brought the machine to a halt right in front of the pits for the most dramatic close of Bonneville racing action to date.

Sporty Cars Endure

After the hot rodders went home, the British came back to the salt with BMG's EX-219. For the straightaway runs, driver Phil Hill set five new Class E records in a car without a roll bar or safety har-

nesses and with his legs kinked over the front axle.

Austin Healey trotted out a souped-up, fully streamlined Sprite powered by a 950-cc four-cylinder engine. It was driven by the international trio of Gus Ehrman of Greenwich, Connecticut, Ed Leavens of Canada, and Tom Wisdom of the United Kingdom. They managed to capture nine international Class G and 40 American records during a 12-hour assault. Ehrman then attacked the 1-hour international records, and while he was throttled up at 150 miles per hour

on the 10-mile circle, the hood flew up and he spun seven full revolutions. Unfazed, he restarted and spun again, but didn't quit until he had secured 18 records.

Going His Own Way

Late in November of 1959, former Mormon missionary Athol Graham ran his crudely built *City of Salt Lake* streamliner to an astonishing 308 miles per hour. Graham, much like Jenk-

ins had done years ago, tested the car privately with friends from Salt Lake City because SCTA safety officials had sent him home twice with a shopping list of things to fix before he could safely run at their meet.

Surprising his critics, the *City of Salt Lake* pushed up to 344 miles per hour in December. Graham was now on par with Thompson's *Challenger* and suddenly a contender for the ultimate record. Fitted with a V-12 Allison engine, the runs made him the fourth fastest man in landspeed history. Graham claimed the idea for the car came in a dream of Divine origins.

The following year, on August 1, 1960, with his wife, Zeldine, and crewman Otto Anzjon assisting, Graham disregarded all pleas for caution from seasoned salt pros Mickey Thompson and Nathan Ostich and roared down the course at over 300 miles per hour. The car got sideways, pencil rolled, lost its tail, and then launched into the air before pitching end-over-end. Graham died before the ambulance arrived at the hospital. As the first of six cars scheduled to use the salt to exceed 400 miles per hour, it was a tragic beginning toward the goal. An August 3 editorial in the *Salt Lake City Deseret News* said:

> Mr. Graham in his inexperience and anxiety to succeed took risks that should not have been taken. He paid the fullest price for those risks. We mourn his passing and hope other such deaths can be avoided—without, however, ending the probing of the unknown and the challenging of the difficult.

The speed search continued with only the briefest of pauses. Fortune turns like leaves in the wind, and a few days later Bob Bowen, driving the *Shadoff Special* streamliner, set five new national and international records under the scrutiny of USAC timing.

The Shadoff Special driven by Mal Hooper was the pride of the high-performance crowd in 1953 when it nailed six international speed records, proving to the international motorsports community just what a hot rodder was capable of doing. Co-owner Ray Brown built the 303 CID V-8 Chrysler engine with Hilborn fuel injection and spent three solid weeks dyno testing a bushel full of cam and other speed secret combinations. The work paid off when the streamliner consistently ran above 230 miles per hour. *Tom Medley*

Chapter 8

The Jet Age

C obb's caustic comments find support among staunch defenders of the wheel-driven sect. It is the considered opinion of the hard-core, piston-popping, gear-grinding crankshaft crowd that a race car needed to be wheel driven before it could expect respect—the only way to an honorable record. For those purists, the idea of jet or rocket power is abhorrent, and worthy only of scornful ridicule.

Politely ignoring such thinking are those unfettered visionaries who pursue speed on land by any means available, from steam to frictionless magnetism. For them, the only restriction is to stay connected with the ground. Good thing too, as flying race cars usually stop with disastrous results.

HOT ROD magazine Senior Editor Gray Baskerville sneers at the mere mention of jets and labels them "blowtorches on wheels." For him, the quintessential Bonneville car is a 1929 Model A Ford body. He explained, "It started out as something that was originally designed to go 50 miles per hour tops, and because of the hot rodder, now goes 300 miles per hour; that's an achievement." Many also reference Mickey Thompson, who had earned unquestioned respect as the Senator of Speed with his quad motor *Challenger*. (Note: The car was recently restored by rodders Jim Travis and Bob Opperman and is on display at the NHRA Museum of Drag Racing in Pomona, California.)

The early 1960s saw a shootout for the World Land Speed Record, in which the piston motors would forever be separated

> *A jet-propelled vehicle would not be a motor car; it would be a sort of aeroplane dragging its wheels along the course.*
>
> —World Land Speed Record Holder John Cobb

from the ultimate speed fight. Regardless of how much horsepower is produced, there comes a point where wind resistance equals tire adhesion and that's when things start slipping, or breaking, or both.

Dr. Nathan Ostich, a slow-talking man with speed on his mind, understood both points of view. He was the racer's doctor that had not only cured their ailments and delivered their kids, but had raced among them for years at Bonneville. In 1958, the 47-year-old doctor contracted severe salt fever. To "heal himself," the physician spent more than $50,000 to build the world's biggest lakester. On the salt in 1960, the *Flying Caduceus* was the first jet-powered car to blast across the salt and the third car of six locked in a struggle to reach 400 miles per hour. Powered by a J47 turbo jet engine, the body had been shaped by wind tunnel tests at the California Polytechnic College. Designed and built with the help of *HOT ROD* Editor Ray Brock, mechanical wiz Ak Miller, and crew chief Allan Bradshaw, the 28.5-foot-long brilliant red car was an imposing sight. Firestone Tire and Rubber built two sets of 48-inch tires and aluminum billet wheels.

After an assortment of experimental teething problems spanning two years, the good doctor finally clocked 331 miles per hour on the salt in 1962. Sadly, the front wheel came off at the same time and the big car spun three times before Ostich could pop the parachute. "That was fast enough," he told Miller, and he parked the "weinie roaster" permanently.

Art Arfons kneels next to the red, white, and blue *Green Monster* powered by a 17-stage J79 jet engine, which he rebuilt from practically scrap. The driver's cockpit, trimmed in white leather, is visible over Arfon's left shoulder on the side of the car. Together, they set three World land speed Records. *George Callaway*

This monster-size lakester is actually the *Flying Caduceus*, the first jet-powered car to run at Bonneville, built by Dr. Nathan Ostich. Physician to many racers, he is seen here above the left front wheel, wearing sunglasses, in August 1960. *Wilford Day*

Out of the wheel-driven crowd came a hot rodder, Norman Craig Breedlove, a skinny kid with the hee-haw laughter of a mule who had it bad for the "way-fast" groove. Driving *Spirit of America*, he first claimed a World Motorcycle Land Speed record in 1963. Atop "hero-hill," he had plenty of august company taking the world speed crown for automobiles in 1964 after Donald Campbell, Tom Green and Art Arfons.

Donald Campbell, the British speed heir apparent, came to the salt in 1960 with all the bravado of a military operation. His huge entourage shocked the locals and dwarfed Mickey Thompson's contingent in comparison, but all the chaps involved were utterly polite. Oddly, after carefully ramping up to speed from 170 to 240 miles per hour, he suddenly got "ants-in-the-pants" and sprinted to 345 miles per hour. It was his undoing. Visually, the accident was a mirror-image of Athol Graham's misfortune, but Campbell only suffered a fractured skull, a pierced eardrum, and a few cuts. He made scrap metal out of the multimillion dollar car. "Campbell simply was in much too big a hurry and is alive solely by the grace of God," wrote respected journalist and on-site observer Griff Borgeson in a January 1961 *Sports Car Illustrated* report. Clearly Borgeson was sending a veiled message to others about taking their time about going fast.

Thompson, on the salt at the same time, went to visit Campbell at the hospital. Get well wishes arrived from Queen Elizabeth, saying that she hoped he would be able to resume his speed quest soon. When Campbell asked what Thompson had heard from President Eisenhower, the hot rodder didn't have an answer. In that awkward moment, it became painfully apparent to both men that the United States did little to support the efforts of its amateur swashbucklers.

Thompson then took *Challenger* onto the unusually hard, rough salt, convinced he had the answer to the 400-mile-per-hour barrier. The course proved too malicious for Mickey and his thundering, unsprung *Challenger*. After only one run, the severe pounding of his internal organs required immediate medical treatment. From his hospital bed he asked that a new, smoother course be prepared. Trouble continued when USAC pulled a petty political/publicity stunt and revoked his sanction for participating in an "outlaw" event (the 12th Annual Bonneville Nationals, with whom USAC was fighting about timing rights).

Just as he resolved the USAC problem, the 15-ton oil truck that lays the essential black guide line got mired down to its axles in the mud flats. Thompson opted to run without the line. Embracing his wife, Judy, with all the emotion of a final farewell, Thompson then bade goodbye to Fritz Voigt, who growled, "Goodbye, crap! I'll see you in 10 minutes at the other end." Off Thompson went to shift four transmissions by moving a single lever through three speeds and make those 32 synchronized throttle butterflies obey his command.

A few days later, on September 9, 1960, Mickey Thompson and his optimistic illusions sailed into reality as he tripped the USAC clocks at 406.60 miles per hour. He was the first hot rodder to do so (Cobb was the first ever), but was denied a record when a driveshaft broke on the return run.

Return of the Jets

In 1962, Craig Breedlove's first test sessions were chaotic. The car failed to perform, and his whole program was on the verge of total collapse because of internal fighting. Some accused him of not being able to drive the car properly. Breedlove decided to return to California and sort out his problems.

As *Spirit of America* was on the way home, Romco Palamedes and Vic Elischer were on their way to the salt with the voluptuous *Infinity* jet. Powered by another J47 engine and driven by drag racer Glenn Leasher, things went terribly wrong after a few runs and Leasher was killed as the car became a twisted, ripped heap in seconds.

Breedlove found salvation for *Spirit of America* with Lockheed engineer Walt Sheehan, the only other man to ever drive the *Spirit*. Sheehan had played a major role in the design of the ducts for the F-104 Starfighter and was an expert in charming every possible erg of energy out of a jet. After revisions were made, *Spirit of America* bore little resemblance to the backyard creation the hot rodder started with years ago. From the proverbial knee, Breedlove learned about critical aerodynamic and thrust nuances from Sheehan, training that empowered him to chalk up five World Land Speed Records by 1965.

Breedlove also faced the sanctioned ostracism from the FIA in Paris, but like Ostich, he put his faith in the public, not in a foreign group of faceless people. Part of the problem was ignorance. Horsepower had long been the measure of strength for hot rodders,

so when the jets arrived with "thrust ratings," confusion abounded until the simple conversion formula was understood. Using Ostich's J47, which is rated at 5,200 foot-pounds, the calculations work out to 6,930 horsepower, more than three times that of Mickey Thompson's meager 2,000-horsepower *Challenger*.

On August 5, 1963, Breedlove unleashed 85 percent of the available 4,000 pounds of thrust stored in the three-ton three-wheeler that looked like a jet fighter with amputated wings. Breedlove zipped through the mile in 9 seconds, and USAC's Joe Petrali announced the speed was 388 miles per hour.

Taking no chances with his fire-breathing toy, Dr. Nathan Ostich has a crew member standing by with a fire extinguisher after a run. Note the spent parachute line extending out from the top of the afterburner. *Utah State Historical Society*

It had taken 16 years to break Cobb's record, but 1964 would see the record change hands six times. The only other time that had happened was in 1904, when Henry Ford scared himself half-crazy driving on frozen Lake Saint Clare in the middle of winter.

Walt Arfons started the high-speed game of "musical records" when he brought the Goodyear-sponsored *Wingfoot Express* to the salt in late September of 1964. Engineer and builder Talmage (Tom) Green, from Elmhurst, Illinois, was also the driver. Arfons had been the first American to adapt a jet engine and aircraft parachute packs for a drag-race car in 1959. In all, he campaigned nearly 25 race cars in his career. "I always studied everything very carefully before doing something," observed Arfons of his racing years. "There were a lot of sleepless nights."

The *Wingfoot Express* car hadn't been a consistent performer, and the pair were not considered serious contenders until Green knocked down 406 miles per hour. The USAC timers were stunned. Green was more amazed because he had heard an ear-shattering explosive jolt before he ran out of fuel in the mile. The engine had ingested a small, threaded nut that had been lost in the cockpit upholstery. When it passed through the engine it severely bent 14 compressor blades and decreased engine power by 25 percent.

"On the second run I knew we needed to start closer because of the fuel problem and diminished engine power, so we used a 2-mile approach to the flying mile," explained Green. One hour before sundown, Green squirted out a 420-mile-per-hour pass, and became the new "Fastest Man on Earth" on October 2, 1964.

"Walter was upset," laughed Green. "He thought I turned off the burner in the middle of the measured mile, but I had run out of fuel. It was a tremendous feeling of power and I was fully prepared to see how fast the car could go."

Other than a couple of stock car heats, Green had no high-speed driving experience. "When I broke the record, I'm sure Craig Breedlove and Arthur thought to themselves, 'If Tom Green could do this, then I better get back out on the salt and prove myself to the world again,' " he said mirthfully.

Younger brother Art Arfons showed up with the *Green Monster*, powered by a J79 capable of outputting 15,000 pounds of thrust. Unlike the previous jets, Arthur's had the driver's cockpit on the left side of the engine. Engine manufacturer General Electric wanted no part of the land speed racing business and did its best *not* to help Arfons rebuild the very damaged, surplus motor. When the mechanical wizard Arthur overhauled the beast into perfect working order, GE even tried to buy it back. Arfons just laughed. On October 5 he ran with a vengeance, ripping off a

Donald Campbell's *Proteus* on the course at Bonneville in September of 1960. The car flipped and crashed at 345 miles per hour. The wreckage is seen in the upper left-hand corner, sitting in a Wendover Air Field hangar. Campbell was lucky to escape with his life, since there was no roll cage protecting the driver. *Richard Dixon Collection*

"Not fast enough," Breedlove worried to himself. In the timer's stand were FIM and USAC official observers, who stood ready to declare a new World Land Speed Record if the California kid could get the job done.

The return run was 428 miles per hour, for an average of 407.45 miles per hour. *Spirit of America* was the fastest car on Earth, and the record was safely back in the United States—the first time since 1928.

Cycle World magazine publisher Joseph Parkhurst was surprised that the FIM would give top motorcycle honors to Breedlove instead of Bill Johnson, who ran 230 miles per hour on a Triumph at the salt that same year. "It is even a bit ironic that every shred of advertising and publicity attached to Breedlove's folly refers to the vehicle as a car, not a motorcycle," he wrote in the November 1963 issue.

434-mile-per-hour average that booted Green off the top of the pile after just three days.

Walter Arfons and Tom Green were driving back to Chicago for a big bash with Goodyear executives. While stopped at a traffic signal in some small town, Walter heard over the car radio that Arthur had broken the record. Tom recalled, "Walter got out of the car, even though the signal had changed, and came back to my car to tell me what had just happened. After that, we just went home and never went to the celebration party, but I never felt any animosity toward Arthur."

Come Back Here, Kid . . .

Breedlove wasn't sitting on his hands—he reclaimed the crown on October 13 at 468 miles per hour and then again on October 15, when he burst through the 500-mile-per-hour barrier and notched a new world record at 526 miles per hour! The tasty fight could have gone on longer that year if Breedlove hadn't gone swimming on his return run. After running through Petrali's USAC clocks at 513 miles per hour, Breedlove made the return run with the engine at 100 percent power.

SPEED DIVINE; SPEED DEFINED

Salt fever is an unmerciful "speed itch" more powerful than the lunar pull on Earth's oceanic tides. It is a disease for which doctors have no cure. Only temporary relief is possible, obtained by traveling as fast as possible as many times as possible in a given racing season. What is speed?

At Bonneville, speed is . . .

"A sensation of euphoria punctuated by momentary terror at any given time." —Skip Higginbotham, racer.

"The roaring sound, the gears and engine screaming behind you, the wind beating your head into the roll bar, the sound growing stronger, louder, incredibly louder all the time." —Alex Xydias, racer.

"Like a violin player playing good classical music. He keeps trying to reach a higher note, and just when you think he's there, he hits a higher note. It is all-consuming. " —Art Arfons, World Land Speed Record holder.

"Purity. It means flat out as fast as you can go with no other consideration than velocity." —John Baechtel, motorhead.

"A sensation unlike anything else. Approaching danger, you feel as though you want to turn the throttle both ways at the same time. You try to balance the risk with the rewards and those feelings develop exponentially the faster you go." —Dale Martin, SCTA chief inspector, motorcycle.

"The ultimate rush. What racing is all about." —Dan Warner, SCTA advisory board/rules.

"Starts over 250 miles per hour. It makes me feel real good. It's a high, but not a drunk high. My adrenaline gets going, but I stay cool, totally focused, and it's the only time I seriously concentrate. I am aware of everything around me." —"Fast" Freddie Dannenfelzer, racer.

"The faster you go, the more you slow down. As your speed increases, you mind must keep up, or you are in trouble. Seconds seem like minutes. With the *Turbinator,* I get somewhere faster than I think I ought to be there in my own mind." —Don Vesco, fearless racer.

"Figuring out how to get the most from the least, how fast you can go on how few cubic inches." —Doug Robinson, racer.

"The common denominator that accommodates the fastest and the slowest." —Wally Parks, NHRA founder.

"Gets in your blood. It makes you want to come back, go faster, do it again." —Glenn Barrett, SCTA/BNI chief timer.

"Gets your heart pumping. The sensation is different under 200 than over 200 miles per hour, everything becomes so quick." —Mrs. Tanis Hammond, racer.

"The f***ing limit." —Gray Baskerville, HOT ROD magazine senior editor.

"Everything in the universe vibrating, like a time warp. It is when you see telephone poles squirt up out of nowhere. I am jealous of Andy Green." —Jim Fueling, racer.

"Never having to look in the rearview mirror." —Elice and Bruce Tucker, racers.

"Money. If you romanticize a technical term, you forget the human ability to think, reason, and discern." —Barney Navarro, speed parts manufacturer.

"Without it, life is meaningless." —Ron Christensen, Salt Radio disc jockey.

"A natural high. Once you have been there, you have to do it again, but go faster each time. The first time you get to 150 miles per hour, it's a high, but then you get to 175 and 150 becomes ho-hum." —Ken Walkey, racer.

"A moment of truth" —William Scace, Speedway Manufacturing Company.

With Arfons' record in its cross hairs, *Spirit* steadily accelerated through the measured mile until the temperamental parachutes came out while the car was till under power. Engineer Sheehan was astonished that Breedlove would have fired the chutes so soon. "They were not made to be used at 500 miles per hour," he said, hoping that it was instead another malfunction that caused premature deployment. "The canopy area was heavy webbing, not lightweight nylon," noted crewman Nye Frank. "The chutes were so heavy that when they came out, they would sometimes fall to the ground without opening."

Not this time; the afterburner saw to that. His parachutes gone, Breedlove then stood on the giant rear brakes, burning them to a useless crisp. He slid between the first set of telephone poles, but snapped off another pole with the right rear outrigger axle, still traveling around 200 miles per hour. He shot through a shallow lake which helped slow *Spirit*, but he was headed for the dike that had so troubled Sir Malcolm Campbell years ago.

"He went by me at about 200 miles per hour," said *HOT ROD* magazine photographer Eric Rickman, who was parked down at the far end hoping to snap a parachute shot. Breedlove's problems got worse when Spirit walloped the 4-foot mud dike. "The car popped up and over the dike," observed Rickman, "but by now had slowed to under 100 miles per hour when he landed in the canal. It was right over the underwater trench cut by the mining company." Invisible from above, the ground sharply dropped away, but *Spirit's* rear wheel track was slightly wider than the trench and only the car's nose tipped in and sank.

Breedlove had the good sense to remove the canopy before the car plunged into the water. He swam to safety, but the car was finished. The next time it would roll would be as an artifact in Chicago's Museum of Science and Industry transportation collection.

"We had overcome a variety of problems on the salt and achieved our goals," concluded Frank. "It's easy to make the required power, but being alive at the end of the program is what it's all about. Craig was scared shitless of the car at times, but he still went out there and got the job done. That's courageous."

Arthur Arfons had the last word in 1964, ending the speed parade on October 27 at 536 miles per hour. It had taken 16 years to lift the record 13 miles per hour, and now these backyard boys had batted it about for three weeks and parked it at a stunning new level.

"Craig was always friendly at the Salt," recalled Arfons, "but he wasn't about to help me out of a jam. A true competitor is someone who is your equal, someone who pushes you to do your best to better him."

Driver Craig Breedlove poses in front of *Sonic I*, the second of his jet-powered land speed race cars. Breedlove had upped the ante to 600 miles per hour in September 1965, nabbing his fifth land speed title in two years. *Goodyear Tire and Rubber Co.*

Schematic of Art Arfons' *Green Monster.*
Art Arfons

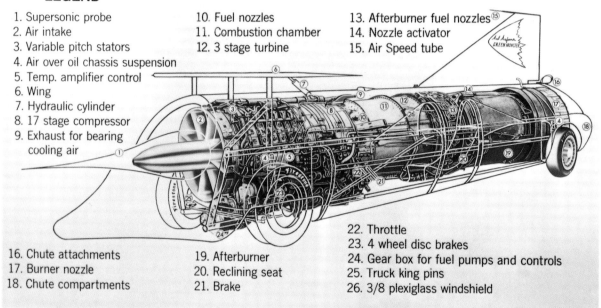

SCHEMATIC VIEW OF ART ARFONS' "GREEN MONSTER" 17,500 H.P. JET ENGINE

LEGEND

1. Supersonic probe
2. Air intake
3. Variable pitch stators
4. Air over oil chassis suspension
5. Temp. amplifier control
6. Wing
7. Hydraulic cylinder
8. 17 stage compressor
9. Exhaust for bearing cooling air
10. Fuel nozzles
11. Combustion chamber
12. 3 stage turbine
13. Afterburner fuel nozzles
14. Nozzle activator
15. Air Speed tube
16. Chute attachments
17. Burner nozzle
18. Chute compartments
19. Afterburner
20. Reclining seat
21. Brake
22. Throttle
23. 4 wheel disc brakes
24. Gear box for fuel pumps and controls
25. Truck king pins
26. 3/8 plexiglass windshield

"Is this thing safe?" wondered Paula Murphy, the first woman to drive a jet, when she first set eyes on Walt Arfon's *Avenger* in 1964. "The open cockpit allowed a lot of wind to buffet around, but as the acceleration gradually built up, I was pasted back in the seat until the parachutes hit," she said, "and then the force was so great it wanted to pull my eyeballs out of my head." Despite the bad weather and wet salt, USAC clocked her runs at 277 miles per hour average without the afterburner. Unlike her male jet-driving counterparts, Murphy was snubbed by the 200 MPH Club and was not invited to be a member. *George Calloway*

He added that because he had Firestone sponsorship, but Breedlove and his brother relied on Goodyear, it not only made for a great media battle, but brought attention to the sport. "Every time the record went higher than mine, it was my greatest personal challenge to try harder," concluded Arfons of the speed chase. "It was all-consuming." That same month, the FIA joined reality and amended the International Sporting Code, establishing a category called "International Records for Special Vehicles." Arfons' 536 record was the first they acknowledged.

Woman Driver!?

By 1965, Breedlove had built another jet, called it *Spirit of America-Sonic I*, and set two more WLSR records. The first came on November 2, 1965, with a 555-mile-per-hour record. He then told his wife, Lee, to get a babysitter for a few days, and plunked her into the hot seat as a stall tactic to keep Arfons off the salt. Knowing full well that his wife could easily exceed his own record driving the more than capable car, Breedlove restricted the engine power to 60 percent, and she recorded a paltry speed of 308.56 miles per hour, which the press agents puffed up as some vacuous "women's record," as if the car knew, or cared who drives it.

This publicity stunt had been concocted to "demote" aviatrix and auto racer Betty Skelton, who had driven Arthur Arfons' *Cyclops* jet at Bonneville on September 28. She ran a one-way speed of 315 miles per hour, but averaged 277 miles per hour. Skelton had exceeded the record of Paula Murphy, the first

Walter Arfons watches a crewman make last-minute adjustments to Wingfoot Express, powered by a Westinghouse J46 jet, before driver Tom Green blasts off toward the history books as the first man to break the World Land Speed Record on October 2, 1964. The car was 24 feet long and required 14 men working for nearly a week to shake out the race car's problems on the salt. In the end, it was a mere 1/16th of a turn for the idle adjustment and simply opening up the afterburner opening that put the car into the big speed numbers. *Goodyear Tire and Rubber Co.*

The Wingfoot Express Jet was several years in the planning and building stages with Walt Arfons building the frame and installing the J46 jet engine before moving the car to designer and body fabricator Tom Green's shop in early 1963. After Arfons suffered a heart attack, Green also took on the driving chores. Green is shown here (inset) working on the driver's cockpit. Not a hot rodder, Green had the reputation of being "as cautious as a grandmother" when it came to street driving. *Goodyear Tire and Rubber Co.*

woman to drive a jet on the salt, who had gone 226 miles per hour the year before in Walter Arfons' *Avenger*.

Arfons had also turned down the engine power on Skelton. At 39, she was a more experienced and well-rounded driver than Arfons and Breedlove combined. This was a gal who had soloed at 12, got her pilot's license at 16, nailed 426 miles per hour in a P-51 Mustang, drove Indy cars, set NASCAR records, was a test driver for Chrysler, was chosen by NASA to test for the Mercury astronaut program, and had flown upside down cutting a ribbon at only 10 feet off the ground!

At great personal peril, Arthur Arfons recaptured the record on November 7 at 576.553 miles per hour. The right rear tire blew on the return run, flipped, and rolled the car, but miraculously, Arfons only suffered swollen eyes and a skinned forehead and cheeks. He was more worried about how he was going to square things with his wife, June.

On November 15, very late for salt speed runs, Breedlove returned amid threatening weather and raised the WLSR to 600.601 miles per hour. In two years he had taken the record up 306 notches. Whew!

Sadly, despite a wide variety of other racing activities, Breedlove never again rose to racing greatness as he did in the early 1960s. He managed to reinvigorate a couple of old sponsors, pick a few new ones, and take a crack at the WLSR again,

but his 1996 and 1997 runs were bitterly disappointing and oddly disorganized for a five-time world champion.

Breedlove's accident tally is equally, if not more, impressive than his speed marks. No one has crashed faster than he, or more times than he, and lived through each one without so much as a scratch—the last one at 677 miles per hour. Whether he is a consummate hero or complete nut case is a matter of perspective. Breedlove shared his rarefied speed experiences during a 1996 interview:

Speed is also something that I do alone. It is a very personal, intimate experience. When I'm strapped into the cockpit, I don't feel forsaken, but I am alone in the experience. Speed is also the exhilaration of self-gratification; I don't need group approval. I feel good about accomplishing a difficult task, but the reward is staying alive.

Speed can also be menacing. All my crashes share the sensation of losing control, and a healthy dose of fear shoots through me. To survive, I must calmly remember to remain just a good witness while surrounded by violent speed. Pure speed, like pure light, is a spectrum of vivid experiences that happen in an instant but stay with you for a lifetime.

With so many afterburners and flash bulbs popping out on the salt, the remarkable achievement of brothers Bob and Bill Summers was practically ignored. In the middle of the jet war, with their ultrasleek, 32-foot golden streamliner, the brothers accomplished what Mickey Thompson had tried so valiantly to do; they set a new wheel-driven record of 409.277 miles per hour. On November 12, 1965, driving *Goldenrod*, hot rodder Bob Summers, 28, erased Donald Campbell's name from the top of the speed list. As far as piston people were concerned, it was the only record that counted on the salt that year. The brothers' creation was brilliantly engineered and executed—four fuel-injected in-line Chrysler Hemis, coupled in pairs, back-to-back together putting out more than 2,400 horsepower.

It was a hard road to hoe for the brothers. They battled a variety of parts failures, chased back and forth to their shop in Southern California making changes, performed numerous engine tuning tricks to sweeten the power output, and frustratingly waited as the rain poured down. The season was almost over when Firestone, one of their sponsors, offered them some of Art Arfons' salt time. With days left, Bob spun the 210-inch driveshaft fast enough to record a 404-mile-per hour run, but both rear wheel bearings were junked in the process.

Pulling an all-nighter, the fellas had *Goldenrod* ready for battle the next morning. In a light, misting rain, Bill pushed off his brother, who only shifted up to third gear before the Summers Brothers became the champions of hot rodders everywhere.

"We never doubted ourselves, or the car," remembered Bill Summers. "We were young, strong healthy lions, but it was such

Craig Breedlove stands at the tip of the team lineup in early 1964. Long before the days of fancy, color-coordinated uniforms with elaborate embroidery, the dapper dozen *Spirit of America* crew made do with clean white T-shirts and blue jeans. Third on the left, with his hands on his hips, is Lockheed engineer Walt Sheehan, the only man to ever drive the *Spirit of America* other than Breedlove. The car is now part of the permanent collection of Chicago's Musuem of Science and Industry. *Craig Breedlove*

a lot of work and a great deal of stress. When I saw Joe Petrali already talking to Butch when I drove up in the push truck from the other end of the course, I knew he wasn't there to talk about the weather. When he finally told us our official speed, I broke down, softly crying in a combination of relief and joy."

For the racer, once the record is broken the adventure is practically over, but for the fans the excitement is only beginning, because they view the accomplishment as only starting when the record is set. The young hot rodders had taken the record away from

Donald Campbell and his million-dollar car. (A plane crash in Salt Lake City at the same time the *Goldenrod* set the World Landspeed Record overshadowed the brothers' great achievement in the news.)

The next day, Bill and Bob removed the Chrysler engineer's air scoops and fitted their own hot rodder versions. *Goldenrod* ran faster than ever, at 425.99 miles per hour. Chrysler then wanted its engines back. "We took them out and gave them back to their representative, Keith Black," said Bill Summers. "November 13 was the last time the car ever ran."

Driver Bob Summers confers with his brother, Bill, before setting off on record-breaking runs to capture the World Land speed Record for wheel-driven cars. Although the public had become enamored with jets, to the hot rodder, these two men were champions, chalking up a 409.277 miles per hour average on November 12, 1965. The record still stands today. *Bill Summers and Richard Dixon/LandSpeed Productions composite*

Chapter 9

Losing Ground; New Fun Found

In reflection, it had been quite a traffic jam on the salt throughout the 1950s! Friendly competition got kicked into high gear with every description of car, bike, and truck, powered by a great variety of engines, old and new. What had started out as mundane passenger cars had been reshaped into remarkable, high-performance machines. The early modified cars had also been street driven, but as speeds increased, purpose-built cars forged a new motorsports heritage, all happily sequestered on the salt.

Salt racing encouraged and promoted family-style participation, yet the "family" was not necessarily defined by blood lines. At one meet, Kent Enderle spent so much time helping others solve problems that he missed out running his own car. Later, he and his brother, Pete, built a hydrometer that would forever solve the vexing problem of accurate nitromethane fuel blending. Enderle's story was one of thousands told in the decades to come. As the extended families grew and matured, the relationships proved to be stronger than Velcro pulled sideways.

Records Established, Let the Breaking Begin!

SCTA, staffed entirely by volunteers and the occasional paid clerical staff member, proved it could police its own while having a whale of a good time. The group had its exasperating political moments from time to time, but overall the organization moved

Future, n. That period of time in which our affairs prosper, our friends are true, and our happiness is assured.

–Ambrose Bierce

forward and evolved with dignity and grace. However, for as good a job as had been done, nothing could stop the steady loss of participants to drag racing. Instead of unparalleled growth, SCTA spent the 1960s struggling to maintain the status quo.

Furthermore, where in the past racers designed and produced the parts needed to improve Detroit's iron, the car makers had caught on and were now selling high-performance parts of their own making. They found plenty of new customers on the drag strips and cashed in, luring many away from the salt. This winnowing process, painful at the time, proved to be very healthy in retrospect. Those who went drag racing did so first for the variety, but later stayed to lap up the big money after discovering they could make a living off the sport. The hot rodders who remained true to the salt were not motivated by cash awards or the chance to win valuable merchandise, but for the sheer satisfaction of doing something well.

1960 / 12th Annual / Sizzling Seed

Bursting with new vehicles, SCTA expanded to 57 competitive classes in 1960, and the entry fee had risen to $28. The trend was toward small, diminutive streamliners and compact cars. The slickest little flyer was Bill Burke's fiberglass streamliner nicknamed *Pumpkin Seed* because of it shape. A brand-new design for Burke, it delivered him into the 200MPH Club with a 205 average from a dainty 156-inch Ford Falcon engine tuned by Bill Stroppe and crew.

Twin brothers Charlie and Robert Markley packed a pile of punch into their belly tank lakester. Salt racers since the late fifties, they were a threat throughout the 1960s, pushing speeds near 300 miles per hour. Beginning in Class C with a DeSoto mill, they switched to a blown Dodge in 1960, and then moved to Class D with a Chevrolet in 1962. *Ron Christensen*

Nicknamed the *Pumpkin Seed*, the diminutive streamliner was entered as Burke and Laster's *Golden Commode*, due to its bilious gold-green color. Driver Bill Burke qualified for the 200 MPH Club, using the Bill Stroppe-prepared Falcon engine. *Bill Burke Collection*

Bert Munro's 1920 Indian Scout Motorcycle Streamliner set the SA 1000 land speed record at 183 miles per hour in 1967. The record still stands and is the oldest on the motorcycle record books at Bonneville. Pictured here is the restored bike, completed by Steve Huntzinger. *Dave Howe*

Highly regarded for his success on the NASCAR circuit, Stroppe's engine performed well the entire week. Burke demonstrated how beautifully a land speed record could be orchestrated, running better each time he flew through the traps; not even the formidable Vesco-Dinkins team, running 196 miles per hour, could keep up.

Another bit of tiny thunder was the elfish *Wee Eel II* driven by Els Lohn. Clever and classy, Lohn had rigged up an ingenious snap-coupling that included a two-way intercom in the car so he and the push truck crew could have a dignified conversation as the car was being pushed up to speed. The supercharged Morris engine nabbed a new record in Class G at 135 miles per hour.

Still passing on fancy and new was Texan Karol Miller, who, with only one non-stock part (Isky camshaft), jolted the observers when he qualified for a record run with mufflers still connected. Other eyebrow raisers were the Granatelli Brothers, proving the value of their Paxton blowers, and chipping away at the GMC brand monopoly. Fred Larsen and Don Cummins shoved their wedge-shaped modified roadster up to 212 miles per hour.

Several big parts manufacturers set up booths on the salt and offered free technical assistance and parts (or fairly priced) to competitors. Firestone debuted a new "low profile" tire that would run on 100 psi. Less bulky, the new rubber simplified streamlining challenges while at the same time increasing the contact patch so critical for good traction.

On the Autolite payroll for the week was Bill Stroppe, who in addition to the well-stocked race trailer and machine shop, made a big hit with the *Bonneville Trolley*. The vehicle was the salt's first "bus service," hauling people back and forth to the starting line and around the pits. Attached to its back was an immaculate white, triple-door toilet, with each luxurious compartment individually labeled: Ford, Chrysler, and General Motors.

1961 / 13th Annual / Sad Salt

Only nine motorcycles showed up for the August 20–26 Speed Week, but among the 119 cars entered, 100 ran in a single class, 8 brought different size engines for two classes, and speed wrinkle Norm Thatcher, 64, lugged enough engines to be top qualifier in three!

The salt was in sad condition, the result of not enough rainfall during the winter months to fuel the natural surface regeneration. The water table, normally just a few inches below the granite-hard surface, had sunk to almost 5 feet. Dirt from the surrounding mountains settled on the surface and made the salt dirty. This produced fluctuating surface temperatures that caused the salt to crack, buckle and lift. Utah state highway road crews worked six full weeks, 24 hours a day, continually scraping and patching the salt surface, but could only carve out an 8-mile course, 2.5 miles less than the year before. As a result, speeds were lower, but 20 new class records were recorded. The top speed of the meet was 313 miles per hour. Pump gasoline was used by 83 entries, and the remaining 36 mixed up brews containing nitro, methanol, benzine, alcohol, and other speed secret chemicals.

For streamliners, only the Summers Brothers' *Flying Wedge* and Els Lohn's *Wee Eel II* were able to set records. The Bennett-Rochlitzer Studebaker coupe entry picked up two modified records.

In between frames, *HOT ROD* Photo Ace Eric Rickman uses his "tribal knowledge" of Els Lohn's racing rig to pour himself a cool brew on the salt. Notice he brought his own monogrammed glass. *Eric Rickman*

Called *The Redhead*, or the *Coke Bottle*, the streamliner has been an endearing, stylish favorite among salt racers for years. Seen here at the 1964 Speed Week, the Hammon-McGrath-Whipp entry experienced a streak of bad luck with a new torque converter. *Leslie Long*

By the time competitors reached the front of each line, good racing etiquette required drivers to be ready to run. Starter Bob Higbee, seen here attached to the coiled communication cord, will final check each car for safety before waving it off. *Richard Dixon Collection*

Nestled in line with purloined patio umbrellas to make travelin' shade is the Herda-Cagle-Knapp 999 streamliner patiently waiting. Directly behind is the Chevy-powered Eyres and Willet B/Gas Roadster, later purchased by George Bentley and driven by Al Teague. *Leslie Long*

Roadster records got a little boost from the Larsen-Cummins entry, the Marden-Ohly crew, and the Perry Boys-Quincy team. The once popular competition coupe and modified roadster class was in sharp decline.

Packing a 1,710-cubic inch V-12 turbocharged Allison under the hood was the Arfons-Snyder streamliner that pranced up to 313 miles per hour, but Arfons, a gentle spirit with drawing room manners, was never able to use full throttle due to the short course. Bill Burke came back with the *Pumpkin Seed*, this time partnered with Mickey Thompson and a brace of blown Pontiac Tempest engines, but was beset by problems and only managed a 218-mile-per-hour run in a slide, no less. The sports car classes exploded, and the guy with the biggest barking dog was Knot Farrington. Driving a Chrysler-powered T-Bird, he added 28 miles per hour to his speed from the year before, using streamlining tricks.

A new generation of riders appeared when Gary Richards took over from his father and set a new AMA record of 159 miles per hour on the family's 40-inch unstreamlined Triumph twin. For the Stars and Stripes was Walter Ross, riding his 55-inch unstreamlined Harley-Davidson Sportster to an AMA class record of 142 miles per hour.

1962 / 14th Annual / Indian Man

Mickey Thompson's happiest moments came a month before Speed Week, behind the wheel of a Pontiac Catalina fitted with 421 thirsty cubic inches that got 5 miles to the gallon. Starting on July 25, Mick managed to rack up 104 endurance and straight-away records.

On August 19 the salt was as perfect as any hot rodder could want when 141 cars and 15 bikes started pounding the ground at the Nationals. The fast car crowd inked 32 new records, including one by a jet (the first). The cycle riders penned eight new records into the books, but the one by New Zealander Herbert James "Bert" Munro, 62, on his streamlined 1920 Indian (a bike he bought new!) at 162 miles per hour was the show stealer. He had come all the way from his hometown of Invercargill just to race on the salt. His participation proved that amateurs have as good a chance at setting records on the salt as the pros. Dirt poor, he cut a deal with Wendover's local junk yard owner and slept in the back seat of a different wreck each night. When he ran out of money to go home, the racers took up a collection on the salt to buy him a ticket.

Munro was the king of the biker hot rodders and made an annual salt pilgrimage to crusade against his own records. Munro only bought parts as a last resort. Why buy new connecting rods when old rusty tractor axles can be reworked? Cylinders made from an old gas pipe dug out of the ground and shrunk fit with sand-cast-iron fins worked just fine. Why not just melt down those old tractor pistons and recast them into exactly what you want?

Faster, but not as charming, was Bill Johnson astride Joe Dudek's 40-inch streamlined Triumph. He set an all-time record of 230 miles per hour using fuel, and then switched to gas to nail another record at 205 miles per hour. A new gaggle of stream-liners included entries from Mark Dees-Racer Brown using a GMC-blown Tempest in four-wheel drive, and the *Redhead* of Hammon-McGrath-Whipp and Herda-Hartelt fitted with GMC-blown Chryslers. Ermie Immerso's car packed in four box stock Ford 406 engines.

The Athol Graham's car was back, now the *Spirit of Salt Lake*, and his widow, Zeldine, intended to drive. She was so overtly badgered that she gave up the driver seat to Otto Anzjon, who had helped build the original car. Although it was unknown at the time, Anzjon was dying of leukemia.

Ernest Bennett, Tim Rochlitzer, and Bob Joehnck brought a spiffy new lakester, designed with the driver enclosed at the rear, using a drop tank from a F-86D jet fighter. Over the years, this car would go on to put more racers into the 200MPH Club than any other car on the salt.

The "close, but no cigar" prize went to Nolan White, who missed qualifying for the 200MPH Club by less than 1 mile an hour, setting a sports racing record at 199.203 miles per hour. On the flip side, the fast old man from the San Fernando Valley, Norm Thatcher, showed up with two cars and three engines and went home with three records—again.

1963 / 15th Annual / Block Salt

It was becoming clear that the salt was shrinking, and the worried racers started vocalizing their concerns when the potash company dug a huge ditch at the west end of the salt flat, part of the mineral extraction process. The subsequent drainage from the salt beds forced the Utah State Highway Commission to collect 40 tons of salt from the edge of the beds and spread it over the south end of the 9-mile course in a desperate attempt to smooth it over. The hard work did little for Mickey Thompson, who was pummeled into a hospital bed by the rough course. Stepping up the run pace, new timing lights placement proved ingenious and combined a "short" and "long" course on one piece of real estate for the 169 cars and 18 motorcycles that would complete 1,415 runs.

No racing today: Bonneville is immersed in water. Under the salt bed, a geological percolation process helps to make the salt as flat as a pancake and hard as concrete—God's gift to the land speed racer. *Joe Panek*

Alex Tremulis' Gyronaut, a two-wheeled vehicle, was supposed to be fitted with a pair of gyroscopes to keep it upright and stable at low speeds. It never came to pass. Driven by Bob Leppan, it ran close to 200 in 1965. *Wilford Day*

Wendover's Western Motel parking lot, where in one week more engines were assembled, rebuilt, and torn down than all the local garages combined could manage in months. *Will Scott*

Alan Richards built the smallest car to ever crunch the salt crystals. Aptly named, the 20-pound *Claustrophobia* mystified almost everybody as to how the hell anyone could fit in it to drive. The aluminum bug had a 32-inch wheelbase and 18-inch tread and was powered by a 2.8-inch Garelli engine. Racers knew its top speed was much faster than the recorded 55 miles per hour, because the engine was long past its peak power curve away before the little egg reached the first timing light. It was commendable that *Claustrophobia* could maintain 20 miles per hour per cubic inch!

Another sight straight from the *Twilight Zone* was a Studebaker coupe that blew its right rear tire while running 200 miles per hour. Eyewitnesses reported watching the car do a complete flip, land on its wheels, and then spin a few times. The only damage to car or driver was a little bodywork crinkle where the tire blew!

The Summers Brothers' *Wedge* trotted off with top speed of the meet at 308 miles per hour. Tom Beatty's tank was the oldest car at the meet, making its 13th appearance. Nolan White, Tim Rochlitzer, Don Vesco, Burke LeSage, and Don Johnson were all tickled to join the 200MPH Club.

The mind-blower of the event was courtesy of the Markley Brothers, who jacked up the D lakester class record 39 miles per hour to 258 miles per hour with a perfectly tuned supercharged Dodge. Others thought Fred Golin and Pino Ceccato performed a bit of a miracle by building in 17 days a C gas roadster that picked up a record of 161 miles per hour. Then there was regular Fred Larsen, who went home for the fifth year in a row with a new record. Bill Scace from Chicago, Illinois, terrorized the grand touring ranks with his supercharged Tero Chevrolet Corvette, snagging 175-mile-per-hour record.

Bill Burke got quite an awakening when Earl Flanders measured up his brand spanking new Andy Granatelli-prepared Studebaker Avanti engine to find it was 36 inches short on its reported displacement of 259 CID. Missing cubes aside, riding on new Sears Allstate Bonneville tires, Burke still established a record of 147 miles per hour!

1964 / 16th Annual / We Got Trouble

"Absolutely lousy; a genuine stinker," wrote Don Francisco in the December 1964 *Popular Hot Rodding*. Sadly, the 136 cars and 31 motorcycles were only able to complete 527 timed runs. First, the timing equipment failed for the best part of opening day. The salt was so poor that the SCTA recruited every available passenger car and truck to run over the course to pack and smooth the surface, in addition to continual dragging. The wind blew a gale on

Wednesday, tearing the timer's stand to pieces and prompting officials to close down the meet again. Friday started out great but slammed shut in the afternoon when 90 degree crosswinds preceded a downpour. By nightfall the course was flooded.

It was not a total disaster. The fastest speed of the meet came from the crafty Markley Brothers' lakester, blitzing the clocks at 274 miles per hour. Wilford Day managed a 130-mile-per-hour run in his modestly cubed Plymouth Barracuda. Jack Lufkin and Jim Short made it into the 200MPH Club, joining under new rules. Without explanation, in the 1964 SCTA program, 200MPH Club President Jim Lindsley announced that members must not only be timed over 200 miles per hour, two ways, but must now qualify and exceed an existing record.

Don Vesco sets two new motorcycle records on his 250-cc Yamaha—one accomplished by starting his ride sitting side saddle!

The 1965 Driver's Meeting was held an the empty lot along Wendover Boulevard directly across from the Western Motel, the racer's "official" headquarters. Check out the stylish rags on the STP gent. *Will Scott*

Ford Walters brought what some thought was a moonshine still, but turned out to be a steam-powered car—a first for the salt—but it never ran right.

Focusing on ram tuning principles, Tom Keosababian set a 125-mile-per-hour record, punctuating the silence with a one-of-a-kind exhaust note. Sticking out more than 2 feet from behind his Corvair Monza was a zany set of funnel-shaped exhaust megaphones.

It was hard-running Mickey Thompson's last salt fling, driving a Sears Allstate Corvette. Doctors advised him to give up high-speed driving for a while after he fainted during the event.

In October, Studebaker arrived on the salt and left 10 days later with 349 endurance and high-speed records. Andy Granatelli, with brothers Joe and Vince, not only prepped and sweetened the engines, but took up some driving chores as well. Officiated by USAC and sanctioned by FIA, the majority of the good deeds were performed by two "salt virgins," Californians Paula Murphy and Barbara Neiland. Their runs included a female-only record run of 1,000 miles with a sealed hood. Both gals ran so hard they exceeded previous records set by Mickey Thompson and Andy Granatelli.

1965 / 17th Annual / 91-Hour Race

A raging downpour two days before the Nationals delayed the start for four days until the water evaporated off the course. Some fellows eyed Fred Andrews' Evinrude-powered streamliner with envy; he later managed a 100-mile-per-hour pass! For the hearty souls who waited, there was a luxurious tech inspection and correction process, a "low net" volleyball game played on a tennis court (sponsored by the San Diego Roadster Club, no bad-mouthing of officials allowed), a beer can crushing contest (steel, not aluminum), and, of course, gambling at the State Line.

With only a 5-mile course to use on Thursday, the 19th, others bailed out when it was discovered they would have to drive through 5 miles of saltwater slush to reach the usable course. Those who stayed discovered that where salt thickness had once

Flying Caducesus jet car of Dr. Nathan Ostich was considered the first jet of its kind on Bonneville. The fast doctor was physicisan to many racers during the 50s and 60s. The doctor is seen here with his back to the camera in the white T-shirt with the medical caduceus and checkered flags. *Hot Rod* Editor Ray Brock is next to him and was crew chief for the car. *Wilford Day*

Never give up the race! That was the battle cry in 1965 when a late storm delayed racing for four days. Here the crew of the Kurtis-powered *Fireside Inn* sports racing entry tries like the dickens to push the yellow duck up out of a low spot on the salt. The brine is highly corrosive, especially to vehicle electrical systems. *Will Scott*

been measured in feet, it was now only a few inches in spots. The overall available area was shrinking as well, and many believed the continual pumping away of the salt brine for potash mining activities of Kaiser Chemicals, a division of Kaiser Aluminum, was to blame. Kaiser angrily disagreed, saying the loss was entirely due to variable weather and humidity. By late November, state officials quieted everything down by announcing that a geological study would be done. Unfortunately, the fox was allowed to guard the henhouse, and the study was paid for by Kaiser, putting the objectivity of the report in question.

Only 91 hours of racing took place, once Chief Starter Bob Higbee let the first car go down the course. SCTA crammed in 589 qualifying runs, yet miraculously knocked out 10 records in between high wind shutdowns. Of the 141 vehicles entered, 97 made at least one run.

The Herda-Knapp-Milodon Engineering streamliner, which had established an International record of 311 miles per hour in 1964, was the fastest of the meet, at 272 miles per hour. An absolute engineering marvel, the car easily could have passed aircraft-quality building standards. The only flathead powered car of the meet was Bob Westbrook's modified roadster, which went to the top of his class with a 136-mile-per-hour run.

Art Chrisman, now president of the 200MPH Club, tried to clarify the rules for entrance to the club with an article in the 1965 program. But the only clear thing was that qualifying for membership was more complicated than it used to be.

International Records

On September 5, 1965, Bob "Butch" Summers drove a 1966 Plymouth Satellite to improve the USAC American closed-car Class

B records. He set a new 156 flying mile and 155 flying kilo to retire Mickey Thompson's standing marks.

Walt Arfons was back in late September with a multirocket-powered *Wingfoot Express* driven by Bob Tatroe. Although interesting, the car nearly burned to the ground from the combined heat from the rockets, but Tatroe escaped unharmed.

Quiet and amiable Bill Martin, after rolling over three times, blasted to bits the Hans Muller/NSU-held record, clocking a 174 miles per hour average over the standing 150-mile-per-hour record. Martin's streamliner was powered by a Yamaha RD-56 two-stroke.

Renowned car designer Alex Tremulis exercised his Gyronaut, a motorcycle powered by 2 650-cc Triumph engines and driven by Bob Leppan to speeds close to 200 miles per hour.

1966 / 18th Annual / Tiptop Salt

The salt surface was in terrific shape, better than it had been in years. The Bonneville Nationals started the racing season with 164 car entries and 24 bikes. Of the 62 new records, six brought new members to the 200MPH Club. On Friday, a lusty tailwind shut down competition early because some cars were registering almost

There were not many 1964 Plymouth Barracudas that could knock out 130-mile-per-hour runs in 1966. Wilford Day, 34, had the magic figured out in F/Production, running a slant-six Dodge to a record-setting average of 143 miles per hour. Utah Oil Company provided free Beeline Gas to all racers for more than a decade. *Wilford Day*

This was once the ultimate transfiguration of the stock machine. La Mirada, California, resident Fred Larsen (of Larsen-Cummins streamliner fame) tucked a 398 Chrysler under his blue bonnet and pulled out a Class A record of 228 miles per hour in 1962. Larsen joined the 200MPH Club in 1959. *Ron Christensen*

This must be the "pit area of brotherly love!" The Markley boys' lakester is surveyed by the curious in the background as the Summers brothers unload their new red liner. Energized by a 302-inch mill, the narrow nymph cranked out a 309-mile-per-hour run. The teardrop styling was possible because "Butch" and Bill tiptoed around the international rules, demanding four wheels. They aligned the rear two and let the front two tend to steering and accepting driveline power. *Ron Christensen*

20-mile-per-hour increases over previous runs. All the suspect times were eliminated as a gesture of fairness.

Ginnie Geisler puts the woman's role at Bonneville into stark perspective with her gentle but painfully naked assessment of how "salt fever" can affect family life. She wrote a "Raceitorial" in the 1966 SCTA Bonneville program:

"With salt in his blood and victory in his heart, each driver slides behind the wheel of his powerful machine. The constant nagging question tears at his heart; after months of sweat, sacrifice and sleepless nights building this car, will he be rewarded with a record? Once on the salt, they [the women] are neglected, rejected and become the bang board for the tension and pent emotions of their men."

Her timing was uncanny. After seven years of bewildered trying, Geisler's hubby, Bruce, with partners Cook and DeHaan, posted a record of 171 miles per hour with their two-door Studebaker named, of all things, the *Hanky Panky Special*.

The fastest car of the meet was the gorgeous *Redhead*, shaped like a Coke bottle. The McGrath-Hammon team posted a 331-mile-per-hour speed, set with the 464-CID Chrysler, Potvin

immediately for induction. On the pristine salt wilderness, it was easy to forget President Johnson had escalated the Vietnam conflict to a war earlier that year.

Ted Gillette, who had driven Toole County's only ambulance for years, also served as the standby medical transport since 1956. He passed away in January 1967, but left behind a summation of long association with the racers:

> I have experienced many horrible accidents on the highway. This year, I have picked up (to date) 14 fatalities plus numerous injuries. This proves to me that, under the rigid safety inspection and supervision of the Bonneville nationals, it is safer to travel 200 miles per hour on the salt, than 70 miles per hour on the public highways.

1967 / 19th Annual / New Road

In comparison to other forms of racing, sponsorship was sparse on the salt, making those that helped very dearly appreciated. For the past 19 consecutive years, Bell Auto Parts had made the difference for racers by setting up and stocking a parts store on the salt during Speed Week. Cool water could always be found in Bell's "Palm Tree Oasis." Harvey Crane, of Crane Cams, was an instant friend when he picked up the tab for the orange-colored "little stinkers" strategically placed throughout the pits for "women" and "men" in need. In addition to the "daily" sponsors like Champion, Isky Cams, Autolite, STP, Beeline Gas, and Grant Piston Rings, almost 60 other businesses or individuals picked up the tab for class trophies.

The event got under way on Sunday, August 20, 1967, with 155 cars and a whopping 57 motorcycles buzzing the clocks. When it ended, on Saturday, August 26, the record books had 32 new names extracted from 1,152 qualifying runs and five new members for the Grant 200MPH Club. Top speed was again the Herda, Knapp, and Milodon streamliner, at 326 miles per hour. After the SCTA event, the car would set a new International Class B record of 357 miles per hour.

The surface conditions were generally good, but the 10-mile endurance track was unusable because there wasn't enough salt surface area to plot a course. This year also saw construction start on Interstate 80, replacing the well-worn "Victory Highway" that had opened in 1925.

Bob Joehnck, who thought the shape of a Corvette Stingray was like trying to shoot an arrow backward, was pleased when lawyer pal Mark Dees became the world's fastest mouth. With the help of a giant pile of experimental headers, Dees ran his normally aspirated, small-block Chevy 203 miles per hour. Dees then jumped on his Velocette Thruxton Elite 30-inch motorcycle and nailed another record. Other vehicle jumpers were veterans Don Vesco and Ron Benham, who also found the time to test, tune, and have some two-wheel fun. Jumping the Class X record 20 miles per hour, veteran 1932 roadster man George Morris brought a car he has been racing since 1946 and spit out a 144 miles per hour average.

Classes for flatheads were re-established in 1966 when the hard-core salt racers clamored for more speed opportunities. Bob Westbrook was one of the first to step into the record books with a 157-mile-per-hour average. This choice 1927 ran on deuce rails and drew its strength from a 1948 Mercury flathead with a Potvin 400 cam, triple Stromberg 97 carburetors, Harman and Collins magneto, and Schiefer button flywheel and clutch assembly. Note Mrs. Westbrook's colorful clothespins holding the parachute covering to the quick-rig pole and line canopy. *Will Scott*

cam, and 6-71 GMC blower. The fastest bike of the meet was the *Gyronaut*, driven by Bob Leppan and wrenched by Jim Bruflodt. The bike set a new AMA 245-mile-per-hour average.

The obsolete flathead and inline engines got another chance for glory when Class X was added to 10 of the 13 categories. The antiques accounted for six records, and the winners included Fred Lobello's four-banger lakester, which had competed annually since 1951. Another golden oldie was the fuel roadster of Mardon-Ohly-Bentley, built in 1958, which eclipsed the Quincy-Perry boys' 1960 record of 182 miles per hour.

Mario Andretti drove a tachless fastback Mustang, stuffed with an unblown Indy engine to run 175 miles per hour. Old sage Ak Miller told Andretti, "Just wind it up until you feel something float, and then back off a little."

Orangecrate, the tiny, 9-foot, rear-engine streamliner of Louie Bonesio, that weighed 500 pounds with driver, went home the owner of the Class I record at 129 miles per hour. Not bad for 30 CID. Bug fans had to root for the little 1956 Volkswagen Beetle driven by Dean Lowry and built by Engineered Motor Products, Inc. The highly modified 118-CID engine pushed out a 121-mile-per-hour qualifying run, but failed to nab the record.

Poppy red and sanitary describes Fred Holmes' and Judy and Kim Kugel's '32 gas roadster, which set the Class E record at 165 miles per hour. Relying on the grunt from a 1964 Ford 260-CID V-8, the car was the envy of pit row.

Bill Burke drove his aluminum-bodied *Rapid Transit* streamliner, and sons Bill Jr. and Steve traded driving chores in a 1963 Avanti with 427 Ford under the hood. Together, the boys set a 175-mile-per-hour record in Class B gas coupe and sedan. That evening, Bill Jr. was served notice by his local draft board to report

Ak Miller drove a six-cylinder street-worthy Mustang up to the salt and then mashed the throttle to register 148 miles per hour on pump gas. Miller employee Jack Lufkin ran his modified sports car in three classes and obliterated the records by up to 29 miles per hour in two of the three. Don Torgeson learned about air flow with his AA Altered coupe that got stuck at 185 miles per hour. He thought the supercharger might need more air, so he chomped out a few holes in the body and picked up an astonishing 25 miles per hour—good enough to join the "2 Club."

Ed Iskenderian personally spun wrenches on his son Ronnie's and Jerry Spotts' 1962 Corvette. The "cam father" was impressed by the boy's ability to boost the existing record by 30 miles per hour on their first trip to the salt. The Markley Brothers showed up with a new threat in the shape of a lakester that ran 260 miles per hour, thanks in part to a 55 percent reduction in frontal area using the wing tank off a T33 fighter. Warner Riley from Illinois and Bob Mauriallo from New Jersey both brought Harley Sportsters and notched new records without a lick of help from sponsors.

Bureaucratic Jungle Bungle

While the racers were busy stirring the speed pot, Utah state officials blindly sold a plot of land from the Bonneville Salt Flats basin that included a portion of the speedway. Local Tooele County Commissioner George Buzinais discovered the error and repeatedly tried to warn the State Land Board and Gus Backman, chairman of the Bonneville Speedway Association. Backman and the Land Board simply thought the local guy was mistaken. After the sale, Buzinais came forward again, this time with tax assessment proof that the speedway was in jeopardy, but again he was ignored. Not even results from the 1960 Utah Geological and Mineral Survey that had measured the thickness of the Bonneville Salt Crust were believed.

"MmMMmm, MMmMmm, good!" This E/Gas Roadster of Judy and Jim Kugel and Fred Holmes ran under the Road Runners Car Club banner. It was a classic configuration of an open-air deuce. The 260 CID Ford mill relied on a Clay Smith 300B flat tappet cam, Forged True pistons, Hilborn injection, and Doug Headers. For its 1965 salt showing, the car clocked a record-setting 163-mile-per-hour average, yet was far from its more than 200-mile-per-hour potential that it attained in later years. *Will Scott*

1961 was a great year for Harry Mardon. He drove the 93-inch wheelbase, tube-frame chassis Mardon-Ohly-Bentley D/Fuel roadster to a new class record of 203 miles per hour qualifying for the 200MPH Club in the process. In 1965, he nudged up his own record to 207 miles per hour legging the blown 258 CID Chevy. Note the odd-ball exhaust pipe exiting just aft of the firewall. The car also sported one of the first all-aluminum tonneau covers used in Bonneville racing. *Will Scott*

Leo Lake, Yamaha USA and Alfred Le Blanc, FIM Representative from Liege, Belgium inspect Bill Martin's 250cc Speed Probe. On September 25th, 1965, Martin screamed across the salt and into the record books with a speed of 173.8 mph despite equipment failure and poor course conditions which eliminated forward visibility and finishing with a full roll when a playful breeze caught the parachute. *Dale and Lonnie Martin*

The alarm finally sounded in 1968, when the 14 owners, led by Herbert Heyman of Los Angeles, brought a trespass action against the Bonneville Speedway Corporation, rightfully demanding $100 per month rent for use of their 640 acres. An injunction was filed, and the racers were barred from crossing the parcel of land located at the north end of the speedway.

The state eventually repurchased the land in 1970 for $22.50 an acre, but had it not done so, any car running in excess of 300 miles per hour would have had to find a new place to race. The salt rodders were grateful to Utah taxpayers for spending $14,400 for desert property they had sold 10 years earlier for $1,600.

1968 / 20th Annual / Rain Out

Rain finally caught up with the racers after 20 years. The original 1968 dates were rained out and Bonneville XX was rescheduled for October 15–21 through the Herculean efforts of SCTA and motivated racers who refused to let the year pass without making a pass down the salt. Of the original 140, only 57 returned to set 19 new records. Top speed for the meet was 291 for those Markley boys, but it was the lakester of Allen-Parker-Griffith-Allen that re-inked record books at 244 for the biggest new record jump.

The crown prince of salty delights, Bill Burke, one of three men (along with Ak Miller and Jim Lindsley) still racing at Bonneville since the beginning, reflected on the past two decades saying,

"This event belongs to each one of us who participates in any way . . . each year I look to Bonneville with greater desire, deeper respect, and more admiration, and I hope each of you does the same."

1969 / 21st Annual / Give Us the Money!

BSA, Triumph, and Kawasaki muddied the amateur waters by offering bonus money for anyone who snagged a record with their brand. The extra bikes clogged up the run lines to the point that some thought this year's event was a bike meet to which cars had been invited. Entries were so numerous that Speed Week seemed compressed; so many more vehicles in line meant longer waits, which translated into fewer runs overall. The salt was in excellent shape, so most didn't mind the wait to have the thin, black, 9-mile line all to themselves.

That included Pete Barker, who whipped his Volkswagen Beetle until it ran nearly 130 miles per hour. Or Clarence Everett, who stuffed a flathead in a late-model Camaro, and Verlin Marshall, who parked his flathead in a Studebaker. Whether you brought a bulky Hudson Hornet or the fastest car of the meet, you were made to feel welcome. If LeVan Prothero's production Camaro could run over 200 miles per hour, why not yours?

Bonneville is surprises, just like the one the Thompson/Frasier entry gave the record books by upping the Class B competition coupe mark from 178 miles per hour up to a whopping 248 miles per hour! Bill Taylor joined the 200MPH Club at 201.916 miles per hour driving an Ardun Ford-powered roadster drinking a solution of 98 percent nitro. Whew! "Big" Bill Edwards (self-proclaimed Mayor of Wells), Jack Lufkin, and Dick Beith were all trying to turn exhaust gases into miles-per-hour experimenting with plenty of pounds of turbocharger boost.

Safety is foremost for SCTA, but how do you predict freakish nightmares like the flash fire that took the life of congenial innovator Bob Herda? Long known for his premiere workmanship, at least he passed into salt history right out on the course that he loved so well.

Some say the Golden Age of Bonneville, an era of radical transformation that had started in 1955, ended in 1969. It was certainly the period of greatest change: engines, techniques, body styles, and of course, an explosion of new faces.

The Coffee Grinder II is typical of a salt racing machine: many hands to make fast work. Entered by the team of Allen-Griffith-Parker-B&N, this cool blue enclosed belly tank lakester ran a 388 CID supercharged Chrysler and was the A Class leader at 250 miles per hour, a single mile per hour slower than the class record held by the Quincy Auto-Brissette Brothers entry driven by Bob Summers. Some of the chassis competing in this class date back to the early years of dry lakes racing. *Will Scott*

Chapter 10

Passing the Wrench:
The Hot Rodder's Kids Go Racing

An official highway sign now marked the turn-off to the flats, "Bonneville Speedway," part of the Interstate 80 project completed just before the hot rodders arrived in 1970. Rolling into town for the 22nd Annual Speed Week, they found a new, paved two-lane road that extended out onto the salt, ending just short of the SCTA registration trailer. "This was a major improvement over the bumpy, kidney-beating, washboard road we had used for decades," said a delighted Ron Benham.

Moving with the times, SCTA formed Bonneville National, Inc. (BNI), which would focus specifically on producing the annual speed week. Administration of the salt was transferred to the Utah State Department of Parks and Recreation through a Special Land Use Permit from the Bureau of Land Management (BLM). The new overseers were enthusiastic supporters of BNI, rather unusual for bureaucrats. Even Utah Governor Rampton got involved, and out went the hated canal that was drying out the salt. The once badly damaged salt surface was being nursed back to a healthy, glistening hard, moist condition.

Of the 300 entries, 170 were motorcycles, lured again by the factories' promise of cash for records. On the high side, the week ended with 27 new record holders. On the low side, three chilling crashes resulted in one man making the ultimate sacrifice for his sport.

Mel Chastain, driving Bill Burke's streamliner with Les Leggitt's blown Chrysler had just nosed into the 300-mile-per-hour realm

To perceive something by way of faith is one thing. To fully understand that perception is another thing altogether.

–Saint Gregory

when the car suddenly began to violently tumble. By the time the 2,000-pound car stopped slamming into the ground, all four chrome Anza wheels were square and the frame was bent up into a sickly "U" shape.

Noel Black, driving the twin-engine B&N Automotive streamliner, *Motion I*, had set top speed of the meet on Monday, thundering through the traps at 352 miles per hour. On Wednesday, the pendulum of fortune swung heavily in the opposite direction. After clearing the fourth mile, clocking 380 miles per hour, the car wiggled, slid, lifted into the air, and disintegrated. Flown by air ambulance to a Salt Lake City hospital, Black did not survive the night.

Closing out one of the most horrific of afternoons in all of Bonneville racing, the running gear broke on Mel Hoy's wing tank lakester as he was traveling in excess of 230 miles per hour. The car spun a few times, flipped, barrel-rolled, and landed *back on its wheels* before spinning again. Hoy climbed out unhurt.

The snappy little streamliner of Fred "Put your foot in it" Larsen and Don Cummins choked down a 265-inch V-8 Chevy block to 120 inches and four holes to obliterate the existing E streamliner record of 128 miles per hour by recording a 227-mile-per-hour record—115 miles per hour over the old record. Another sharp streamliner appearing that year was Matt Guzzetta's, powered by a 500-cc Triumph that took the number one spot at 137 miles per hour. Meticulous is the *only* way to describe Chauvin Emmons' modified roadster, running a 360-inch injected Chrysler.

One of the most successful designs in Bonneville Racing history, the Larsen and Cummins Class D streamliner gallops down the course pulling on all 183 cubic inches from the blown Chevy engine that gave the team a decade closing 289.50 mile-per-hour record. *George Calloway*

This is how many of the racers remember the State Line Hotel and Casino, complete with their pal, 'ole Wendover Will, the world's tallest mechanical cowboy. With his waving, pointing arm he bid welcome to all who passed. Will is still on duty today, even though the hotel and casino have been "citified." *State Line Hotel and Casino*

Don't let the conservative attire fool you. This man was a certified motorhead maniac. Tom Senter was famous for working on his race cars while listening to Bonneville recordings of engines blasting down the black line, cranked up to eardrum-splitting loud. The high boy roadster sitting in his driveway was only one of many salty speed projects. *Senter/Telnak Family*

Running for all he was worth, Jim Travis ditched his gas roadster fenders and pushed his little flathead to establish a 133-mile-per-hour X/StR record.

Diminutively weird, but lovable was a good way to describe the 1-cubic-inch tricycle streamliner with dual-CID model plane engines and a 15-speed bicycle sprocket. Dean Lowry of Deano Dyno Soars stomped out the G/Sports racing record at 148 miles per hour driving his animated *Terra Soar* VW. Finding a way to race on someone else's nickel was Ak Miller, who used his vast knowledge and skills to lead a merry band of Chaffey College kids to a D/Production record of 173 miles per hour, driving the fully accredited class project Mustang.

At the annual 200MPH Club banquet, photographic sharpshooter Eric Rickman was blown away when the membership decided he was their "Man of the Year," an honor bestowed annually on someone who has made an outstanding contribution to salt racing. Joining the sacred fraternity of fast men was Elwin "Al" Teague, who had bumped up the C/Gas roadster record to 231 driving the Sadd-Teague-Bentley entry.

The final run of the meet was a numerologist's dream, and a record to the second power. The streamlined Studebaker of Neil Thompson, Don Alpenfels, and Gregg Frazier ran exactly 235.49 miles per hour on back-to-back runs!

As for all those motorcycles, AMA referee Earl Flanders had his hands full authenticating 66 bike records, including Darrel Packard's record 82 miles per hour, set with a modified 50-cc naked Suzuki! Don Vesco became the talk of the salt after exploding a rear tire at 250 miles per hour in his twin Yamaha streamliner and coming back two weeks later all patched up to nail the World Speed Record for motorcycles, running 251 miles per hour.

What a Gas, Man!

The rocket age arrived on October 23, 1970, when former test astronaut Gary Gabelich drove the rocket-powered *Blue Flame* to a 622.407-mile-per-hour record in the flying mile, ending Craig Breedlove's five-year reign as "World's Fastest." Bigger news overseas was the fact that Gabelich was thus the first man to exceed the 1,000-kilometer-per-hour land barrier, at 1,001.639 kilometers per hour.

A flower-carrying member of the "peace generation," Gabelich festooned himself with multiple sets of love beads and good luck charms, then had an intimate talk with the 5,000-pound car before blasting off on his fateful ride. Don't snicker, because just as he was counting down to run, the dark, foreboding sky parted, lighting the course, and only the course, with a brilliant stream of sunlight.

On August 20, 1973, Dr. Allan Abbott, 29, of San Bernardino, and his $2,000 bicycle broke the land speed record on the Bonneville Salt Flats. The pizza-sized gear prevented the bike from being pedaled under 50 miles per hour. Abbott was towed up to speed and released. Abbott's speed was 138.674. It was the first time a bicycle had raced for time on the famed Utah course. *SCTA*

the obligation onto me. I wrenched the motor; the responsibility was now on my shoulders, and it was then I realized what a burden my father had carried to put me into the '2 Club.' "

There were plenty of big, bratty bikes at Bonneville that year, but applause was in order for 21-year-old Phillip York, from Albuquerque, New Mexico, who bravely climbed aboard a poked and stroked 100-cc minibike to buzz down the course at 92 miles per hour. York had highly modified the engine, but when he poured in an 80 percent nitro mix, the jaws hit the salt when the clocks recorded a speed in excess of 100 miles per hour. York is a great pal of Dave Campos, the World Record Holder for motorcycles.

On the international scene, NASCAR great Bobby Issacs brought one of his obsolete Daytona Chargers to the salt and scooped up 28 new straightaway and endurance records. The poor, loose, and wet salt conditions didn't bother the veteran dirt tracker one bit. The good old boys went home with two of Ab Jenkins' marks that had been set in 1951.

1972 / 24th Annual / Biker's Year

In an effort to keep Bonneville the last frontier of raw speed, a place where fair competition can flourish, the SCTA made a variety of Rule Book changes that caused quite an uproar. The move instantly obsoleted some cars and drastically altered the way others would compete within a class.

One of many caught in the changes was attorney Mark Dees, who involuntarily retired his Austin Bantam to buy the Markley Brothers' belly tank fitted with one of smiling Bob Joehnck's magic 468-inch rat motors. Dees was determined to reach 275 miles per hour, or sue the guy who beat him.

In the damnedest bit of bad luck, the 16-year-old car of Nick Sadd, Al Teague, and George Bentley, the pride of the roadster

1971 / 23rd Annual / The Younger Generation

When Larry Lindsley drove the family Super Bird to a 210-mile-per-hour record and qualified for 200MPH Club membership just like his dad, a new era dawned for the sodium speed seekers. The young men who had pioneered salt racing were now all over 40; most were in their 50s and a few were over 60. The children who shared their father's love of the speed chase were donning helmets and strapping into adventures of their own.

Not yet, but soon wives would also join the ranks, and even grandchildren would want their turn down the long, black line. The roster for the fast families of the first order would grow to include, among others, names like Lindsley, Kugel, Burke, Miller, Cook, Martin, Arnet, Vesco, Thayer, Rochlitzler, White, Stringfellow, Fergusen, Temple, Arias, Batchelor, Hammond, Dolan, Jeffries, and Sable. Some would step out of the driver seat, and others would just build more cars or share the seat time with their kids. Either way, the second generation would get a "running start" at the salt's challenge.

"For me the whole experience of Bonneville was getting into the '2 club,' " said Bill Burke. "I wanted that distinction for Steve. I felt so strongly about doing this for him because we were so deeply immersed in the sport. It was like sending him to Harvard and graduating with honors." The Burkes are a family that have more records than they have race cars, and they brought dozens of cars to Bonneville.

"When Josh and Jason, my brother Bill's sons, qualified for a record in the Avanti, we were looking at a three-generation legacy," observed Steve Burke. "Dad built the car, then passed

Noel Black and Bert Peterson owned the B&N Automotive *Motion I* twin-engine streamliner, also called *The Rhinoceros,* due to the bumps in the bodywork where each engine was located. Driver Noel Black lost his life when the car got out of shape, violently tumbled, and destroyed itself in 1970. *George Calloway*

1973 / Silver Anniversary

To help celebrate a quarter-century of sodium sizzle, 170 cars and motorcycles showed up August 17. Champion Spark Plugs, Bell Auto Parts, STP, Kawasaki, Moon Equipment, Isky Cams, and Top Gear stepped up to help sponsor the silver milestone. BNI managed to get FIA sanctioning for the last two days of the meet, saving racers wads of dough and adding to the anniversary fun.

A special, quarter-century banquet at the State Line Hotel and Casino was attended by pioneer saline citizens. Utah Governor Rampton showed up and presented the SCTA/BNI officers with a plaque of appreciation. The weather fell down and delivered a rainstorm followed by a land-locked hurricane that halted racing for two days.

On Thursday, Ken Walkey nailed a new FIA record down and bagged the SCTA fuel lakester record as well—or so he thought. He changed engines, only to discover on Friday morning that the record had been disallowed. Back in went the first engine, instant replay was engaged, and then Walkey swapped engines, *again*, to finally grab that darn record on Saturday.

Although spectators saw a 1955 Chevy on the course, it was the bicycle rider pedaling behind enclosed in a wind-draft box at the rear that made people squint. Fitted with a sprocket the size of an extra-large pizza, Dr. Allan Abbott cranked out an impressive 138-mile-per-hour run.

Back from the dead was the Sadd-Teague-Bentley fuel roadster, rebuilt with the help of Steed Oil Products. Demon driver Teague ran with seeming impunity, clicking off a jaw-dropping 268-mile-per-hour run! Bill Snyder drove the slab-sided, Thermo-King-sponsored streamliner *College of the Redwoods* to a record to become the first diesel-powered pilot in the 200MPH Club.

Salt Fever can be devastating to the racer, inducing an almost rabid need for speed. In this case, Ron Benham was affected so badly that he actually accepted U-Haul's request to pull a trailer behind his modified roadster at high speed. Don't laugh; he got it up to 142 miles per hour—maybe the fastest trailer on the planet?
Robin Richardson

fleet, was severely damaged in a head-on return road collision that hospitalized two people. It happened AFTER a safe run at 250 miles per hour. Think about that for a moment. That's 4 miles a minute in a car shaped like a barn. The roadster came to life only because all three partners threw in together; none of them had the money to build one on their own.

By screwing in one of Les Leggitt's raucous Chryslers, Chauvin Emmons finally sailed into the 200MPH Club to dock the B/Modified Roadster record at 240 miles per hour.

1974 / 26th Annual / Brownieville?

Where once the surface had been hard and clean, compact enough to lay down some rubber off the starting line, the saline expanse was cracked and chipped like scalloped potatoes left in the oven too long. The hot rodders had watched the slow demise for a quarter of a century, and Ab Jenkins had voiced serious concerns 20 years before that, but such complaints were largely ignored.

That summer, 1974, the Utah Geological and Mineral Survey performed a second set of measurements of the thickness of the Bonneville salt crust, and then the State of Utah backed away from the salt issue by simply not renewing its Special Land Use Permit. Like a hot potato, administration was transferred to the BLM. The good-intentioned, budget-conscious Utah State Highway Commission scooped up 500 tons of mud-mixed salt from the edge of the salt plain, and then spread the filthy salt over the course trying to smooth the damaged race surface, making it a distinctly dingy brown that year. For the first time in all of salt racing, the rooster tails unzipping from the tires were billowing clouds of dust, growing as the cars and bikes got up to speed. Disgusted, SCTA President Elmo Gillette directed some core samples be taken around the pit area and discovered that while the salt was approximately 18 inches thick, the upper portions were heavily mixed with dirt.

Any record set is a right fine achievement. Despite perfect assembly of top quality parts tuned to perfection, a crew that operates with drill team precision, and a driver with reflexes of a tiger, the weather can quash all hope. Gary Gabelich set a new World Land Speed Record of 622.407 miles per hour on October 23, 1970, and this photo was shot the next morning. *Richard Dixon*

The team had made 19 runs over 600 miles per hour, but ran out of fuel each time on the return run. As a last resort, Dana Fuller used his hopped-up truck to push the *Blue Flame* to 120 miles per hour before Gary Gabelich lit the rocket motor. "It's like nothing else," gushed the rocket man. Inset: Emily Gillette, longtime member of the Bonneville ambulance crew, gets a hug from the world's fastest man. *LandSpeed Productions composite*

Mustachioed Mike Cook's steamy 295 miles per hour in Leggitt's *One Way Special* became the fastest-ever recorded time for an open-wheel car. Don Vesco's 248-mile-per-hour hot-hauling of his Yamaha streamliner boosted one of his two new records by more than 155 miles per hour. Dave Campos cackled his twin Harley Ds at 231 miles per hour for two new gas and fuel records.

Mike Corbin, riding a partially streamlined bike powered by dual A4B-Xf jet starter motors fed by 20 Yardney batteries costing $5,000 each, steadily tickled more amps from the setup throughout the week. He ended with an electrifying 171-mile-per-hour run.

As for the cars, Vern Anderson pointed the silent but deadly *Pollution Packer* rocket to a 4.9-second quarter-mile record before the *Clean Air Corvair*, running on turbocharged propane, made a case for camping stove fuel by upping the class record to 173 miles per hour. Back to simpler things, wily old Harold Johansen, after years of trying, legged his black, G/roadster through the traps averaging 208 miles per hour and found himself the first new member of the 200MPH Club that year. Clyde Sturdy followed in his AA/gas roaster, popping out a 218-mile-per-hour average.

In September, attempts at Ab Jenkins' endurance records by North American Racing Team (NART) had little success. All that actor-racer Paul Newman, Luigi Chinetti, Jr., Milt Minter, and Graham Hill could manage were three national and international records before conceding defeat.

"I don't care how much horsepower he had, that Ab Jenkins had guts, and he deserves his records," said an exhausted Chinetti.

Al Teague started racing with his brother, Harvey, but his driving and mechanical talents hit the limelight when he teamed up with Sadd and George Bentley in 1968 to build an open cockpit 1929 Model A red highboy roadster, powered by a blown Chrysler Hemi. During the 1972 Bonneville Speed Week meet he set the B/Blown Fuel Roadster record at 250.805 miles per hour, including a one-way pass at an incredible 268 miles per hour. *Jane and Al Teague Collection*

It was very humble before it made a world record-setting rumble, but this is the *Spirit of 76* sitting in the alley behind Al Teague's mother's house in 1976. The open-wheel, high-speed lakester was based on a design by Lynn Yakel and made from the mold of a motorcycle streamliner by Denis Manning. Teague later turned it into the 409-mile-per-hour streamliner. *Jane and Al Teague Collection*

He was referring to the 20 records Jenkins set back in 1940, while driving the *Mormon Meteor III*. NART director Dick Fritz showed as much familiarity with how to run on the salt "as Napoleon did with Russian winters," remarked *Deseret News* columnist Lee Bensen.

All the racers went home a bit saddened by the news that Firestone was leaving racing. Suddenly, every available Firestone Bonneville tire was as valuable as gold.

1975 / 27th Annual / Mr. Cool

Vera and Multy Aldrich kept contestants well fortified prior to their record runs all week. The pair estimated they served 750 cups of coffee during the 1975 Speed Week along with 125 cookies, two watermelons, two gallons of hand-cranked ice cream, and one pie. All this was in addition to pumping more than 1,000 gallons of gasoline during a generally wet and gloomy Speed Week. So cherished are these two that in the program, under "hospitality," they are simply listed as "Multy & Vera."

Burke LeSage had the proverbial racing ants in his pants, not only driving his first professional race car at age 16, but winning the season championship as well. Years later, the boy wonder would squeeze 139 miles per hour out of this Volkswagen-powered lakester built by Ron Benham, whose cars have put 15 people in the 200 MPH Club. *Burly Burlile*

Don Vesco's hero was wild Jim Hunter, a tiger of a guy who rode the *Brute*, and any other motorcycle he pleased. Hunter would have been pleased with Vesco's 252-mile-per-hour run, upside down with the parachute out. The timers wouldn't give him an official record because he didn't have the rubber side down. A few weeks later he shared the salt with the *Blue Flame*, averaged 253 miles per hour, and inked his first world motorcycle record, surpassing Don Leppan's mark. *Burly Burlile*

Daryl Smith endeavored to pick up where J. Otto Crocker left off, when failing health forced the longtime chief timer to retire. Almost poignant, on Monday, Smith and his new clocks got sick at the same time, delaying the time trials in the process.

The high point of the meet was Bob Noice finally getting the *One Way Special* to huff it hard two ways for a new record in A/Lakester. Tearing off a 311-mile-per-hour average, the terminal speed on one run was a howling 317 miles per hour.

Car owner Les Leggitt now had the world's fastest open-wheel car, pumping up the old record by 41 miles per hour. The engine was the first late model blown fuel Chrysler motor, based on a Keith Black aluminum block, to run at Bonneville. "I still have Black's original $2,200 receipt and the 18-page instruction manual explaining how to put the engine together," recalled master motor builder Leggitt. He believed drivers are like spark plugs: "If one doesn't work, you pull 'em out and screw another in."

Sandbagging is for other motorsports. In five classes, the record rose 20 miles per hour over the previous mark. The F/Modified Roadster record shot up 50 miles per hour, from 140 to 190, by a crowded entry named S&H Speed Enterprises, Volk, Mattinson, Hasselwert.

Don "Have Bike, Will Ride" Vesco, also known as "Mr. Cool" for his enviable ability to ride or drive anything with wheels, salted away a new FIM World Record aboard *Silver Bird*, his 21-foot Yamaha-powered streamliner. The 900-pound, 1,500-cc, aluminum-skinned speed tube posted a two-way average of 302 miles per hour and snagged an AMA 303-mile-per-hour average.

Removing the stain of private industry-funded studies, the BLM finally responded to the controversy over salt deterioration and asked the U.S. Geological Survey to conduct a detailed investigation beginning in 1975. Spanning two years, to 1977, it focused on the hydrology and surface morphology of the Bonneville Salt Flats. This survey was sparked by a Utah Geological and Mineral Survey, which had confirmed what the racers knew all along, that "11 million cubic yards, or 13 million tons, had been lost between 1960 and 1974." An earlier survey had found that "there was 20 million cubic yards of salt over four inches thick; in 1974 there was no salt of that thickness."

Among the study's conclusions, Howard Ritzman, assistant director of the U.S. Geological Survey stated:

"If the race track is to be preserved, then some means must be developed to stop depletion of the salt, or to restore salt at the same rate it is lost. The evidence we have appears to show a connection between the withdrawal of potash and the thickness of the salt," stated Howard Ritzman, assistant director of the U.S. Geological Survey.

Fingers were pointed at two major suspects, the weather and Kaiser Chemical Company, and the geologists were more suspicious of Kaiser. For years to come, government authorities would continue to have feet of clay with regard to saving the salt. This was the last year the Utah State Highway Commission would be involved with maintaining the speedway, ending a 23-year mission.

1976 / 28th Annual Hello USFRA

Wanting to broaden the racing schedule for landspeed racers as well as to keep a closer

When racing at Bonneville, fire suits are mandatory! *Burly Burlile*

Some of the most precious moments a person spends at Bonneville are in the early morning quiet. It is then that everything takes on a celestial glow, and a sense of peace and well-being can be found by those who take the time to look. Here, the competiton coupe of Jim Travis awaits its first firing of the day. *Burly Burlile*

eye on what was happening out on the salt, a group of stalwart speeders founded the Utah Salt Flats Racing Association (USFRA) in 1976. Some members began to spend long hours on salt during the spring and summer, grooming the course. Others were trained in the latest rescue procedures, and still others hunkered down to develop a timing system and technical inspection procedures. Eventually the group was ready to venture into hosting a few hot laps of its own, and began holding "warm-up" events before and after the SCTA Speed Week. Salt Racers were delighted, since it meant additional opportunities to flog their metal mounts.

SCTA dedicated the 1976 event to the new USFRA, but wind and rain pretty well trashed a lot of serious racing hopes. Those who did get it all together on the shorter course were able to spool up 24 new records that included eight open classes in which no record had been established.

Ermie Immerso resurrected his voluptuous streamliner, returning with two Lycoming T-53 turbines in place of the big Ford mills, and set the first mark for AA/streamliner at 197 miles per hour. Brand new was the Teague, Bentley, and Bisetti B/lakester, the product of an 18-month initial build process. A scruffy duckling, this vehicle was destined for salt racing's throne, but started out in the "spin-out club" before Mr. E. Teague could vector a path to a 261-mile-hour run.

More tasty vintage was on hand, with the J. D. Tone and family entry prancing to 142 miles per hour, setting the pace in X/Vintage Altered. Zacherson's daughters and sons set two records: XX/Fuel Coupe at 108 miles per hour and XX/Fuel Altered at 97 miles per hour. In the slippery streamliner that always could, Rick Vesco joined his big brother in the mighty "2 Club" after posting a 211 average driving the "family" car.

Tom Senter had 'em on their toes craning to look at his 258-inch Ardun-capped Mercury mill dropped into Mark Dees' modified roadster. The car ran 177 miles per hour on its maiden outing and was taching 197 miles per hour when the stinking water hose let loose. Mechanical problems and poor course conditions spoiled a new World Land Speed Record attempt by Bill Frederick's rocket-powered "SMI Motivator" in October to close the racing season.

1977 / 29th Annual / Pesty Weather

Most people were highly pleased with the 1977 event despite the pits being relocated 5 miles from the end of the road for better viewing of the racing action by all. The shortened, 5-mile course made things tough for the big motor vehicles, but racers managed 18 new records, half of which were former "open" records. The wind was mischievous and malevolent again, not only interrupting the racers, but toppling the port-a-potties throughout the pits.

The *Fullhouse Mouse* tried, but failed, to catch the *Flying Fliver* driven by local Utahan and founding USFRA member Hugh Coltharp, who puffed his four banger to the lowest speed of the meet but established a new record in V4/Street Roadster. High-speed duties were performed by Ermie Immerso's Thunderbird Turbine, at 236 miles per hour. The fastest motorcycle record was set by ole' hand Jack Wilson at 180 miles per hour with—what else—a streamlined Triumph. Shari Vickery of Denver, Colorado, climbed onto her 250-cc Yamaha and put the feminine touch to a record—twice, inking one and then improving on it before the week was out.

1978 / 30th Annual / Motorcycle Land speed Record

Salt Racing intelligentsia came to understand that whatever record Don Vesco wanted, Don Vesco got. This year, on a twin-engine Kawasaki streamliner, he set a motorcycle land speed record of 318.598 miles per hour.

"I used to bend the firewall pushing on the pedal trying to go faster," remarked Vesco of his high-speed fun. "The faster you go, the more you slow down. As speed increases, seconds can seem like minutes and your mind has to keep up, or you are in trouble. When I don't keep up I crash, or fall off the bike."

Most guys trying to catch the eye of a pretty woman would use flowers, perfume, or jewelry. Not Vesco. He just waved his blown 1,300-cc Kawasaki streamliner at Marcia Holley. She climbed on and set a record of 229 miles per hour that also earned her the right to wear the colors of the up-to-then all-male 200MPH Club. You go, girl! "The bike was hard to balance," recalled stunt woman Holley, "and it took me all week to learn how to ride it."

(Right to left) Driver Jerry Collier, Steve Cantelli, and Steve Garcia met in the fourth grade of Our Lady of the Holy Rosary Catholic School and were still making mischief well into middle age when they met Mike Manghelli (far left). With a four-cylinder air-cooled three-liter VW, the quartet roared to a 189-mile-per-hour speed, the fastest a VW had ever gone on the salt up to that time. *Burly Burlile*

It was a big year for the "2 Club." Besides Miss Holley, 14 gentlemen joined the ranks, the biggest load in one year. In the next year's program, president Monte Wolfe stated there were now 135 members. Although he enumerated many professions of the 200MPH Club membership, he chose not to mention that the club's first lady had earned a spot—on a bike, no less, the hardest type of vehicle to control on the salt!

The colorful spirit of "Bert" Munro "high-sided" in January of 1978. This had been a guy who got the idea for streamlining his bike from a New Zealand fish and then convinced the venerable Rollie Free to help him! As of 1999, one of his records, set in 1967, remained intact.

1979 / 31st Annual / Lady Man of the Year

The weather was gorgeous, and after a few rough years the salt was back in excellent shape, allowing a 11.5-mile course. Motorcycles accounted for 125 entries, and a major discussion on rules continued throughout the week.

SCTA President Gordon Hoyt remarked it was "best we've seen in 10 years." He was one of nine men who joined the 200MPH Club that year. After 30 years, Duane McKinney, a man who raced at the first event in 1949, joined the 200MPH Club, legging a record in B/Grand Touring at 210 miles per hour. Interestingly, the "2 Club" voted Emily Gillette its *"Most Valuable MAN of the Year."*

Nolan White, driving the *Spirit of Autopower,* picked up the *HOT ROD* magazine trophy for "Fastest One-Way Car Time," cranking out a 319-mile-per-hour run. Don Vesco picked up the motorcycle counterpart for his 261-mile-per-hour clock screamer. Jim Lattin, competing in the XX/Altered Class, heaved the record 57 miles per hour upward, the biggest jump of the meet, from 101 to 157 miles per hour. In total, 30 new records were set, but most were by just a few miles per hour, reflecting the high degree of class competitiveness.

In September, Bill Fredricks was back on the salt with a rocket car, dressed up in shiny red paint with a beer sponsorship. Stunt man Stan Barrett was at the controls, but the salt proved too tough for the unsprung car, and the crew departed without a making a return run, abandoning any chance of setting a record on the salt.

Ignoring the state study, Kaiser Chemical refused to acknowledge that any salt erosion problem existed. This infuriated the racing community, making life miserable for the BLM and Utah State officials. After much consternation and debate, a compromise was reached whereby the race course would be moved to another location, one that wouldn't be so vulnerable to mining activities.

"The BLM can't act until the U.S. Geological Survey completes its study," explained USFRA Vice President Larry Volk to Dave Wallace, writing for *HOT ROD* magazine. "After two years, it looks like we are still on the back burner." Through his editorial feature, "Endangered Species," Wallace appealed to racing enthusiasts to get involved to save the salt for the sake of posterity. He reminded readers that if Bonneville racing ended, the kids "won't have far to look to find the parties responsible."

The heart of Bonneville racing is the venerable roadster, the original hot rod, the car that started it all. Zeke Zacherson and his daughter's red roadster line up with the persimmon Piner and Eastwood entry alongside an unidentified but well-shaded white highboy. *Burly Burlile*

When you see the name Dave Campos, expect to see Harley-Davidson as his powerplant. Campos drove the Easyriders streamlined bike to 322 miles per hour in 1990. Here he is pictured a decade earlier in a 1980 ride. *Burly Burlile*

into high, but he still lifted the record to 269 miles per hour from 229 miles per hour. More stunning, the 40-point spread was produced with only 90 turbocharged inches of a four-cylinder Ford.

Rick Vesco can tell you about life at 320 miles per hour—upside down—in a streamliner! Or maybe the bigger story is how he got that gas-drinkin' small-block Chevy to go that fast in the first place. *The Jammer* and its keeper, Dave Campos, rode together at 226 miles per hour for top bike honors.

Moiling for speed gold, the great salt prospector Al Teague clinked out a new record of 308 miles per hour in an A/Lakester—just one more step on his way up the hill. Jim Deist, the man with the flying stopping power, was named "Most Valuable Man of the Year." The Carter family drove home knowing it was the "Best Appearing Crew" on the salt that year.

In September, try as he might, Englishman Richard Noble was foiled from making a serious attempt at the World Land Speed Record driving the jet-powered *Thrust2*. The solid aluminum wheels turned the jet into an ice skate on the moist salt surface, and Noble repeatedly slid off the track and into the dreaded "crunchies," the potato chip–like blistered salt chunks that were lifting off the clay base. The crew was sure rookie driver Noble needed some driving lessons, until he recorded a 418-mile-per-hour run.

1982 / 34th Annual / World Speed Record Farewell

The meet was a complete washout, not helping the SCTA/BNI financial woes, but in September, Richard Noble and his upgraded jet car *Thrust2* returned to the salt and were rained out for the second year in a row. Frustrated, Noble abandoned Bonneville and embraced the Black Rock Desert in Nevada. With him, he took Bonneville's crown racing jewel, the unlimited World Land Speed Record.

"Peter Moore, an accountant who had come to watch us run, told me of the alkali playa known as Black Rock," said Richard Noble. "Within 24 hours, Peter and I were on the playa, and I had renewed confidence that the compliant surface would provide the essential flexible link between the car's hard, aluminum wheels and the track." He was right; the car ran 615 before the season finished.

1980 / 32nd Annual / Slush Run

The salt got a dandy bath late in the summer of 1980, dumping 9 inches of rain onto the course. Still, 275 entrants (the largest meet to date) were able to stab 'n' steer down 3 miles of buildup and two miles of shutdown, inking 36 new records into the books and adding four new 200MPH Club members by week's end. Long or short, it still required more than 5,000 hours of planning, operating, and cleanup to produce the event, relying heavily on a volunteer staff.

The fastest one-way time for a car was posted by Al Teague in the Teague-Bentley-Bisetti lakester, at 280 miles per hour. A Vincent Black Shadow steered by Dave Matson claimed the motorcycle top-speed prize at 195 miles per hour. Just as happy on the other end of the scale was Ziggy-Toe and Ben Jordan, who improved the Class I/grand touring record to 120 miles per hour, the slowest time of the meet.

1981 / 33rd Annual / Long Course Returns

It had been a loooonnng time since the hot rodders had 11 miles of salt to pounce upon. The 241 entries wasted no time racking up 43 new records, set by 29 cars and 14 motorcycles. An estimated 200 runs per day, or 28 runs per hour clicked off, but reducing long lines gave the board a challenge before the next event, along with a growing financial crunch.

Larry Monreal squeaked into the books by the hair on his chinny chin chin, raising the H/Fuel Coupe by the slimmest of margins, only .735, to 130.735 miles per hour. The stubborn Fiat five-speed of Don Debring's *Longshot* H/fuel streamliner refused to shift

1983 / 35th Annual / The Big Flood

Unusually high precipitation levels from late 1982 and early 1983 created a 20-foot-deep Lake Bonneville and flooded the surrounding lowlands. There was no racing for the season, and the SCTA/BNI was in grave financial trouble.

Meanwhile, at dry-as-a-bone Black Rock, Richard Noble, driving for England, set a new World Land Speed Record of 633.468 miles per hour piloting *Thrust2* across the friendly, alkali playa. Bonneville, like Daytona Beach before it, had "been replaced" as the site for ultimate LSR (Land Speed Record) attempts. More than just weather, the Interstate and nonstop mining had long conspired to bring this day to pass.

1984 / 36th Annual / Shorty Aborty

"It's a helluva way to run a desert," lamented Utah's governor after two years of rain. The racers struggled to lay down three days of wet and wild racing in a short but sweet speed meet. The push vehicles were slathered with cottage cheese make-up.

Hungry for speed, the racers galloped through the course, knocking off 40 runs for every hour of time trials. The modest success comprised 126 car entries and 45 motorcycles that managed a remarkable 1,370 runs in three days, to produce 18 car and 9 bike records.

Fast Fred Dannenfelzer's modified roadster had started life as chalk lines scrawled on the cement floor in the family garage. A little over four months later, the car was put on a trailer for Bonneville.

The kids have vivid memories of nightly ceiling-high fireworks as Dad welded the car together. "We're talking about Peter Pan," reveals wife, crew, and partner Patty Dannenfelzer about her husband. "He is never going to grow up; he's always going to be a boy. It's just that the toys get more expensive." Hubby banged out a 251-mile-per-hour run, but broke a rod. Ouch! Can you hear the cash register calling? Patty's favorite part of the car is the blower; she looks at it fondly and sighs, "That's my new carpet up on the manifold."

Rich Fox used straight Jimmy power to be the "Big Bumper" in XX/Vintage Altered by blowing the record up to 144 miles per hour from its paltry 97 miles per hour. Hooker-Graham-Hooker, whose battle cry was, "Why do it once, when twice is more fun!," bumped the mark from 100 to 129 miles per hour driving a step-side pickup

The rain might frighten away the neophytes, but old salt shoes know that the race course will usually dry up if they have a little patience. Over the past 50 years, only six Speed Weeks have been total washouts. *Burly Burlile*

It's the dawn of a new race day. Although the salt flats look waterlogged, for those brave souls willing to splash through the brine for a few miles, a dry set of race courses awaits in the distance. *Burly Burlile*

fitted with a turbo 212 Detroit diesel. The Scotty's Mufflers street roadster showed up for the 25th year in a row. Whoa!

In January of 1984, World Land speed Record holder Gary Gabelich, 43, died in a traffic accident while riding his motorcycle. He left behind a wife and young son.

1985 / 37th Annual / No World of Speed

High water levels from the previous four years rejuvenated the salt to a prime condition; nature had healed itself. The USFRA was so stoked at the restored salt that it planned to hold its first "World

of Speed" event in September, but too much standing water on the course forced the cancellation of the event.

Things dried out in time for the SCTA/BNI meet in September. Joining Nolan White, Al Teague brought his lakester-turned-streamliner to record the first ever runs in excess of 350 miles per hour. Chairman Monte Wolfe commented on the feats, "It is one of the highlights of my life to see those cars go through the 4-mile timing light and still be accelerating."

Of the 172 pre-entered vehicles, an astounding 72 records were set, with 14 runs exceeding 300 miles per hour. Burke LeSage gave the meet only a "four-star" rating, as rain and hail shut down

Marcia Holley, the first woman to "officially" qualify for lifetime membership in the 200 MPH Club by averaging 229 miles per hour riding Don Vesco's blown fuel streamliner motorcycle in 1978. That record was still intact after the 50th anniversary of SCTA's Speed Week. *Marcia Holley*

the racing on Thursday afternoon. Included in the event results were "LeSage's Pages" recapping the action:

With Lester half-way around the world, Susan Leggitt's boys, K.C., 18, and Thomas, 15, along with pals David Penstone, 18, and David Alexander, 15, accept the responsibilities of operating a 300-mile an hour machine. Driver Papa Smurf, otherwise known as Bob Noice, expressed 100 percent confidence in the young foursome.

Standing within the walls of time, 267 years, or four drivers, on a brilliant Monday morning, line up to take off down the 7-mile course. Keith Burkdoll, 66, 170 miles per hour; Bud Morrill, 61, 140 miles per hour; Bill Brooks, 69, 220 miles per hour; Charles Scott, 71, 213 miles per hour.

Tom Burkland and Jeff Carroll, both 20, are part of our growing list of father/son combos for the 2 Club.

Pattie Lindsley narrowly missed the 200 Club regalia, third generation accolades and so forth. A bridesmaid by a scant 1.1 miles per hour.

Imagine letting your sister-in-law take your rod for a cruise! Marcia Holley-Vesco checking Rick's No. 444 out at 272.014 miles per hour, average.

Classic salt ingenuity was reflected in a V-8 Chevy engine sitting alone on an engine stand. In reality, it was an inline four, the left bank shod with head and shiny valve cover, the right bank of empty holes covered with a flathead!

Sally the Salt Dancer neon sign at Jack Mendenhall's Museum of Gas Pumps in Buellton, California, also the site of the Dry Lakes Hall of Fame. *LandSpeed Productions*

Gale Banks tipped the money can along with *Popular Mechanics* Stringfellow and Geisler to produce a AA/Gas Coupe fitted with a turbocharged GMC 456-inch big-block. Wrangled by Stringfellow, he slammed the standing record into the next galaxy, from 201 to 260 miles per hour!

At first blush, a D/Fuel Coupe seems a likely ride for pops Fjasted, but no, Roy brought the gas-burning Pontiac Firebird punching out a 205 run on a 202 record. Son Carl and partner Vic Enyart are responsible for the traditional rod.

1986 / 38th Annual / Everybody Out!

Times were a-changin' as 200MPH Club president Ermie Immerso pointed out that the 185 membership would certainly swell with the advent of onboard computer technology. "Beware of the finely tuned family sedan," he warned.

"I can foresee a wholesale invasion of new members through this 'dial-a-ride, dial-a-speed' method. We must prevent this from happening . . . to think that someday a member will be presenting a hat and T-shirt along with a handshake to a robotic driver scares me, and I am fearless."

Wendover had a little scare of its own 30 minutes before midnight on Monday, August 18, when a carbon monoxide leak emptied all 248 rooms at the State Line Hotel & Casino. More than 300 people (mostly racers) ended up on the lawn of the Silver Smith across the street. The slumber party was rousted yet again when the sprinklers powered up in full view of TV news crews.

Pauline Fergusen made life a whole bunch easier for Chief Timer Gary Cagle and his crew when she spearheaded a successful

Greg Bennett (right) and Kenny Lyon stand beside their 150-cubic inch twin-engine turbo fuel-injected Harley in a V-4 configuration. Lyon rode the bike to 190 miles per hour in 1981. Lyon was also part of Dave Campos' record-setting *Jammer* at 294 miles per hour and the Easyriders World's Fastest Motorcycle project at 322 miles per hour. Lyon has set 11 Bonneville World Land Speed Records with his Honda GoldWing-powered streamlined motorcycle known as Project GoldWing. *Easyriders Magazine*

A few of the old salts get together. Left to right: Jim Lindsley, Larry Volk, Multy Aldrich, Eric Rickman, and Burke LeSage. *Daniel Hostetter*

fund-raising campaign to purchase three separate timing systems, including a spiffy Chronomix Computer able to process official record data along with spectator and announcer data.

The father and son routine spread to the motorcycle classes, and this year saw Glen and Mike La Follette join Lou and Steve Nauert and Keith and Jim Burkdoll. The dads mainly spun wrenches, while the kids twisted the grips.

A few "roundy-d-round" cars showed up and found the Bonneville Salt Flats a gracious hostess. All the way from West Virginia came news correspondent Gordon White, towing his post–World War II Offenhauser-powered midget; he built speed to 134 miles per hour by Wednesday. Mark Dees and Bruce Johnson both ran vintage sprint cars into the mid-150s before a vicious rain squall slammed the door on the time trials. There were only four days of qualifying and three days of record runs, but 28 cars set new records along with 10 motorcycles. In between, Charley and son Cliff Clupper chalked up a three-wheel mark of 165 miles per hour, and seven new members were inducted into the 200MPH Club.

The USFRA meet was rained out just before opening day. Painfully apparent to all concerned was the beautiful weather just before and after both SCTA/BNI and USFRA dates—an endless string of hot days and cloudless nights. Sigh.

1987 / 39th Annual / 3 Gals 4 the 2 Club

Hot rodders, once the scourge of highways and byways, blinked and were celebrating the 50th Anniversary of their efforts to legitimize their sports. The SCTA was a half-century old. SCTA President and Director of Racing John Helash sweated out a cancellation of insurance which would end the salt racing until Bill Hill of K&K Insurance secured a new package of coverage.

In July, Art Arfons and his son, Tim, came to the salt with a jet-powered motorcycle. Securing some test time after the USFRA meet, things went very wrong and Arfons, 64, went airborne and crashed at 300 miles per hour. Arfons was unhurt but shaken.

"Mrs. Hospitality," Vera Aldrich, who for 15 years greeted every racer who came to the salt with a smile, lost her battle with cancer on February 5. It was revealed that in all those years, she never left her post to see a car run. "The racers are my family; I just love being part of it all," she was heard to say many times.

On Monday afternoon, hailstones the size of golf balls put an immediate halt to racing until Wednesday morning. Full-tilt racing unfolded the rest of the week and 11 new members joined the 200MPH Club, including an unprecedented three women! They were Tanis Hammond, at 251 miles per hour, Sylvia Hathaway, at 202 miles per hour in a Citroen, and Courtney Hizer, at 215 miles per hour in the Miller American D/Altered Coupe.

"My very first run in the car brought a wave of fear," admitted Hammond. "I thought, 'What *am* I doing here? I have three little kids at home,' and then 'I'm having so much fun.' The fear came and went just that fast, like a wave washing in-and-out on the shore." Husband Seth added, "Tanis is our 'Shift Queen.' According to the computer, she is faster than anyone, and I am the slowest."

Sylvia Hathaway considered her "2 Club" trip a multifaceted sensation of great speed. After many delays, she left the line thinking,

A pair of second generation racers, Steve Burke (left) and Mike Cook in front of the GT40 Red Valkerie *at the 1976 Speed week. The fiberglass body put the No. 90 car in Class B sports racing, and the 366-CID Hemi engine, running on gas, recorded a 247-mile-per-hour speed.* Bill Burke Collection

Sky Tracker I, the six-wheel, streamlined car of Don Vesco with a Jocko Johnson-designed rear section. Powered by a turbocharged Offenhauser, it ran 318 miles per hour before Vesco flipped and crashed in 1985. *Ron Christensen*

"Push it. Do it. Shift, shift shift, Go, go go! Shift into fifth, mash the throttle, come on boost. Come on . . ." She recalls the car suddenly felt as though it was no longer in contact with the ground. "It seemed very light, and as it drifted about, time itself seemed to change," she said. "Such a sensation is impossible to describe adequately." She and her husband, Jerry, were the third husband/wife team to join the 200MPH Club ranks.

Indy Car driver A. J. Foyt also qualified for "2 Club" honors at 267 miles per hour. Doing it the hard way was Dennis "Spin" Varni, who, on his way to "2 Club" membership, wiped out a set of timing clocks, destroyed a set of tires, and chewed up a parachute driving the Varni-Walsh-Cusack deuce in AA/Gas Roadster. Officials added that he was clocked at over 200 miles per hour through the clocks, backward!

Out of the Pontiac Firebird came the primal scream of Gale Banks' turbocharged big-block responding to Don Stringfellow's silky smooth gear changes, which delivered a thundering 268-mile-per-hour record for production-based cars. The eyeball-popping run used 29 pounds of boost!

The veteran San Diego Roadster Club team of Eyres, Wavra, and Finley trotted out two pretty blue roadsters onto the salt. Consecutively numbered 831 and 832, they turned 154 miles per hour and 202 miles per hour, respectively.

Some people love salt racing more than others, and Fritz and Gayle Kott wore their hearts on their sleeves by getting married right on the salt. They were later seen wandering the pits happily bound together by a set of rather secure handcuffs.

Taking literally the battle cry of "Run what ya brung," Mort Strain and Irv Orth showed up with a lakester powered by a V-12 M48 tank engine. The 1,790 cubic inches was equal to four big-blocks.

At the USFRA World of Speed meet, Al Teague roared to fast time of the meet at 360 miles per hour. But Dave McDonald got serious attention for his A/Gas Coupe record of 237 miles per hour.

1988 / 40th Annual / Hot Pants

The hot rodders were one sportsman short going into their annual speed meet. Al Thayer, a veteran lakes and Bonneville competitor, departed this earth on the Ides of March, leaving behind the legacy of many mentored young men who learned fabrication arts and self-reliance from the highly respected, generous racer.

SCTA officials instituted a variety of changes to improve safety as well as heighten the pleasure of participating in Speed Week. These ranged from having a doctor on-site to streamlined registration procedures. The BLM issued an edict that racers may no longer deliberately dump used crankcase oil onto the salt. Those that did faced disqualification and/or criminal prosecution.

Drag Racing's "Swamp Rat," Don Garlits, found the salt to his liking, running an XX/gas streamliner to qualify for 200MPH Club status with a modest 217-miles-per-hour average, using a supercharged flat head. At the Club's banquet he remarked, "I should have done this 15 years ago."

On his way to owning the World's Fastest Modified Roadster record, Fred Dannenfelzer described his "Hot Pants Run," which vividly explains why many drivers in trouble on the course are just too busy to be scared:

A water line broke 1 mile off line, spraying hot water everywhere in the driver's compartment, but the Donovon engine was running good, oil pressure was up and I could still see so I thought, "lets stay with it." Many parts of my body got quite warm, but thankfully didn't blister. At the 5-mile mark, a header bolt came out, which started a blinding oil spray. I shut off the car, but knew my first 'chute squidded just after it flowered because the car didn't slow down. I threw the second chute and it worked fine. Then I ran over a surveyor's stake and ripped off the belly pan. When things start going wrong, you don't think of anything in particular, just what you have to do next, go to Plan B, C, D, until the car stops. The realization of what could have been always comes afterward; it catches up with you later. I was on Plan F before the car stopped.

Joe Teresi came to the salt with the Easyriders streamliner motorcycle to break the existing land speed motorcycle record of 318 miles per hour. A tire blew at 280 miles per hour and the liner crashed, but driver Dave Campos walked away to ride another day.

Jack Mendenhall, owner and curator of the Museum of Gas Pumps/Dry Lakes Hall of Fame, and Paul Vanderley from Biloxi, Mississippi, built *Sally, the Salt Dancer* and ran 213 miles per hour. Sally raced nine years, was always first in her class, and set two records in her day.

The USFRA World of Speed brought 19 new records into its record books. The fastest came from the lakester of hard-hitting "No Nitro" Hammond, at 251 miles per hour.

1989 / 41st Annual / Save the Salt!

Speed Week is akin to Brigadoon; a temporary city that rises from nothing and then disappears annually, leaving behind no trace from year to year. Unlike the enchanted Scottish city, Speed Week's magic comes from hundreds of volunteers devoting thousands of hours attending to millions of details so that a select few may have the time of their lives for seven short days. Entering its fourth decade, the SCTA has elicited a life of its own. It is a heritage that will continue to evolve beyond the control of any one man or board of directors, because it is the sum total of efforts from everyone involved. Nowhere else on Earth does such a form of racing occur: A rare piece of thriving Americana that embraces a wide cross-section of the population, it will remain an evocative slice of American life for as long as the amateur racers, their kith and kin, continue to contribute.

This year's competition started with great promise: an 11-mile long, 100-foot-wide course, 255 entries, FIA recognition, and more media attention. It all nearly came crashing down with a Wednesday night deluge that ended a wind-swept first three days.

Roy Creel matched mile for cube and turned a record-setting 216-mile-per-hour run driving the lakester he and Terry Burian entered. The feat also plastered a "I'm in the '2 Club' now" smile on his face.

Petersen Publishing Librarian Jane Barrett took on the SCTA/BNI program chores, starting with a dedication of the event to

"up from nothing" racer Dick Miller, who tragically had lost his life in a crash on the El Mirage Dry Lakes. Barrett crammed the program full of tasty reading material, making it the best-ever program and giving the racers something to read while waiting in line on the salt.

Bruce Crower contributed an article examining the virtues of belt tires that could provide up to 20 square inches of contact patch on the rear wheels. Crower noted the setup, held in place by teeth, had been tested smoothly up to 517 miles per hour. Ro McGonegal offered "The Engine That Ate Detroit," outlining the amazing story behind the development of the Oldsmobile Quad four-cylinder head, a design steeped in Formula One racing technology and the child of Cyril Batten and Gordon Dollar.

The big story was the results of a massive letter writing campaign initiated in 1988 by USFRA which adopted the motto "SAVE THE SALT." Using the 1977 Recreation and Management Plan from the BLM, racers discovered the once 96,000 acres (in 1926) had withered to 25,600 in 1976. Utah Senator Jake Garn responded, and a contingent of racers went to the State Capitol to bring the issue to the attention of legislators. The club also made appeals through the media in enthusiast magazines, gathering grassroots support and funding to keep the issue fresh and demand action on the part of the government.

The USFRA World of Speed meet was one of its best yet. Nineteen speed records were set, including one laid down by a blind driver at 128 miles per hour. Al Teague was again top speed at 392 miles per hour, ever inching closer to that magic 400 door.

It was only after Vesco installed pneumatic tires that he crashed the *Sky Tracker* at 60 miles per hour. Originally, the car was fitted with hand-cast urethane belt tires bonded to the six aluminum wheels. Note the chain drive hooked to an Indy-style Hewland transaxle. *Ron Christensen*

Chapter 11

The Nineties and Beyond

A s land speed racing turned the corner into the last decade of the century, the racers hoped that by using the Bonneville Salt Flats more often it would call attention to the plight of the shrinking resource. Growth was evident everywhere in the sport except for the salt itself. Speeds continued to rise as the racers developed better driving skills, using improved engines, chassis, parts and body styling, but emphasis shifted from record-setting to ramping-up pressure on the government to take corrective action at Bonneville.

The glistening saline surface is the Holy Grail of landspeed racing, the last great bastion of amateur motorsports, the place to which you must come every year lest you lose the faith. Such faith has allowed thousands of ordinary people to accomplish extraordinary feats.

Broadcast television and cable show producers followed the swelling number of spectators that provided a colorful, mile-long line backdrop watching the cars out on the course. Burly Burlile, organizer of the Bonneville Nationals Cruise-In, a street rod road trip culminating on the salt, reported increased participation.

The original hot rodders inspired hundreds of additional devotees, many from their own families, but would their numbers be enough to save the salt? Where a shortage of good racing tires may have hampered the sport, the loss of the Bonneville Salt Flats would signal the sport's ultimate destruction—very unpalatable to those with a need for speed.

> *The purpose of life is not always to be happy, but to have it make some difference that you have lived.*
>
> —Ralph Waldo Emerson

As part of a unifying thrust, SCTA/BNI added another event to the racing calendar in 1990, the World Finals, a four-day meet in October, bringing the total number of sanctioned racing events to four annually. SCTA President Gillette points out:

"Most of us have already used up our vacation time, and we're taking the true 'red-eye' express to Wendover to put on this meet. If it helps *Save the Salt*, and gives racers what they want, all our work will be well worth it."

Save the Salt got a major lift when new mining owner Thomas Reilly of Reilly Industries came forward to join the effort in preserving the salt flats. The racers were delighted with the mining companies' willingness to help. The BLM formed a special advisory committee to investigate salt loss in a three-year study. No action, just another study.

Meanwhile, there was racing to be done. The Fourth Annual USFRA World of Speed (WOS) grew stronger, racking up 25 new speed records in 1990. Rick White led the pack, peeling off a 384-mile-per-hour run.

At the 42nd Annual Speed Week, the pedal-to-the-metal racers found an additional course on the salt. The brainchild of Chuck Kalbach and Jerry Bates, it was a short course for vehicles running 175 miles per hour and below, and is now used for rookie drivers and slower licensing runs. Although more labor intensive for the SCTA/BNI staff, the extra course slashed waiting time in line for each of the 369

Without the annual winter flooding, the Bonneville Salt Flats would not be able to rejuvenate itself each year and produce the marvelous flapjack-flat playa so treasured by the land speed racer. This precious natural resource has been constantly threatened by mining activities for the past century. *Bill Taylor*

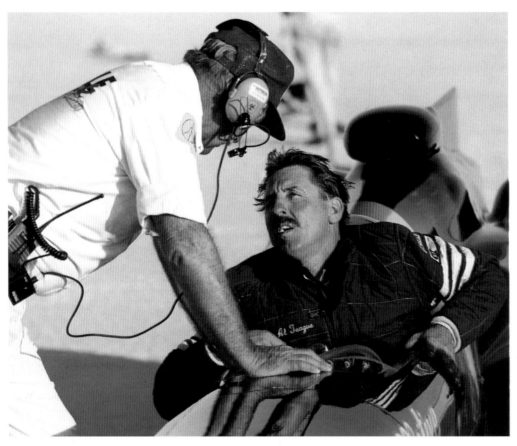

entrants. At week's end 1,644 runs had been timed, and a whopping 80 new land speed records were set, despite a rain shower that caused a slipperier than usual track.

Both USFRA and SCTA/BNI welcomed the formation of the Land Speed Authority to create a common record keeping and certification system. Initially heartily supported by both groups, it unfortunately fell victim to politics and quickly faded from prominence.

Dennis Dalton, husband to SCTA/BNI Chief Starter Bob Higbee's daughter, Joyce, and father of 12, was killed in a head-on collision in July 1991. He had proposed to Joyce during a Speed Week in 1980, and had joined his father-in-law on the starting line the following year. Dalton had been a master at getting drivers to forget about sweltering in a hot fire suit when the action was stopped.

In his honor and memory, the 43rd Annual Speed Week was dedicated to Dalton. And it was a stunner. One of the best weather weeks the racers had seen in some time, some 350 entries set 122 records. The racing season came to a chilling halt as snow canceled the Fifth Annual World of Speed. But not before a new World Land Speed Record unfolded.

Unlike those who might bluster about what they expected to do out on the course, unassuming, almost bashful Al Teague just let his actions speak for themselves. On August 21, 1991, those actions lifted the entire landspeed racing community into a state of giddy euphoria. Driving his hand-crafted *Speed-O-Motive* streamliner, Teague posted a 409.986-mile-per-hour average to become the fastest hot rodder of 'em all.

August 15, 1991: the moment of truth. Chief starter Bob Higbee is just about to tell Al Teague that he has broken the World Land speed Record, averaging 409.986 miles per hour in the wheel-driven class. The last time that occurred was in 1965. *Bill Taylor*

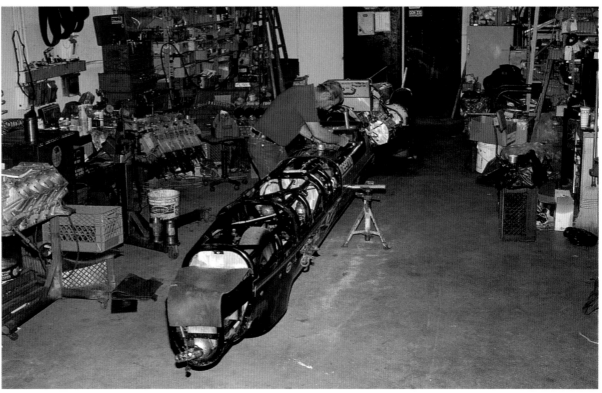

Does Al Teague know how many gazillion hours he has put into his race cars? Does he care? Probably not. For a few short days of unlimited, flat-out speed, any hot rodder will spend countless hours bent over a race car chassis and engine or stand in a cold, lonely garage, just for the chance to thunder across the salt. It is reward enough. *LandSpeed Productions*

Bruce Crower's 300-mile-per-hour-plus streamliner that used Kevlar cog belts instead of pneumatic tires. Mounted on notched aluminum wheels, they permit a larger contact patch for traction and are capable of 800 miles per hour according to Crower. *Bill Taylor*

When he fires up the car, everyone stops, watches, listens. The throaty, harmonious song of controlled explosions trails behind the car for 5 miles and remains audible at the starting line long after Teague has shut down the supercharged Chrysler engine, popped the parachutes and disappeared over the horizon. People shake their heads in awe.

As an added bonus, because the FIA had recently created a separate category for supercharged engines, *Goldenrod's* long-standing record of 409.2 miles per hour remained intact. Teague used just one supercharged bullet, but *Goldenrod* had four normally aspirated pentastars.

The hot rodders couldn't have asked for a better, albeit reluctant, hero in Teague. Not only was he self-deprecating when it came to his accomplishments, but he was also a humble statesman for the sport, a veritable poster boy of American know-how. Teague is to salt racing what Jimmy Stewart was to acting, or what George Gershwin was to music—simply put, inspiring.

There was no shortage of racing opportunities for the straight-line acceleration crowd, with four separate events scheduled for 1992. USFRA kicked off the season in July and held another event in September that dovetailed with SCTA/BNI's 44th Annual August Speed Week, and then the World Finals season closer in October. Such interest put further pressure on the authorities to rectify the unconscionable and unchecked deterioration of the salt. The racer strategy seemed to be working.

Nolan White and son, Rick, built this four-wheel-drive streamliner and drove it in August 1990. It was the first single-engine car to run over 400 miles per hour. The very next day, Al Teague, driving his single-engine streamliner, also ran over 400 miles per hour. *Bill Taylor*

When Maryann and Ron Benham started married life in 1957, it was in a modest, two-bedroom home with a small garage. Since then, the garage has been expanded into a 24x60-foot shop, where Ron has built race cars that have enabled 15 people to join the 200 MPH Club, including Ak Miller, who was 70 years old at the time. "Bonneville is a fraternity whose clubhouse has no walls," said Benham. "It's a volunteer organization in which dedication surpasses that of paid military forces, a close-knit group of people whose membership dues are paid in full each time a car makes it safely down the long black line." *LandSpeed Productions*

The *"Bingham Report,"* an independent engineering analysis released in 1993, outlined a very promising methodology that could revitalize the salt crust over a 10-year period. The cost was estimated to be $600,000, primarily for power to run the pumps. The project would reactivate existing wells but require high-volume pumps to relocate a six-foot-deep buildup of salt in the potash recovery ponds. During the winter months, a 20 percent brine solution would be pumped from Reilly's property back onto the speedway acreage—approximately 18 square miles. The racers were informed they would be expected to pay half.

Shocked but determined, the racers developed a line of commemorative merchandise as a fund-raising mechanism, and SCTA/BNI inserted a special fund-raising form into all its membership renewals. Media reports also generated funds, but even the smallest of gains came only with a tenacious struggle. At the helm of *Save the Salt* was racer Rick Vesco, younger brother of bike racing champion Don. With a business to run, a family to raise, and racing program of his own, somehow he found time to continually beat the drum about the deplorable salt conditions.

After nearly a decade of trying, Fred Dannenfelzer joined the "2 Club," driving his modified roadster in 1985. It was dubbed the "hot pants" run when a water hose came loose in the cockpit. He upped his own record a few more times before selling the car in 1993. "Patty cried harder when the car got sold than when our daughter left home," recalled Fast Fred. *Dannenfelzer Family*

Sometimes the hobby consumes the hobbyist. That was how it was with Bruce Johnston since the 1930s. Involved with racing all his life, he was a highly skilled machinist. This is a glimpse of his "toy box" out back in the garage where he built many racing machines. He and wife, Helen, devoted 13 years of volunteer service to the SCTA. *LandSpeed Productions*

Just as some progress was being made, area BLM chief Greg Morgan was reassigned. Morgan, a big supporter of the racers, would bring a trailer onto the salt during Speed Week and camp out. In effect, he had a de facto field office in operation, which proved very helpful when issues would crop up requiring government input. After the BLM commented it would like to remove itself from the race course preparation business, the racers took over the responsibility and saw their use fees reduced as a result.

The first three events of the 1993 season were canceled because the Bonneville Salt Flats was trying to revert to its former self: Lake Bonneville! USFRA managed to get a few days of racing in at the Seventh Annual WOS. Veteran racer Bobby Unser came to the salt and joined the 200MPH Club.

Giving kids a chance to experience the thrill of salt racing, the USFRA instituted a Junior Salt Flat Racing League. The multifaceted program was designed to give youths from 8 through 17 years of age the opportunity to race with their peers in near-replica models

of adult competition vehicles. The half-scale lakester/dragsters would compete in four classes on a half-mile track with standard timing traps at the end of the course. Although the youth program was heartily embraced, the time-eating attention required for *Save the Salt* forced the USFRA board to suspend the youth program for several years after the 1995 Speed Week.

Salt samples were taken in 1993 from various locations on the speedway to determine why some areas were crumbling into small pieces, yet in other places the salt remained hard and resilient as ever. Chemical analysis showed the strong areas were composed of a minimum 94 percent sodium chloride. The problem areas were only at 86 percent sodium chloride, with a blend of magnesium, sulfur, calcium, and traces of potassium. This blend of chlorides has an extremely weak crystalline structure that breaks down easily under heavy loads.

By 1994, Dean Zeller was the new BLM District Manager. He penned an open letter in the SCTA Program commending the

After more than 40 years, the *Mormon Meteor* got its tires salted up once again, thanks to Ab Jenkins' son Marvin. Starting a frame-off restoration when he was 72, Jenkins brought the record-setting car back to the salt in 1998 when he was 79. Having helped Augie Duesenberg build the darn thing in the first place, who was better qualified to fix up the old charger? *LandSpeed Productions*

In 1988, Ed Rannberg of Eyeball Engineering showed up with *Kawashocki*, a 1,000-amp/240-volt electric-powered motorcycle that had ripped off 11-second runs over the quarter-mile. A founding member of the Electric Vehicle Association of Southern California, "Eddy Current" was a remarkable statesman for the ampere crowd. *Ron Christensen*

Gourmet speed secrets have been known to increase driver reaction times on the salt. Here, the roadster and motorcycle power pancakes of BWS Racing's driver John Wright sizzle on the grille. The team makes him cook to keep him out of trouble. *LandSpeed Productions*

cooperation among the racing groups as well as the relationship between the racers and Reilly Industries. In a postscript, he wrote, "Help preserve the Salt Flats. Support *Save the Salt*."

The racers wanted more than just words on paper. To that end, attorney racer Mark Dees reported that a proposal between Reilly and the racers had been drafted but remained unsigned because both sides were awaiting the release of a pivotal U.S. Geodetic Survey which might further define responsibility. Regrettably, the report was delayed for the same reason the 1992 and 1993 races were canceled—rain.

The engineers were hampered in making scientific measurements and observations critical to the analysis. The racers believed the report would place the responsibility squarely on industry's shoulders. The BLM also stirred the pot with a land-trade offer, but again, it hinged on the outcome of the U.S. Geodetic Survey, postponed indefinitely until the weather improved.

Salt veteran Ray Brock and the NHRA got together in 1994 to produce a short but very persuasive video documentary on the salt loss problem. As Dees aptly put it, "The outlook is fairly good, but so far we really haven't saved a teacup full of salt."

The weather bamboozled the 46th Annual Speed Week in 1994, and when the SCTA/BNI applied for a date change, the BLM denied the request, stating it was too close to the scheduled 8th Annual USFRA WOS meet. Trying for a joint meet with USFRA, the southern California group was again denied. As spokesman Wes Potter stated, "There simply isn't enough time to resolve all the problems of combining the events. Also, the salt is too fragile to allow more than a four-day meet."

The BLM confirmed there was an odd crust on the track but would not comment on its "raceability," saying that it was up to the racers to decide. The 104 entries saw new Brockmeyer Timing equipment, wire, cones, and signage at the 1995 USFRA Ninth Annual WOS and were impressed with the new addition to the safety arsenal—the metal slicing "Jaws of Life"—purchased with donations from many of the racers.

A controversial "catch net," designed to trap cars that have lost the ability to stop short of the interstate on return runs, was unveiled. The 80-foot-wide, 4-foot-high net was held in position by 50-foot

chute lines located 1 mile from the interstate. For years, drivers of high-speed cars had fretted about making the required return runs, but not all believed the net was the answer. Erected without damage to the salt, the net was owned by Stroud Safety Company, who stated it would loan the net to all salt racers. SCTA/BNI declined the offer.

Since 1980, the USFRA has promoted the 130-mile-per-hour club, which focuses on street-driven cars and motorcycles. Aside from normal safety and good mechanical condition requirements, the drivers need only to have a Snell-approved helmet, with motorcycle racers also required to have full leathers, including gloves and boots. By 1995, there were 39 recognized members, 3 women and 36 men, in the 130MPH Club. For faster vehicles, there is the 150MPH Club, but it has more restrictive rules and safety requirements. Ed Van Scoy was the only member listed in the 1995 program, squeaking in at 151 miles per hour. The 200MPH Club now stands at 320 members strong.

The long-delayed US Geodetic Survey was released in 1995, and although it did not place blame squarely on industry's shoulders,

George Fields is an awfully nice fella. He let Bob Nakonieczny drive his *Trackmaster Fabricator's Special* competition coupe during the 1997 Speed Week. Would that we all could have such nice, generous friends. *Bill Taylor*

the conclusions pointed a number of fingers at the mining operations as being responsible for the salt loss. This information caused *Save the Salt* attorney Robert Pruitt to convince Reilly Industries to absorb the entire amount, not just half, of planned restoration costs.

"The racers have no duty at all to assist Reilly in restoring the salt," revealed Pruitt. Citing the Bonneville Salt Flats National Register of Historic Places designation, he explained, "There is a law that says you can't wreck a Historic Register property, even if you own it." Pruitt also pointed out that 25 percent of the land Reilly used in its operation was federally leased land, which carried a reclamation stipulation as part of the lease, yet Reilly did not view the laydown project as part of its restoration responsibilities.

Save the Salt Chairman Rick Vesco knows the job is not complete. He understands that only with a monitoring process firmly in place will any measurable results be possible. "Since the salt laydown program may take 30 years to complete," he wisely observes, "it is essential that the racers be able to track net salt gain, or salt loss." Unfortunately, people are weary from the long battle and react ambivalently. Clearly, much, if not all of the concerted restoration effort could evaporate right along with their salvaged salt if the monitoring aspect is left undone.

Taking further steps to protect the salt from further contamination, the BLM informed racers that an impervious tarp must be placed on the ground under the car to prevent the "littering of fluids

Called a maverick and old sage, Chauvin Emmons is hard on the throttle of his modified roadster in the 2.5-mile point. He boosted his own record by 30 miles per hour, to 291 miles per hour, in 1997 with the help of his wife, Sharon, and his totally stoked crew's tuning of the nitro-drinking 483-CID Hemi. *Bill Taylor*

Don Vesco is all smiles looking over Turbinator's new paint scheme for the 1999 season. Posing with the *HOT ROD* magazine perpetual trophy, Vesco's name was etched into the brass plate on the base that reads as the "Who's Who" of land speed racing. *Menzie Studios Photo*

Even the World's Fastest Man, Andy Green, has to attend the Rookie Class at Bonneville. Although he drove past the speed of sound, Green was a salt virgin and was required to take the orientation class before he could run on the course. *LandSpeed Productions*

Jack Costello, driving the orange streamliner, gets a push off from his elated T-roadster starting crew. *LandSpeed Productions*

When it fires up and heads down the black line, there's no missing the *Phoenix*, the 200-mile-per-hour green diesel truck of Carl Heap. *LandSpeed Productions*

It's just another afternoon for the boys and their noisy toys. Jim Travis demonstrates to Lee Kennedy just how hard driver Dan Warner's head really is, while Jim Miller lounges over the car and Kerry Hart provides a little shade. *LandSpeed Productions*

and foreign materials." It must extend out at least 3 feet from the car. A number of other edicts are also in force, but the bottom line is: if you pack it in, you must pack it out, and that includes cigarette butts and nutshells.

SCTA/BNI and USFRA entered into an agreement to jointly prep the salt for racing, integrate the records of both clubs, and dump the minimum speed requirements for a given class. New also was the vehicle log book, which must be kept with the vehicle, regardless of owner, so that inspection notes may always be accessible. Chief Inspector Lee Kennedy implemented a new inspection process, which met with great success.

Mike Steed, Dennis Perrin, and Terry Nish masterminded a *Hot Salt* Street Rod event set for the 1995 Independence Day weekend to allow participants to experience the black line. There would be no times recorded, only certificates to say you were part of the happening. The event was to include a car show, swap meet, concessions, music, BLM tours, and several cruise events, but bad weather killed the great idea.

The 47th Annual Speed Week got 252 entries that ripped off 1,200 runs and set 80 new records, proving the thirst for speed had not yet been quenched. The 1995 salt was in poor shape. Event organizers prepared several courses in advance so that as one track showed signs of deterioration, the speed trials were shifted to virgin salt with minimal downtime. Taking no pleasure in banning the new, belted tires, officials knew they must protect the now fragile salt surface.

Jeff Williams slowly lets the clutch out as starter Bill Taylor bids him onto the 50th Anniversary race course. His father, Bob Williams, hand built the low-slung motorcycle using a Honda 350cc (21 CID), SOHC engine for a powerplant. A custom mechanical fuel injection system and a turbocharger from a Honda 650 delivers the fuel. Williams recorded a top speed of 156.52 mph running after a record of 156.92 mph, only 4/10ths of a second off the pace! This is remarkable, considering the pair had only first come to the salt as spectators in 1997. Despite being confined to a wheelchair, the elder Williams was so fired-up about land speed racing that he built the pictured bike in less than a year. *LandSpeed Productions*

Master motor man Charlie Hamilton tweaks Al Teague's supercharged engine prior to the team's 366-mile-per-hour record-setting run in class C, blown fuel streamliner. Living the unequaled Bonneville competitive spirit was Charley Markley, who also helped the crew defeat his own record, held by the Hoffman-Markley car. *LandSpeed Productions*

Tanis Hammond, dubbed the "Shift Queen" by her teammates because she can shift the car faster and smoother than any of her male contemporaries, including her husband, Seth, and son, Channing, is hoisted out of the lakester at the end of another well-driven run. *LandSpeed Productions*

It takes great nerve, amazing confidence, and loads of experience to name your race car the "Raspberry Rocket," let alone paint it howling pink. "I told the painters 'any color but pink' and of course they painted it pink," chuckled owner and builder Tim Rochlitzer. As the fifth car he has built and campaigned, he has set a dozen land speed records over the years. Powered by a 255-CID small-block Chevy with GMC blower, the car holds Class E gas and fuel records. *LandSpeed Productions*

Sue Christopherson beams as she poses alongside her Chevrolet Camaro, a car she has worked on ever since her honeymoon. She ran 214 miles per hour and earned a spot in the male-dominated 200 MPH Club, only the sixth woman to ever do so. *LandSpeed Productions*

Rain pinched the course down to 4 miles instead of the customary 5, but Al Teague was still able to clock a 365-mile-per-hour run on wet salt. The proboscis-predominant Simca Coupe from Trackmaster Fabricators Special posted a 304-mile per hour run from a 468-CID nitro-breathing Rodeck TFX Hemi. Jeff Kugel averaged 228-mile-per-hour in the family roadster, joining his dad and brother Joe in the 200MPH Club along with six other happy haulers.

The BLM got yet another district manager; Joseph J. Jewkes took the helm and commended the efforts of all involved with protecting the salt, which the BLM finally considered a "threatened resource." Save the Salt's Vesco reported that engineer Brent Bingham had completed field testing of the pumps and construction of the salt berm, and had determined that the salt brine quality was higher than hoped: 98 percent pure sodium chloride! If all

goes well, one-half inch of new salt will be flowed back onto the speedway each winter. The test project term is five years.

It was obvious that the racer strategy of conducting additional speed events, along with the constant pressure of Save the Salt, was making positive progress. USFRA's WOS event celebrated its 10th anniversary, and SCTA/BNI dedicated the 1996 48th Annual Speed Week to Lee Clancey, Tom Ruddy, and Don Watkins.

Good ole' fashioned racing was thundering along with highboy roadsters, still true to their original hot rodder design, and now well over a half-century old. The Wilson and Waters entry in C/Fuel Roadster nattily averaged 225 miles per hour, and driver Greg Waters qualified for 200MPH Club membership with 16 others that year.

Hard-charging Chauvin Emmons got the job done in an A/Fuel Modified Roadster by tickling the record up to 263 miles per hour

Ron Cook nailed four records at Bonneville before taking a pair of high-speed tumbles, one at over 200 miles per hour while trying for another record at El Mirage Dry Lakes. Miraculously, Cook walked away from one and lived through the other without losing any personal parts himself. *Ron Cook*

It takes talent, teamwork, and tenacity to be successful on the salt. That's precisely how BWS Racing won the 1998 SCTA Points Championship. Here, Randy Speranza (left) and Dave Brant keep driver John Wright company as they wait in line with *Dreamliner*, their diminutive, electric blue streamliner. *LandSpeed Productions*

It's the *Hanky Panky* Studebaker coupe scratchin' and a sniffin' on the starting line. It is said to be one of, if not *the*, oldest gas coupes still competing on the salt. Owner Bruce Geisler has served as SCTA president, board member, SCTA season champion four times, and set 40 records—more than any other racer. *Louise Ann Noeth*

with his injected Keith Black bullet. J. Arthur Urciuoli learned a salt lesson the hard way when he brought his rare GT40 Ford to compete for best time in Class B/modified sports. Shod with road racing tires, the car lost its grip at the 2-mile lights and spun out after it qualified at 180 miles per hour.

The Burkland family unveiled its new streamliner with a 285-mile-per-hour run showcasing the car's twin-engine, all-wheel-drive approach to speed. On the other end of the aero scale was Matt Marsac driving the Joint Venture Freightliner Semi Tractor. Always a spectator wonder on the track, Marsac nudged his record up to 221 from 220 miles per hour, coaxing the power out of a quadruple-turbocharged 1,472-CID Detroit Diesel.

Told she had life-threatening cancer, no one raced with more courageous enthusiasm than Ellen Christensen in the 11th Annual USFRA WOS in 1997. No stranger to things fast, Ellen had already spent time off-road racing, played with stock cars, and earned a couple of salt records driving *Salted Peanut*, a three-cylinder supercharged Chevrolet Sprint.

Admiring Christensen's resolve, Manette and Bill Ward put their record-setting Chevy-powered Opel GT at her disposal to first run in excess of 200 miles per hour and then attempt a new record in Class C/modified sports. Devoted hubby Ron Christensen was ecstatic but jumpy when Ellen clocked 213 miles per hour, but the parachute failed to open at the end of the third mile. With only two-wheel drum

brakes left, she wisely spun the car in order to avoid overshooting the course. Whatever else one may say, Ellen did not "go gently into her good night, but raged, raged against the dying light" on June 4 the following year.

The district manager chair at the BLM changed for the third time in three years, causing an inevitable "*Save the Salt*" slow-down, as new man Glenn Carpenter acquainted himself with his new post in 1997. The BLM salt loss study report was now four years overdue. For reasons unknown, the state of Utah vacillated on granting water permits for the salt recovery test program. However, the salt restoration project did make some progress. A new power line that would service the three newly dug wells and new pumps was installed. Ditches were dug and a 30-inch-diameter pipe laid that will connect the existing pumping network.

The SCTA's dedication list was longer for its 49th Annual Speed Week. Honoring the memory of their departed comrades, the racers dedicated the program to Jim Duncan, Dave Halopoff, Jerry "Bear" Jones, Robert Markley, Ed Rannberg, and Mark Dees.

The late-model production classes had seen a lot of activity in the 1990s. Sometimes called "door-slammers," for the obvious reason, driving these full-bodied cars has been likened to controlling a bear with a sore head on the end of chain. The sheer weight of the vehicle makes controlling it a formidable task that requires nerves of steel to match the body. Among the more gutsy wranglers have

After 50 years, these speed wrinkles came back to their salty roots. In 1949, all these men took a chance on an unknown race course hundreds of miles from home and found a new home with more room to race than they had ever imagined. Some never quit and are still racing. *LandSpeed Productions*

Ellen Christensen's eyes are wide with elation after hearing she has exceeded 200 miles per hour. Battling cancer that would soon take her life, she whipped up the 200-mile-per-hour run to fulfill a lifetime goal. *Ron Christensen*

been Mike Cook, Juris Mindenbergs, John Lingenfelter, MacDonald and Pitts, Jim Fueling, and Don Stringfellow. Cars have spun out with such force that it has blown out windows and sucked off hoods. One even pirouetted on the rear bumper at 290 miles per hour.

"We had to sort out lots of aerodynamic problems," explained Mike Cook. "It being a short-wheelbase car, when I shifted, the torque was so severe it blistered the right front tire. The hardest part of driving an assembly-line car is the first 2 1/4 miles, then it's fun until the 5th mile, at 295, when the car starts to fight the air. We can't sneak it through the air like the streamliners."

Bob Higbee, chief starter and volunteer for more than 50 years. He has spent thousands of hours all alone out on the course, more than any other racer. He's the one who drags the course smooth, pulling heavy weights up and down the 12-mile course at 25 miles per hour.
LandSpeed Productions

The fascinating "Kugel Klan" sold their familiar orange roadster to buy the MacDonald-Pitts Pontiac TransAm and joined the 300-mile-per-hour door-slammer chase. With Mike Cook's 1989 Thunderbird already in the hunt with a 298-mile-per-hour pass, the Kugels wicked up the competitive heat when their twin-turbocharged small-block Chevy knocked out a 295-mile-per-hour run at the SCTA World Finals.

Save the Salt had lobbied long and hard until the salt's caretakers, the BLM, finally acted. In the winter of 1997, after years of bitter arguing, the racers, government, and private industry implemented a cooperative plan to resalinate the racer's playground and nature's twinkling jewel. The outlook was guarded, but hopeful, as 1998's surface conditions translated into marginally higher speeds, fewer spin-outs or accidents, and milder injuries.

August 1998 marked not only a century of landspeed racing, but coincided with the 50th running of Speed Week, with more than 200 cars, motorcycles, semis, and even a motor home vying for honors in 350 classes. In six days the racers clicked off 1,520 high-speed runs down a 7-mile straight-line course to ink 77 new automobile and 33 motorcycle certified speed records. The first event, in 1948, had run with 45 entries, all but one from southern California.

Today, participants come from all over the United States, Australia, New Zealand, Canada, England, and Japan just for the chance to streak across the magical mecca. They reserve more than 1,000 hotel rooms a year in advance, and the local market stays open around the clock when the racers are in town. For half a century they have done it for nothing more than a timing slip and maybe a trophy. Among them are more than 60 families with two

A surrealistic view of Al Teague's streamliner, the fastest wheel-driven car in the world. The jet black car sits under a multicolored tent casting the wild colors onto the paintwork. The air scoop with its rubber insert is seen on top, located just aft of the driver's compartment.
LandSpeed Productions

Don Fergusen, Jr., points out a few switches to driver Jim Travis, 64, who will be making his inaugural run in the family XXO/fuel lakester. Travis ran 203.502 miles per hour to earn entry to the "2 Club," a long-term goal he set for himself in 1952. He raised seven kids before he could start making honest attempts in 1986. *LandSpeed Productions*

You just can't stay clean when you are tuning a record-setting nitro-snorting 5-window coupe. Former top fuel pilot Doug Robinson (in dirty belly T-shirt) listens as driver Will Handzel fires up the BMR (Berg, McAlister and Robinson) racer. Normally supercharged, but at the 1998 SCTA event they went after the 151-mile-per-hour normally aspirated record and pumped it up to 188 miles per hour. The BMR Racing holds seven other salt records. *LandSpeed Productions*

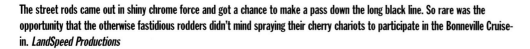

The street rods came out in shiny chrome force and got a chance to make a pass down the long black line. So rare was the opportunity that the otherwise fastidious rodders didn't mind spraying their cherry chariots to participate in the Bonneville Cruise-in. *LandSpeed Productions*

It's big, real big. It's red, real red. The 10,000-pound machine is 36.5 feet long and 7 feet at the tip of the vertical stabilizer. Powered by four 540-CID normally aspirated Rodeck engines with an estimated total output of 6,400 horsepower, the car has run 365 miles per hour in 1992. Hoping for a longer course to improve on the car's top speed and capture the long-standing Goldenrod record, driver Clayton Steen said the car drives, "Like a Cadillac through the park on a Sunday afternoon." Father Roy Steen built the Chet Herbert design with Dan Soran. *LandSpeed Productions*

and even three generations of race car drivers, backyard builders, or engine magicians. Clearly one of this nation's richest examples of kinetic Americana, Bonneville's "Pit City" is full of youngsters, grandparents, and other assorted relatives.

"The heroes are the people whose names you never see in the record books, the cars that may never get a trophy," observed Golden Anniversary BNI Chairman Mike Waters. "They are the people who are simply racing on the salt for the supreme pleasure of being there and having a ball doing it. Our little 'backyard' event took on a life of its own. We hoped it would be special, but it came out the other end magnified beyond anything we could hope for." Waters also noted that the weather was absolutely perfect and the salt racing surface was the best it had been in years.

Well, at least until Thursday. A brief but dandy thunder and lightning storm played havoc with the electronic timing equipment.

The sensitive, infrared photo cells went nuts, even though the cloudburst was miles away, because the system uses the salt as a giant ground. According to Chief Timer Glenn Barrett, lightning struck as one car was running through the multiple speed traps, and the clocks very prosaically reported a speed of more than a million miles an hour.

Adding a special patina to the Golden Anniversary proceedings was the attendance of 42 of the original 49 racers from the first event. Salt racing is an elixir of youth for those whose visions unfold along a 7-mile salty liquorice-colored line. The years have not dimmed their determination to go fast, then faster and faster, though each is eligible for Social Security. A driver's age is meaningless; the only thing that counts is speed. Insulting senility with brazen bravado, a few "speed wrinkles" still race, making high-speed passes right alongside dozens of "salt virgins," rookies burning up with lead-foot desire. How many sports can boast that?

White-haired Don Vesco, 59, who is blind in one eye, was the fastest of the meet, registering 405 miles per hour driving *Turbinator*, a turbine-powered streamliner. Many believe he will soon topple the World Land speed Record for wheel-driven cars. The admired are not necessarily the fastest. Consider Harold Johansen. Considered a mystic when it comes to coaxing horsepower out of a four-cylinder engines, he has never been a big record setter, but he is as much a part of the scene as Vesco.

People marvel at the commitment of Bob Higbee, or "Mr. Salt," as Chief Timer Glenn Barrett calls him. Higbee has attended every Bonneville meet since 1949. For decades he has been part of the advance team that preps the course, chief starter, and an SCTA board member who has attended practically every board meeting for a half a century. On race days, Higbee has been the last to snug down the safety harness, check the helmet chin strap, and make a final inspection before letting the car go onto the course. Racers have lost count how many lives he has saved by catching something they forget. "The racers are my family," he said. "I do what I can to see that they are safe."

Few Bonneville racers get sponsorships, forcing most to dig down deep into their own pockets. But the lack of "big money" is acknowledged among the veterans as being a major reason the sport has endured in its "pure," amateur form and ensures that the average person can still be competitive.

Just ask John Wright, Dave Brant, and Randy Speranza, aka BWS Racing. This middle-aged trio turned a boyhood dream of racing on Bonneville into a surprisingly successful reality. *Dreamliner*, a diminutive, breathtaking streamliner that began as a Dustbuster with four peanut can lids for wheels, was the 1998 SCTA Points Champion and holds four class records, including the distinction of being the world's fastest single-cylinder car, at 128 miles per hour. Their hearts are set on 200 miles per hour record on the salt.

Bonneville junkies have come to understand that from the moment they committed themselves to the salt, Providence moved with them. All sorts of things occur to help that would otherwise never happen. A stream of events is released from that

Left to right, drivers Eric Luebben, Randy Rannberg, and Mark Sterner put on their finest Superman pose with the 24-foot electric streamliner, *Lightning Rod*. The creation of Eyeball Engineering masterminded by Ed Rannberg (in the sky), it is now the world's fastest record-holding electric streamliner. *LandSpeed Productions*

decision, raising unforeseen incidents and meetings, and securing material assistance that none could have dreamt would ever come their way.

Early Bonneville racer Bill Kenz summed up his many years of salt racing in such a way that his comments might serve to describe what has resonated through every salt racer during the past half-century. It is a fitting way to conclude our historical account and focus on a faster future. In the 1958 SCTA Bonneville program, Kenz wrote:

I have enjoyed every moment spent on the salt flats and even during the years when we had troubles.... I was just thrilled to be part of the great sport and to meet so many wonderful people who also live cars and speed.... May the Bonneville National Speed Trials go on and on and on, until we become old and have to stand aside to watch the next generation of hot rodders.

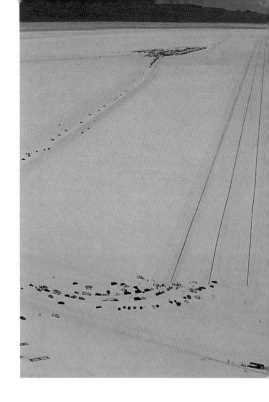

More than 50 racers wait their turn in line for short course access. The two rectangular I-beam sections lying near the bottom of the photo are the drags used to smooth the course and return roads. The heavily populated pit area is at the top center of the photo, 2 miles away. *LandSpeed Productions*

It takes a whole village to put on Speed Week. This happy pile of people were responsible for making the 50th Anniversary Bonneville Nationals rise from nothing and disappear from view 10 days later. The all-volunteer staff, from all over the nation, is the backbone of the racing organization. No other motorsports segment has a more finely tuned grassroots program that permits amateurs to compete equally with seasoned professionals. *LandSpeed Productions*

Speed Reading

The following reference sources were used in compiling the racing history of the Bonneville Salt Flats:

Print

American Institute of Aeronautics and Astronautics.
Aerodynamics of Sports and Competition Cars
North Hollywood: Western Periodicals Company,
1975.

Batchelor, Dean. *The American Hot Rod* Osceola,WI:
MBI Publishing Company, 1995

Eyston, Capt. G.E.T. *Fastest on Earth*, London: John
Miles Publishers, 1939.

Eyston, George and W. F. Bradley. *Speed On Salt,* Los
Angeles: Floyd Clymer Publishing, 1947.

Irving, Washington. *Adventures of Captain Bonneville*.
Portland, OR: Binford & Mort, Pub., 1954.

Jenkins, Ab and Wendell Ashton. *Salt of the Earth*. St.
George, UT: Dixie College Foundation, 1945 and
1993.

Jennings, Jesse D. *Speed and Salt.* Wendover, UT:
Wendover Lions Club, 1964.

Lepp, George. *Bonneville Salt Flats* Osceola, WI:
MBI Publishing Company, 1988.

Medley, Tom. *Hot Rod History,* Osceola, WI: MBI Publishing
Company, 1990.

Shapiro, Harvey. *Man Against the Salt.* London: Minerva
Press, 1997.

Tremayne, David. *Fastest Man on Earth* Harrow: 633
Club Publishing, 1986.

Wendelboe, Lee, *A Will To Live*. Providence, Utah:
Watkins & Sons, 1981.

Electronic

www.roadsters.com
www.scta-bni.org
www.members.aol.com/beanracers/
www.fia.com/
www.metrogourmet.com/crossroads/G_HR_Tea.htm
www.teamvesco.com/
www.pro-blend.com/lsrpage.html
www.alteague.com/index.html
www.motorcycle.com/mo/mcracing/bonneville96.html
www.reillyind.com/
www.sscycle.com/
www.sltrib.com/
www.utah.com/
www.weatherlabs.com/city/fore/ENV1.htm
www.ce.ex.state.ut.us/history/index.html/chicagotribune
.com/splash/article/0,1051,SAV-
9902210388,00.html#top
www.crosslink.net/~gewhite/
www.the-rocketman.com/landspeed.html
www.nitronic.com/
www.spacestar.net/users/kytec/content_2.html
www.si.edu/newstart.htm
www.motorcycle.com/

Appendix

Members of the 200 Mile Per Hour Club as of 1998

Dennis Aase	1992	211.071	Dave Campos	1974	208.000	Jim Duke	1966	250.454	Andy Granatelli	1984	213.322
Reese Adams	1989	205.977	Don Carr	1978	221.899	Gary Eaker	1989	293.608	Roland Gravel	1979	245.805
Bill Aldridge	1987	217.284	Leonard Carr	1990	221.608	John Edmunds	1962	232.782	David Green	1996	204.724
Dennis Allen	1974	273.860	David Carroll	1974	235.839	Howard Eichenhofer	1957	229.666	David Green	1991	213.246
Don Allen	1967	256.521	Jeff Carroll	1985	269.089	Tom Elrod	1979	200.022	Dick Griffin	1978	203.722
Duncan Allen	1986	282.633	Ed Carter	1979	208.997	Leonard Emanualson	1989	221.663	Leon Griffith	1968	244.410
Joe Anderson	1980	212.703	Glenn Carter	1978	205.997	Chauvin Emmons, Jr.	1972	240.780	Roger Griffith	1990	217.934
James Angerer	1973	201.432	David Casteel	1991	258.378	I.W. "Knot" Farrington	1960	200.620	Lee Gustafson	1985	233.389
Art Arfons	1964	536.710	Mel Chastain	1963	206.251	Don Ferguson Jr.	1988	207.369	Scott Guthrie	1988	203.357
Nick Arias, III	1998	265.989	Oz Cheek, Jr.	1998	233.682	Duane Feuerhelm	1978	200.546	Ed Hagarty	1996	232.604
Ron Armstrong	1978	208.471	Art Chrisman	1952	235.910	Jim Feuling	1990	221.994	Harvey Haller	1953	206.778
John Baechtel	1990	217.270	Steve Christophersen	1992	229.750	Leigh Fielder	1998	242.099	Channing Hammond	1996	261.865
Bret Batchelor	1996	237.000	Sue Christophersen	1998	214.847	George Fields	1990	231.285	Seth Hammond	1981	259.731
Steve Batchelor	1990	204.861	Casey Clark	1992	283.747	Bill Fisher	1981	207.287	Tanis Hammond	1987	251.750
Amos Beard	1991	208.706	Dick Clark	1962	208.638	Roy Fjastad	1989	226.975	Ed Harding	1971	209.950
Tom Beatty	1955	211.260	Don Clark	1957	248.410	Paul "Slick" Fontenot	1991	254.856	Brett Harris	1994	220.932
John Beckett	1992	210.180	Robbie Cohn	1989	201.201	Gary Foster	1990	212.109	Jack Harris	1993	200.750
Norm Benham	1989	245.803	Ron Cohn	1990	212.482	Jim Fox	1994	225.575	Jerry Hathaway	1985	200.002
Robert Bennet	1977	203.847	Victor Colvin	1990	260.599	A. J. Foyt	1987	267.399	Sylvia Hathaway	1987	202.301
Ernie Bennett	1967	221.426	Tim Confal	1988	220.615	Greig Frazier	1969	248.473	Holly Hedrich	1990	230.853
George Bentley	1955	203.338	Mike Cook	1981	237.049	Jim Fredrick	1978	206.371	Chris Hill	1988	262.467
Art Bigiogni	1990	225.690	Jack Costella	1992	239.696	Bob Freed	1991	204.552	Phill Hill	1959	254.910
Bob Bowen	1954	248.460	Roy Creel	1989	216.077	Phil Freudiger	1958	214.959	Cortney Hizer	1987	215.539
Bill Brandenburg	1991	243.430	Bill Crossley	1957	205.488	Willie Freudiger	1978	219.510	Harry Hoffman Jr.	1988	209.595
Craig Breedlove	1966	600.601	Don Cummins	1969	289.508	Gary Frost	1995	212.594	Marcia Holley	1978	229.361
Bob Brissette	1957	205.344	Robert Dalton	1990	298.340	Ted Frye	1957	216.750	Leroy Holmes	1953	201.015
Bill Brooks	1985	220.282	Fred Dannenfelzer	1985	265.557	Don Fuller	1989	213.442	Kenny Hoover	1979	225.374
Kelly Brown	1990	236.409	Leonard Daughterty	1992	238.811	Ted Gansberger	1985	201.752	Jim Howe	1991	307.555
Tom Bryant	1990	217.236	Les Davenport	1996	314.536	Don Garlits	1988	207.947	Gordon Hoyt Jr,	1979	239.336
Benjamin Burkdoll	1996	215.359	Dave Davidson	1998	228.000	Patric Gary	1994	207.223	Jack Iliff	1985	216.312
Jim Burkdoll	1988	203.719	Michael Dawson	1992	231.028	Roger Gates	1975	248.242	Ermie Immerso	1956	212.900
Juli Burkdoll	1990	204.586	Paul Dearth	1962	213.580	Bruce Geisler	1969	201.060	Marvin Immerso	1977	236.000
Bill Burke	1960	205.949	Don DeBring	1980	224.405	John Gillespie	1990	253.526	Doc Jeffries	1989	201.710
Steve Burke	1972	221.840	Brian De Vries	1988	223.276	Greg Gillette	1978	216.365	Harold Johansen	1974	208.860
Gene Burkland	1978	255.863	Tom Doll	1991	215.987	Denny Golden	1978	206.315	Bill Johnson	1962	230.269
Tom Burkland	1985	294.868	Mike Dorgan	1987	218.930	John Goodman	1995	205.179	Don Johnson	1963	255.501
Rick Byrnes	1998	204.952	David Dozier	1992	221.095	John Gowetski	1995	221.183	Howard Johnson	1969	270.880

Name	Year	Speed	Name	Year	Speed	Name	Year	Speed	Name	Year	Speed
Bob Jucewic	1990	203.371	Gary Matranga	1971	224.806	Donald Rackemann	1958	200.173	Bill Taylor	1969	201.916
Dennis Kahler	1988	204.133	Dave Matson	1985	202.947	Ron Ragsdale	1996	211.292	Elwin Teague	1970	250.800
Barry Kaplan	1979	206.858	Nick Mays	1990	215.629	John Raines	1998	209.218	Greg Temple	1981	241.848
Robert Kehoe	1970	205.206	Michael McCombs	1992	223.083	Les Ranger	1987	212.721	Jess Thomas	1958	214.470
Don Kehr	1988	213.438	Mike McGhee	1996	232.099	Gary Richards	1969	221.742	Tom Thomas	1986	241.881
M. Lee Kennedy	1998	251.261	Jon McKibben	1992	232.717	Dick Riley	1988	204.761	Richard Thomason	1990	284.968
Patrick Kinne	1990	208.004	Duane McKinney	1979	210.762	Brad Rochlitzer	1992	265.230	Neil Thompson	1966	265.131
Dan L. Kinsey	1990	214.565	Neil McNeil	1995	228.916	Brian Rochlitzer	1996	262.985	Tim Thomssen	1990	231.380
Jim Kirk	1994	253.221	Gary Meadors	1994	223.220	Tim Rochlitzer	1963	226.421	Don Torgeson	1967	210.594
Dave Koskela	1979	263.497	Jim Mederer	1995	242.002	John Rogers	1952	224.144	Charlie Toy	1991	201.223
Sasumu Koyama	1991	246.166	Jack Mendenhall	1991	207.015	Monte Rook	1988	251.134	Ed Tradup	1989	261.848
Jeff Kugel	1995	228.985	Ak Miller	1991	225.760	Gil Ruiz	1970	212.580	Jim Travis	1998	203.502
Jerry Kugel	1967	205.560	Glenn Miller	1990	215.582	Dick Russell	1995	232.402	James True	1996	201.979
Joe Kugel	1990	219.205	Juris Mindenbergs	1984	217.602	Jim Ryder	1996	219.107	Bruce Tucker	1995	205.544
Arley Langlo	1966	209.140	Jon Minonno	1991	221.518	Otto Ryssman	1952	222.570	Al Turner	1992	221.238
Eric Langstroth	1988	215.015	Tom Monroe	1981	217.849	Chuck Salmen	1994	243.556	Bobby Unser	1993	223.709
Fred Larsen	1959	206.950	Bobby Moore	1998	234.162	Frank Salmen	1996	243.697	Paul Vanderley	1992	210.577
Paul La Teer	1990	222.233	Butch Morris	1976	206.267	Don Schellberg	1985	236.840	Dennis Varni	1987	225.012
Bill Lattin	1987	212.040	George Morris	1963	215.957	Tim Schulz	1989	248.688	Don Vesco	1963	222.790
Jim Lattin	1977	210.280	Howard Nafzger	1988	212.893	Charles Scott	1985	213.992	Rick Vesco	1976	211.957
Joe Law	1991	223.657	Glenn Necessary	1990	238.351	Randy Scoville	1987	229.675	Larry Volk	1975	207.645
K.C. Leggitt	1990	282.270	Leroy Neumayer	1953	233.310	Ross Sherburn	1987	216.392	Pat Volk	1991	219.530
Bob Leppan	1966	245.667	Darren Nicholson	1988	227.382	Don Sherman	1986	238.442	Ken Walkey	1990	289.150
Burke LeSage	1963	213.740	Jeff Nish	1986	220.452	Jim Short	1964	201.740	John Walsh	1991	213.853
Roger Lessman	1989	292.719	Mike Nish	1996	304.700	John Simonson	1962	208.394	Tom Walsh	1986	225.377
Jim Levack	1978	204.572	Terry Nish	1994	291.407	R.B. Slagle	1992	212.440	Robert Waddill	1998	243.970
Jim Lindsley	1953	202.070	Richard Noble	1983	633.468	Chuck Small	1955	242.089	Bill Ward	1987	200.961
Larry Lindsley	1971	204.779	Bob Noice	1972	214.680	Bill Snyder	1972	203.740	Greg Waters	1996	221.662
Mark Lingua	1989	213.852	Ray Oberst	1986	226.762	Jim Snyder	1990	220.997	Tony Waters	1958	209.249
Joe Locasto	1958	213.830	Carl Olson	1994	234.276	Dave Spangler	1985	295.802	Don West	1988	247.468
Els Lohn	1964	203.360	Ray Orput	1969	237.302	Jerry Spotts	1974	291.736	Sam Wheeler	1970	208.720
Ed Losinski	1955	236.842	Allen Osborne	1988	201.308	John Sprenger	1975	232.031	Nolan White	1963	213.400
Henry Louie	1992	204.798	George Parker	1991	213.783	Carl Staggemeir	1988	232.198	Rick White	1973	246.840
Jack Lufkin	1964	204.240	David Parks	1996	215.415	Mike Stewart	1980	215.073	Gerry Whitehouse	1991	214.804
Kenny Lyon	1990	211.700	John Paxton	1989	241.338	Mike B. Stewart	1978	205.286	Fred Wiley	1992	200.920
Joe Mabee	1953	203.100	Leo Payne	1969	202.379	Corky Stockham	1990	262.000	Paul Winson	1986	226.762
Dave MacDonald	1987	237.859	Greg Peek	1970	210.500	Jeff Strasburg	1990	255.985	Bill Wirges	1973	241.950
Rich Manchen	1994	253.541	Ernie Pereira	1977	201.367	Lindsay Strasburg	1991	227.718	Monte Wolfe	1972	253.880
Brian Manly	1996	262.520	Tom Perris	1991	255.367	Mike Strasburg	1991	277.415	Earl Wooden	1996	256.142
Harry Mardon	1961	203.318	Tony Piner	1990	226.538	Tim Strasburg	1992	290.953	Ted Worobieff	1958	201.580
Mike Maris	1996	224.874	Lionel Pitts	1988	228.214	Don Stringfellow	1980	209.236	Willie Young	1952	255.411
Charles Markley	1958	207.160	George Potter	1994	223.388	Don Stringfellow, II	1988	224.000	Jim Yriberry	1979	229.181
Robert Markley	1966	260.880	Levan Prothero	1969	202.150	Mel Swain	1971	249.081	Pat Zimmerman	1992	200.355
Tim Markley	1991	210.341	Ron Pruett	1991	222.581	Bill Tally	1990	208.166			
Mathew Marsac	1995	220.919	Kirk Purvis	1959	219.453	Katsunori Tanaka	1990	204.478			

Index